SPIRIT OF ADVENTURE

SPIRIT OF
ADVENTURE
A Journey Beyond
the Whisky Trails

TOM MORTON

MAINSTREAM
PUBLISHING

EDINBURGH AND LONDON

The moral right of the author has been asserted

First published in Great Britain in 1992 by
MAINSTREAM PUBLISHING COMPANY (EDINBURGH) LTD
7 Albany Street
Edinburgh EH1 3UG

ISBN 1 85158 498 6

A catalogue record for this book is available from the British Library

Illustrations by John McNaught

Typeset in Garamond by Saxon Printing Ltd, Derby
Printed in Great Britain by Butler & Tanner Ltd, Frome, Somerset

For Sandy and David

CONTENTS

You see things vacationing on a motorcycle in a way that is completely different from any other. . . you're completely in contact with it all. You're in the scene, not just watching it anymore, and the sense of presence is overwhelming. That concrete whizzing by five inches below your foot is the real thing. . .

Robert M. Pirsig
Zen and the Art of Motorcycle Maintenance

Perhaps we are getting warm, and the drunkenness of the slums, the austerity of the Covenanters, the dreams of the Twilight, are but efforts to reach out to the lost water of life, so that, being bathed therein, we may at last be revealed to ourselves as we are – and as we know we are. Lemuel's mother advised her son: 'Let him drink and forget his poverty, and remember his misery no more. . .'

Neil Gunn
Whisky and Scotland

Inspiring bold John Barleycorn!
What dangers thou canst make us scorn!
Wi tipenny we fear nae evil!
Wi usquebae, we'll face the devil!

Robert Burns

Then he looked up. 'What are you doin' with this motorcycle crowd?'
I explained that I was only a journalist trying to do an honest day's work. . . he tucked his thumbs in his belt and asked me what I wanted to know. . . I shrugged. 'Oh, I don't know. I just thought I'd look around a bit. Maybe write a few things.'

Hunter S. Thompson
Hell's Angels.
The Strange and Terrible Saga of the California Outlaw Motorcycle Gangs

God loves a drunk. . .

Richard Thompson

Acknowledgments

I was aided, and I was abetted: by some who will undoubtedly wish to remain anonymous, by some whose names I forget. Others, whose names I remember and who have not requested anonymity, include the following:

Chief egger-on, friend, confidante and motorcycle *aficionada*, Dr Susan Bowie, bore the whole episode, not to mention John Magnus and James Patrick, with fortitude, good humour and tolerance. The *Scotsman* stretched a point and gave me some time off. Mainstream, again, took a chance. Jimmy at Melven's Bookshop in Inverness gave me the idea and subsequently a lot of help. This book was written at The Sands, Sandness, during the hottest Shetland weather this century: many thanks to Jimmy, Joan and Barbara Nicolson.

Other names, as they occur to me: Iain Abernethy; Stewart and Sandie, not to mention Roddy; Jimmy Sutherland and all at the Saint; Steve, Christine, Mick and Kathy; Big Jim and Evelyn; David Alston; David Ross; the *West Highland Free Press*; Torcuil Crichton; Tandy at Inverness; all at Calmac's Kennacraig office; James Robertson; Doug Scott; Deirdre Grant; Gary Anthony, John Paul and all therein; John McNaught and Gillian Jones; Dad and Ann.

In Shetland: Dave and Debbie; Elaine and Scott; Maisie; Mary; Barbara and Jim; Wilma and Stevie; Peter and Greta; Jonathan and Lesley, Peter, John, Mary and all at Radio Shetland; Cluny and Jill; Tammy and Muriel; Iain.

Prologue

Uisge beatha, usquebae, usquebaugh, ooshkayvar, ishkeevaah . . . ISHkva . . . ISHk . . .

Whisky. The water of life. From Gaelic to English via bad pronunciation. Or was someone just too drunk to say 'uisge beatha' properly? I don't know . . .

Some fat, gout-ridden guest at a deer-slaughtering somewhere in the Highlands, brandy-and-claret-clouded of a hillside morning, accosts a ghillie for a swig of the liquid such serfs carried.

'What the hell's this called, Macdonald old chap?' cries the tweed-swathed monstrosity, his southern vowels slewing and slurring in the remaining mists of last night's rich indulgences.

'Uisge beatha,' comes the reply, pronounced, depending on the form of Gaelic, as something like 'ishkeuvah'.

'Ishky. Ahh,' imitates the would-be stalker, his cherry cheeks flaring through the sullen weather. 'I say, yes, this "ishky" gives one a devil of warm glow, doncherknow? Perhaps we could soften it a teensie weensie bit, bottle it, mount a big TV campaign, hit the glossy magazines, fly up some pretentious wine hacks and get them pissed in a marquee next to a golf course; feed them, bribe them, send them back south . . . it's got possibilities, Macdonald!'

'Yes, sir,' says the impassive Macdonald, the very image of the Highlands, all raw-boned features, bandy legs and bad teeth. ' "Uisge beatha" is Gaelic, sir, a language two or three hundred of us benighted natives still speak, sir, mainly due to the circulation of Postman Pat *videos dubbed patronisingly into the tongue for our lasting benefit, sir. "Uisge beatha" means "the water of life", sir!'*

'Bloody good, man! bloody good! What a brilliant slogan! *"Ishky: The Water For Your Life!" Or maybe, umm . . . "The Drink For Your Lifestyle!" I can see it on billboards from Surbiton to Surinam!'*

'Begging your pardon, sir, but I have a better idea.' Macdonald sheds his Inverness cape to reveal a double-breasted Next *suit, a silk tie and a Marks and Spencer button-down shirt. A cellular telephone peeps from his breast pocket. 'Let's totally colonialise its name. Let's call it, just for the sake of argument, Scotch as opposed to Scottish, whisky as opposed to ishky. Let's castrate its taste, removing most of its distinction for the sake of soft city palates. Let's have different brands all called Glen or Loch something, with labels showing couthy characters in tartan dresses and all the wording in computer-generated Victorian script. Let's invent stupid legends about how it's made, about how it tastes like Harry Lauder's jockstrap, about how it*

conjures up the greatness of Scotland, as in shipbuilding, sheep-shagging, poor old drunken Charlie, the Brandy Prince; Bannockburn, the Sudan, Dunkirk, Culloden, Flodden, Hampden Park, Argentina, Andy Stewart, Moira Anderson, Highland Games, the Queen in tartan, Prince Charles in tartan, the streets of Edinburgh paved in tartan . . . the sea, the brave fishermen, the nuclear power stations, the brave scientists . . . och sir, the Americans and everyone else will love it. Let's sell it, sell it, sell it. Our souls, after all, have long gone. Now there's only the spirit left.'

The fat, florid stalker strips off his tweeds, revealing himself bathed in a shining luminosity, only his crimson cheeks glaring above the awful whiteness. 'Don't you recognise me, Macdonald? Don't you know who I am?'

And Macdonald falls on his knees in the mire, his cellphone tumbling into the peat bog. 'At last, at last you have revealed yourself! Oh great, oh true Spirit of Scotland, spirit of truth, spirit of adventure! I am your slave forever!'

Chapter One

THREE IS TOO FEW

Ishkivaishkivaishkivaishkivaishkiva . . . deep in the engine, below the rip-ping-cotton sound of the single-cylinder two-stroke, somewhere on the edge of my hearing, the hypnotic rhythm continues: lulling, calming, inspiring fantasies and dreams, bending hangovers such as the brain-shrinking, liver-inflating one I'm suffering from into strange visions from the beginning of whisky, or time, or life itself.

It is a dirty Skye morning in what some deluded souls are laughably describing as spring. I am on my way to the Talisker distillery from Portree, Skye's administrative capital – an odd mixture of fishing hamlet, holiday resort and The Village featured in Patrick McGoohan's *Prisoner* TV series.

The previous evening had found me in the Tongadale Hotel, a pleasantly modernised pub-with-bedrooms. My hard-class room had more than a touch of the youth hostel about it, so after a dismal dinner of fried farmed salmon, complete with its suspicions of organo-phosphate and fake pink colouring, I was forced, indeed obliged, to abandon an early bed for the bar. It was not a hard decision to make, especially as the Tongadale's atmospheric howff contained an excellent gantry of malts, some fairly obscure, and a unbelievable number of beautiful women. I ordered an As We Get It, the 57.3 per cent alcohol, direct-from-the-cask Macallan of unknown vintage, and settled on a stool.

Even with water, As We Get It – which is not bottled by Macallan themselves, but by Glasgow firm J. G. Thomson – is ferocious. It doesn't seem that old, but the Macallan hallmarks are there: sherry and wood. Getting drunk on this stuff is like being assaulted with an empty sherry cask, then being left for dead upside down inside it with an open tin of Evo-Stik beside you.

Anyway, one was enough for me at £2.00 a nip. A pint of excellent Beamish stout modified the raw blaze in my stomach to something less ulcer-exacerbating, as the barmaid tried to talk me out of having any more whisky. 'Ach, you're as well with beer at those prices. Anyway, there's no difference between whiskies, is there? It's all a con, isn't it?'

I mumbled something vague.

All around were fit, well-defined bodies, musculature rippling through lycra climbing gear. Skye: The Cuillins; big hills; Munro-bashing, mountain biking, abseiling, orienteering, suicide pacts – the participants in all the healthy pursuits offered by the most homogenised Hebride were gathered in the Tongadale to celebrate their survival in mostly moderate quantities of drink. The exception, as ever, being the rock climbers, a breed whose suicidal tendencies extend to competitive cirrhosis-inducement as a matter of course.

There was a mixture of accents, from multisyllabic educated north of England through Home Counties cheek-chewing to a variety of European dialects. A few homogenised Scots murmured in languid, moneyed tones. People do still speak Gaelic on Skye, but none was in evidence.

There were a lot of women, nearly all partnered by hairy men in furry purple jackets made out of flannelette sheets and costing hundreds of pounds. All the women looked expensively unmade-up, natural, blooming with the conquest of a thousand peaks and the impact of a million sun-lamp hours. The male and female body language on display indicated hours of relaxed wheel-twirling in BMWs, Escort XR3is, Sierra Cosworths, Volkswagen GTs and those cheap Porsches that look like big Triumph Spitfires. None glanced more than twice at the dishevelled figure in the old market-stall leather jacket. I looked so insignificant, so down-at-heel, and so unfit I could almost have been a local.

A blonde woman with a pronounced Spanish accent busily smoked Silk Cut Extra Mild No Death fags while the bleached Australian Surf Mountain steroid machine she was with, quite understandably, kept attempting fairly heavy foreplay in full view of everyone staring, fascinated, at the mirror behind the gantry.

Indescribably beautiful, the Spanish woman also stared at the mirror, catching and loving her own reflection and the antics of her partner, whose hormones could almost be heard panting rampantly above the interminable Dire Straits records on the CD juke box. They were both oblivious to everyone else in the pub. She shook her blonde tresses, pouted and posed like an extra in a sexist rock video, smoking for effect. Her boyfriend, meanwhile, tried to inhale her ear. She took no notice.

I ordered a ten-year-old Glenfarclas, much less hooliganesque than the As We Get It, though still oaky and heavily sherried, as the barmaid shook her head in sorrow at my folly. 'Two quid for that!' Then the door flew open.

Into this sauna-cleansed group of brightish, youngish things stepped a Creature From Another World. Short, rotund, with a crew-cut, thick pebble glasses and a scar running the full length of his face, he stopped in the pool of silence he had created by his entrance. 'Haallaw rare! Hizzit gawn, then, eh?'

It was a cliché Glaswegian drunk, a Rab C. Nesbitt only smaller, more intimidating, less predictably cuddly. There was a collective intake of breath. He went straight up to the Spanish/Australian alliance. 'Take yer tongue oota there, son! Ye dinna ken whaur that ear's been!' The lovely Spanish shoulders were embraced, unsteadily, by an arm clad in a mouldy Millets anorak. A look of utter disdain, complete contempt, was fired at the rolling intruder. His hands flew up in apology. 'Sorr . . . sorry hen. Didnae mean tae intrude. No offence, mate, no offence. Jim's the name.' He extended a hand to be shaken; it was ignored. 'Aw, hell'th you then. Fu'n hell'thye. Amfurra drink . . .'

'Hey, big man!' Jim's palm hit my shoulder. 'My wife, see my wife . . . bar, shit, shut, she's . . . aw the drink, she's away, off, weans an' aw. Know what ah mean?' He pulled out a crushed pack of Embassy Regal King Size and with a clatter dropped his ancient brass Zippo lighter.

Immediately, he turned to the bar manager, a friendly, polite young man in a white shirt, blue striped tie and a side parting. 'Get your act together, pal, awright?' Attempting, with infinite care, to bend down for his lighter, Jim's unbalanced bulk sprawled on the floor, sending nearby drinkers stumbling. He clambered up the side of the bar like a sailor trying to pull himself into a lifeboat.

'No offence, sir', said the bar manager. 'But I think *sir* should get his act together.'

There was no drink for Jim. He wheedled, he fell over again, he shouted and swore and eventually he was escorted off the premises by a posse of three Tongadale employees. 'No offence meant, no offence meant,' he kept crying in a bewildered voice. There was a brief silence when he had finally been put out, broken only by the sound of someone being spectacularly sick over the pub door. Jim's revenge. Doubtless there was no offence meant.

The equilibrium of the assembled drinkers had been upset. They were given no chance to recover. Three times Jim re-entered, on each occasion like a hot blast of hell, the smell of vomit like sulphur in a church, reminiscent of unthinkable horrors. Each time he was escorted out. I missed him. He was the only person, save the bar staff, who had spoken to me all evening.

By some quirk in the Tongadale's computer pricing system, I discovered, Tamdhu and Talisker were only £1.60 for a fifth of a gill. The ten-year-old Tamdhu tasted boringly Speysidish, mild and malty, but by this time my tastebuds were very probably somewhat seared, not to mention my braincells. The friendly barmaid, the one who thought I was wasting my cash on malts, had left, presumably overcome with disgust at my profligacy. The ten-year-old Talisker, however, cut through my inebriation completely: peat, seaweed, smoke and the sea assailed my olfactory organ. One slug, and an explosion of heat erupted in mouth, throat and gut. Harder, sharper than the comparable Islay malts, but with similarities nevertheless: all the wild mountainous grandeur, mist, rain and smelly seaweed of the west as opposed to Tamdhu's prim, proper, nicely cultivated agricultural flavour. Mind you, all those curries in my youth may have ruined my sensibilities as far as the subtleties of booze is concerned. Vindaloo burn-out claims another victim.

'She wants £20 a week to wash the strips. It's too much. Too bloody much.'

By nine o'clock the lycra-and-leggings brigade had started to drift away, back to the hotels and Winnebagos, or to the tents a few foolhardy masochists had insisted upon. At last I met some local Skyepersons, or *Sgiathnanaichs* as they are known in Gaelic. Round-buying set in, malts were abandoned, and the cheapest rubbing whisky became the order of what little was left of the day.

'Tell her £15 a week is plenty, for God's sake.'

If any of my new acquaintances had been Gaels, they would perhaps have ordered 'a wee one' – *te bheag*. Hence the name given to Sir Iain Noble's

Talisker-based blend. Rumours that the rather expensive Te Bheag, the only whisky with a gimmicky all-Gaelic label, had been given that name to ensure that any Gael using the vernacular in ordering a dram would pay a premium price for eponymity are doubtless vicious and untrue.

'Och, what difference does a fiver make, anyway?'

'It's the principle, isn't it? I've got a washing machine, you know. I could do it. Anyway £15 isn't bad at all.'

The conversation, concerning a wage claim by the woman who washes the local football team's strips every week, meandered on for about an hour and a half. The three – Andy, Terry and Calum, all in their early thirties – had been drinking since three o'clock. Andy in particular – stocky, flushed and intense – seemed somewhat the worse for wear.

'He went out for twenty minutes at three o'clock,' grinned Calum. 'Told his wife he'd be back in twenty minutes, anyway. Now look . . . what is it? Seven and a half hours later? I ask you – is this love, or what?'

'Come up to the house and meet the wife,' muttered Andy, who had been explaining about his new business venture. 'Come up to the house and I'll show you the picture-framing equipment. S'brilliant. Have you eaten? I'll phone Cathy and get her to cook us a meal. She's good that way.'

I tried to dissuade him, but he insisted on telephoning Cathy from the call-box outside. He returned to the bar, looking ashen faced. He also appeared to have lost the power of speech. Finally, he turned to me and said: 'One thing, even if I had to get involved with other people, this shop, this bloody business, one thing is, one thing is there's no *bloody* white settlers involved, no *English money!*' He shouted this at the top of his voice. Few health and efficiency tourists were left, and presumably everyone else was used to such displays. The resentment on Skye against the rich Englishmen and women whose purchasing power, especially in the boom of the 1980s, had pushed house prices out of the reach of local people, is immense, if normally hidden.

'My brother's been waiting ten years for a council house. He wanted to buy a wee stupid cottage for him and his wife, just one bedroom, and some fucking stockbroker bought it as a holiday home. Offered three thousand more than anyone else. Now my brother's in a caravan, freezing, and his wife's expecting in July.'

Swaying, Andy walked out of the Tongadale. This time he didn't return. I wondered if his wife was used to such behaviour, if she was sitting at home, nursing her wrath to keep it warm, and harbouring, like Andy, such deep-seated hatred against the incomers who were slowly but surely changing the way of life on their native island.

'Another dram, Tam?' Terry, slightly older than Calum and Andy, balding and with deep lines etched in his face, seemed most remote of the three. I nodded assent. 'What're you doing here, anyway?'

I said I was working. I muttered something about research into the whisky industry. The drinks arrived.

'Good stuff,' I said after a slurp I was hardly in any condition to taste. 'What I'd really like is to taste the real cratur. You know, like from one of the illicit stills, like the one that used to be out at Melvaig . . .'

Calum laughed uproariously, tossing the long dirty-blond hair from a pop-star handsome, narrow face. 'Ach, you don't need to go that far, Tam. I know a place in Vaternish, north of here, a still run by . . .'

'*Shut up*!' Terry didn't shout. He spoke quietly, in the strong, local accent, but with a kind of absolute authority which Calum did not quibble with. Terry turned to me. He hardly seemed drunk at all. 'Just why exactly are you snooping around? What sort of fucking research is it you're doing, chum? Eh?' There was considerable menace in his words and tone of voice, although none in his physical attitude. Terry was thin, slight even, which meant nothing at all. In my condition, an anorexic twelve-year-old could have beaten me to a pulp.

'Whassa problem, man?' I was being slurred, familiar and indulging in obsolete hipspeak as well, like a cliché narco cop trying to be hey! one of the boys. 'Look, I just want to taste the stuff, all right? I'm a reporter, only this isn't for any paper, okay, it's for . . .'

'Listen,' Terry sipped his dram, gazed into his glass as he spoke. 'I'll say this once.'

'I vill zay zis only vunce,' I giggled, too far gone to care that I was totally misreading the increasingly tense situation. Terry fixed me with a glare that penetrated my stupor.

'You're too stupid to be dangerous, so I'll give you a break. I could tell you the name, I could take you to the house, and I could get you the stuff to taste. But I'm not going to. And you're lucky this is me, and not some other bastard. Because what you've just done is like someone walking into Ullapool and asking if anyone knows where he can get some cocaine. Just try that and see how you like floating face-down in the harbour.'

I was beginning to sober up, but not quickly enough. Ullapool's infamy as a centre of drug smuggling was difficult to take seriously, despite the massive houses springing up on Scotland's northern Atlantic shores, reputedly drug-funded, and the incessant customs raids on innocent pleasure craft.

'So . . . listen, Terry. Have another drink. Do they use sugar and water as their base, or what? Beer, or wine or something? Or coke . . . Coca Cola, that is!'

'No,' said Terry. 'Enough. You're getting the benefit of the doubt, but that's enough.' And he got off his bar stool and left. Calum, after a short hesitation, followed. The bar manager looked at me inscrutably. Maybe he thought I was just about intelligent enough to be an undercover policeman.

Yo! Portree Vice! I was beginning to see myself as a West Highland Don Johnson, but when my legs gave way as I hopped off the bar stool to go to the toilet, I knew I wasn't. I was just a little relaxed. Too relaxed. Relaxed, in fact, as the proverbial newt.

The bird hits my goggles with what I can only describe as a splat, the kind of splat which occurs in Tom and Jerry cartoons, along with expressions such as *aargh! blam! keraang!* and *yaroo!* Or is that Billy Bunter? At any rate, this is a real bird, and whereas in a cartoon, the bird would have gone *ow! ow! ouch!*, taken on a mean and vengeful mien and pecked a hole in my helmet, this one doesn't. Instead, it is swept lifeless over my shoulder by the slipstream and on to the tarmac of the A850 north of Portree, where the Toyota Hi-Lux pick-up following too close behind me squashes it into a reddy-brown mess.

I stop the bike, heart pounding in delayed fright, wipe the suprisingly minor, feathery gunge from my oh-so-cool aviator goggles, and thank the Lord the bird didn't fly into my mouth. Raw, unplucked sparrow as a hangover cure doesn't appeal. I turn the unwieldy 250 combination around, bruising my legs as usual. Yes, it is indeed a reddy-brown mess, the poor little bird. Maybe it was a spring rarity, blown off course on its migration route. Now it isn't. I'm not, it has to be said, overcome with conservationist grief at this point. After all, I'm still alive, or approximately.

Still, many's the time on this trip so far that I might have been a reddy-brown stain on the tarmac, surrounded by bright orange steel and fibreglass courtesy of an unexpected meeting between the pre-German reunification workmanship of Messrs VEB Motorradwerk, Zschopau, and an articulated lorry. I count my blessings and proceed towards Carbost, where I hope to find the Talisker distillery, source of a small segment of this morning's hangover.

I'd made it to bed the previous night, apparently without any help. I'd even stumbled down scant hours later in time for a meagre, stomach-quelling breakfast of tea and scrambled eggs. Now there was only the rest of my life to face.

A motorcycle is actually a very good hangover cure, what with all that oxygen forcing its way into your lungs at high – or in my case, low to moderate – speed. But something is not right. Have the DTs set in, or is there something wrong with my steering, which has suddenly taken to wobbling in the most alarming fashion? And here we are in Carbost, but there is no distillery to be seen. What's going on?

I stop the bike in a lay-by, after the usual toe-scraping battle with the gear selector to find neutral. From the top of the heavily loaded sidecar I extract my simplistic Shell Central and Northern Scotland road map. I know Talisker is in Carbost. But Skye, bless its snow-capped peaks and horrid weather, has two Carbosts. The other lies to the south, through the Cuillins, but fortunately more or less on my way to Armadale, where I must catch the ferry to Mallaig at 1.15 p.m. A vicious gust of wind catches my map, which came free with a litre of two-stroke oil, and rips it neatly in two. Is this a sign?

I don't know. I do know something's seriously wrong with the bike. To hold it in a straight line, all my strength is required. Lifting one hand off the handlebars sends it lurching all over the road. I cling on for grim death or life and make it back to Portree in one piece, despite several nerve-wracking veers towards terrified tourists coming the other way.

In the forecourt of a Portree garage, I rummage in my mechanically ignorant way about the steering damper on top of the handlebars. It seems tight enough. Then I feel around underneath, at the nut which keeps the steering together from below, and incidentally holds on one of the main sidecar brackets. It comes off in my hand.

Ah well, I think, that's it then. I'll just have to hire a car and finish the trip that way. My mood is brightening. A hire car is fully allowable against tax. The hail, rain, sleet, snow and mud which have been my lot from Wick through Speyside to Skye will be beyond the windscreen. Everyone will understand. Won't they?

My attempt to answer this rhetorical question ends with me borrowing a shifting spanner from the garage, putting the lower steering nut back on and tightening it until my wrist squeaks. Proud of my technical prowess, I test the steering. It seems a bit stiffer, but the handlebars move. I profusely thank the mechanic, and set off south for Carbost Number Two.

There is a problem. The bike no longer centres itself after going round a turn. Sure, the wobble has disappeared. Instead, brute muscle power is needed for every twitch of the steering. Will I make it to Mallaig, my intended destination? Or is my fate inextricably bound up with the reddy-brown splotch on the road back at Carbost Number One? It starts to rain. Perfect.

Even the most cursory, the most dismissive traveller through Skye has to feel just a little intimidated going through Glen Varragill. On a slow, underpowered motorbike and sidecar, you feel very small indeed: like an insect crawling down the side of a toilet bowl. At Sligachan, bad weather has reduced the usual tented encampment of hill walkers and mountain junkies next to the hotel to the merest flutter of coloured nylon. Cloud and mist chop off the peaks of Sgurr nan Gillean and Bruach na Frithe, rendering their soaring gloom even more overpowering. An emotional chill adds to the bitter cold now seeping through my oilskins, leathers, woollen jumper, shirt, vest, silk longjohns and all-too-thin skin. This is not a landscape to be taken lightly.

'Unfortunately, the rain came down in torrents, and we had to don our waterproofs,' wrote Alfred Barnard in 1887 of his trip to Talisker from

Portree. 'This island is famous for rainy days, even in summer, and from experience we must confess that it comes down sometimes with a heaviness that washes away every particle of dust from your clothes, and pierces your mackintosh like duck-shot through a boat's sail.' I know exactly how he felt.

Up and over Glen Drynoch, with Beinn Bhreac frowning mistily on the left, and the turn-off down the slopes on the edge of Loch Harport is hard going. The perennial difficulty of turning the orange beast left, forcing the bike past the momentum of the sidecar, is compounded by the unbelievably stiff steering. Through the straggling hamlet that is Carbost Number Two, and down to the water's edge for the rather shabby collection of white buildings which make up Talisker. I pull into the carpark with relief. My hangover has reached the sweating, heart-palpitating, never-again stage, and combined with the weather, the handlebar hassles and my darkening mood, I'm not feeling too good.

Locally farmed oysters are being sold from a stall in the carpark at 50 pence each, open or closed. My Tongadale scrambled egg, mixed with the spiritual ingestions of the night before, is lying none-too-easily on my stomach, and my relationship with bivalves being what it is, I gladly and hastily pass by. Maybe Talisker is the ultimate accompaniment for the consumption of cold, slimy shellfish anaesthetised by lemon juice. I have no great desire to find out.

The Talisker reception centre is up a long flight of steps from the distillery courtyard. In the United Distillers mode, it is all dark wood and History with a capital H, but small and rather reluctant. There's a distinct impression that this is a distillery which would prefer to be left to get on with things, rather than be disturbed by hordes of tourists angling for a free dram. I should really pass on the dram, I ponder, given the blood alcohol I undoubtedly still possess. Be responsible, Tom! On the other hand, a wee livener might lift my spirits, the clouds off the Cullins and free my motorcycle steering from whatever demon possesses it.

'Would you like a guided tour?' The woman in the reception centre is recepting, all right, but she seems alone. 'If you do, you'll find Madge, second door on the left if you go back down the stairs. She's just started one.'

I clump off, aware as always in these situations that I appear to unsuspecting distillery guides like Mad Max, only much taller than Mel Gibson and considerably uglier. Still, here's Madge, jangling with lucky-charm jewellery. I wonder whether she's got any of the famous Talisker coinage, once minted by the management to control the workforce's spending, attached to her bracelets.

Madge seems fine, if a trifle over-humorous in a tinkly kind of way, as she leads our dozen-strong party of Americans, Germans, Italians and Spaniards around a distillery which Barnard, that nineteenth-century distillery junkie, should he return today, would undoubtedly find disappointing. Barnard was a man who liked things trim, technically up-to-the-minute and sparkling, and in the late 1800s he described, tediously as usual, 'all the newest appliances and vessels known in the art of distilling', which he found at Talisker. Today the distillery looks like it could do with a good wash and brush-up. Unkempt is the word.

Like Skye itself, the distillery's doings are all up and down. The need for more than a lick of paint here and there makes one wonder if the Talisker management follow the don't-move-that-spider's-web-it'll-spoil-the-flavour code of conduct. At any rate, traditional methods are obviously adhered to, starting with the soft peatiness of Talisker's own water supply.

Like so many distilleries, Talisker no longer malts its own barley. Instead, the barley is malted to the 'special secret Talisker specification' at the industrial Ord maltings next to the Ord Distillery near Muir of Ord. Which is a lot of Ords. Ord is not your actual traditional floor maltings, the kind shown in all the brochures with barley spread out for what seems like miles inside a building resembling a cross between Anne Hathaway's Cottage and St Paul's Cathedral. Ord is basically a modern, corrugated iron and concrete malt factory. I crunch some of the malted barley at Madge's invitation. And sure enough, it tastes malty and er, peaty. The peatiness comes from the heating process, when, traditionally, peat fires were used to stop the soaked barley germinating, and the aromatic smoke flavoured the barley. These days, at industrial maltings, peat will still be burned for a short time, but only to impart flavour. There are dark rumours of 'peat extract' being used as well, a bit like adding Worcestershire sauce to a dish. But it's only a rumour.

I still think it's cheating to have your barley malted somewhere else, but even distilleries with their own maltings tend, with a few honourable exceptions, to bring in the majority of their malt from elsewhere. They just don't tell you that in the advertisements. At Talisker, everything's done pretty much as per normal. You've got a mill to crush the malt, you've got a big tank called a mash tun with a nice copper top to mix it all up with hot water, you've got massive containers called washbacks to ferment the resulting sugary liquid – wort – once yeast has been added. Talisker has five copper stills: two big ones to turn the beery fermented mixture called wash into something as alcoholic as sherry called low wines; and then three small ones to produce something very alcoholic indeed, called spirit. The point with the lovely pot-stills, of course, being that they are inherently inefficient. The end result will only be about 72 per cent alcohol, thus retaining all the flavours from the malted barley and whatever is in the water. After three years in a cask you then have something rip-snortingly strong which can be called Scotch whisky. No one but an Italian or a blender would touch it until it's at least five years old, and in Talisker's case, eight is the minimum you'll find the malt bottled at.

Well, that's the basic story, anyway. There's more to it, but at the moment I'm fascinated by the fact that Talisker's spirit safe looks like it's been painted inside with Hammerite paint, and the smell in the still house is making me feel ill. I can't get those oysters out of my head. I'm also remembering the pristine state of Dalmore back in Alness, just as beautifully situated as Talisker, but mixing state-of-the-art improvements with the best of traditional methods and equipment. That's the application of American cash and influence, though.

Talisker has character, however, and it is much sought after to add depth and distinction to a number of blends. Seventy per cent of production goes into blended whiskies, the point being that just a wee drop of characterful Talisker goes a long way amidst all that nondescript grain whisky. Sherry casks are used for maturing the spirit, Madge explains, although surprisingly she goes on to admit that Talisker uses wine-treated casks as well. In other words, new oak painted with concentrated grape flavour so that the taste rubs off, year in year out, on the whisky. This nifty little practice evolved as a matter of necessity when the sherry producers of Spain, whose second-hand casks were much in demand for the maturing of sherry-flavoured whisky, began using big plastic drums instead. Maturing whisky in big plastic drums is not advisable. You'd then get poncy tasters describing 'a thrilling whiff of polycarbonate, overtones of polythene' when nosing that glass of special single-cask Old Glen Pretentious.

But the salt Skye wind, the reek from the seashore, sea spray – all the Talisker warehouse windows are perforated to allow that heady mixture in. Cut with local spring water from 70 per cent to 63 per cent alcohol, the spirit goes into the casks, losing roughly two per cent of its volume per year in evaporation – the so-called 'angels' share'. So adding a wee drop water to reduce the alcoholic strength spins it out a bit more: good economic sense.

Talisker is bottled at Leven in Fife, where the ten-year-old, the most common of current manifestations, is filtered and watered down again, this time using umm, distilled Leven water. The end result is 45.8 per cent alcohol, and a hell of a dram.

I decide I could do with one, and as the tour nears its end, I look forward to the traditional visitor's dram. But horror! We are shown to the shop, and obviously expected to buy something, like a Talisker tea-towel or whatever. Is this a Skye welcome? Okay, so you don't pay to see around Talisker but . . .

The truth is, at Talisker, you get your dram first, before being taken around the distillery. Maybe they think you won't notice quite how messy it is after a wee goldie. At any rate, temptation has been removed from me, and, increasingly sober, I wander past the oyster stall to the orange beast. Climbing into my yellow oilskins, I wonder if I'll make it to Armadale. If the engine starts first time, I superstitiously decide, I will. Six kicks later, 250 Stalinist cubic centimetres spit petulantly and snarl into reluctant life. Oh well.

It's thirty or so miles to Armadale, down from the mountainous wastes of Glen Drynoch and Glen Sligachan to the lovely, wooded coastline between Knock and Ardvasar. Through Broadford, cutting off down the single-track A851 at Harrapool, my shoulders are aching, and the bike's steering is still near-lethal. I keep stopping to make sure the steering nuts are still tight. The thought of the sidecar taking off in one direction and the bike in another is not exactly inspiring.

The weather varies between icy showers and threatening grey gloom. At Armadale there is a clutch of odd little shops and stalls, not to mention an inn which advertises cheap food and open fires on painted boards and looks like something out of Twin Peaks. I'm cold and starving, so in I go. There is no open fire. A tiny old woman peeks over the bar. Has she any food? A menu is clearly visible on the wall.

'Ah well, *she*'s not here, you see, and I don't normally work here, and maybe in fifteen minutes, I don't know, no, I don't.'

What about the menu?

'Ach well, yes, that's right, but you see the kitchen is closed.'

It's 12.30 p.m. I order a low alcohol beer.

'*Low* alcohol? Can you get that these days? Well, I never!'

At this point I decide I may have left the keys in the bike's ignition. I explain that I have to go and check, and leave the little old woman blinking over the top of the bar, doubtless relieved to have lost another customer.

Two minutes up the road is the Clan Donald Centre, where Americans with Macdonald connections go to check up on their Scawts heritage. There is a museum, gardens, a shop and a restaurant, all set in the beautifully converted remains of Armadale House and its stables. I putter slowly up to it, feeling a bit too scruffy for its Americanised Brigadoon realisation of Scawttishness. Still, hunger conquers my shyness *de couture*.

Inside the 'superb licensed restaurant', portion-control rules. Shepherd's pie is tiny and expensive. The award-winning building is impressive in its pseudo-baronialism, but the service is appalling in that classically Scottish dour, I'm-too-good-for-this-job-really kind of way. I'm almost glad that Americanisation hasn't spread to such an important aspect of the Scottish character. But I wait half an hour for coffee and change my mind.

Back to the pier, where a rather toffee-nosed second-hand book, craft and upmarket huntin'-shootin'-and-fishin' clothes store bears some unexpected fruit. A 1957 Chatto and Windus first edition of Compton Mackenzie's *Rockets Galore* for £3.50. The day's dreichness lifts for the first time. I buy a ticket for the crossing to Mallaig, take my place in the queue of cars, and buy a coffee from yet another oyster stall. What is it with folk who come to Skye on holiday? Do they flock to these oyster peddlers in the hope of a libido-lift? Bizarre. I perch on my for-once-dry saddle and immerse myself in Mackenzie's wonderfully funny grasp of Hebridean modes and manners as they clash with militarism gone crazy:

'Ah, come in, come in gentlemen,' said genial John Farquharson. 'What can I offer you? I have a rather special bottle of malt here.'

'Malt?' Colonel Bullingham, a button-headed man with pale-blue prominent eyes, echoed in surprise.

'Malt whisky.'

'Thanks very much,' said the Colonel. 'I'll try anything once. Fill it up with soda, please.'

A Yamaha GPZ sweeps into the queue with a dry burble. Off gets a serious motorcyclist, in Gore-Tex wet-weather gear and leather breeks. He spares me not a glance, on my orange combination with the prominent L-plate on the back. Besides, I am reading a book, and obviously a dilettante pretend biker. However, I am keen to affirm my membership of the company of lone bikers. After all, haven't I travelled more than a thousand miles in dreadful conditions? Am I not an adventurer? Am I not wearing a leather jacket with a Vincent badge? I go over and say hello.

Bob is feeling a bit sorry for himself. 'I came up from Glasgow for a supposed British Motorcyclists' Federation camp, and half the tents got blown away the first night,' he shakes his large, extremely hairy head. 'Soft bastards checked into hotels and bed-and-breakfasts. This morning I was the only one left on the camp site.' I tut-tut in agreement. Imagine that. Soft bastards.

In comes the MV *Iona*, and the long process of loading cars via the old-fashioned lift-and-turntable begins: Bob and I are last on, Bob's powerful GPZ almost sent flying by a car's careless acceleration off the turntable, which spins violently to the left. I'm happy to be relatively stable on three wheels, despite my muscle-building steering. But then, I'm not a member of the Institute of Advanced Motorcyclists, and Bob is.

Mallaig is half an hour away, and the sea seems smooth. I leave the orange beast with the GPZ and Bob for company. 'I'm not leaving the bike,' he declares grimly. 'You never know what might happen at sea.' I jam the MZ in gear and squeeze through the serried ranks of cars to the stair which leads to the cafeteria. That shepherd's pie might never have existed. My hangover has all but disappeared, and the smell of frying bacon and bad Calmac coffee from the galley is seductive. As Skye slips away behind me, I bite into a cholesterol special, and promise myself that I will become a teetotal, vegetarian, physical fitness freak. But not just yet. There's still a long way to go.

Making Whisky the Easy Way (with common errors listed)

WARNING: Attempts to follow these instructions may result in

(1) Inebriation, or
(2) Prosecution, or
(3) Sudden death.

Steeping, Sprouting, Smoking

First, grow some barley. For Scotch whisky, you'd think this should be in Scotland – and Scottish barley is probably the best, producing more whisky per tonne than that from any other country. A few distillers recognise this, but some cheapskates are interested only in cheapness. 'Come on,' they'll say, 'where the barley comes from doesn't really matter.' Some lie in their advertisements and say it comes from Scotland when it doesn't. Most of it comes from wherever there happens to be a barley mountain, with maybe a little Scottish stuff being mixed in for 'character'.

To make alcohol you need sugar. To get the sugar out of barley you need an enzyme to break down the starch. That enzyme, or rather a mixture of enzymes called diastase, can be released through the malting process. Traditionally, you steep the barley in water for about 48 hours, then spread it out in a big, well-ventilated space to germinate for a week or so. The barley warms up, starts to sprout, and you know the starch has been turned into sugar. You've got to stop the stuff growing – but how?

Here is what you do. You heat it over a peat fire, and the smoke sticks to the grain, giving you a source of sugar which tastes of, well, barley, smoke and peat.

That's what you're supposed to do, but hardly anybody does exactly that anymore. The honourable exceptions include Glen Garioch, Laphroaig, Bowmore, Balvenie, Highland Park, and Springbank/Longrow, and some of them don't use peat exclusively for the drying. Everybody else gets their malted barley delivered from giant industrial maltings (although Glen Garioch do a rather secretive trade in small quantities of their much-prized malt), and because peatiness in whisky is no longer considered universally attractive, some malt is hardly peated at all. It is arguable that this despicable centralisation of malt production has – quite deliberately – robbed some whiskies of their former smoky characters, and some distilleries now pay little attention to the malt they use. Only Glen Garioch and the purists at Springbank have gone for the exclusive local-barley, traditionally-malted-on-the-premises-and-turned-into-whisky approach in recent years. Some deluded souls advertise their whisky as unpeated, which is a bit like advertising smoked salmon which doesn't taste of smoke: Glengoyne, the nonsensical whisky.

One little and potentially very nasty problem which has reared its little head in recent years has been the presence in some strains of barley of an enzyme thought to be highly carcinogenic. Some distilleries now insist on their barley being screened for its presence, while others have sulphur burned in the malting kiln to kill this nasty little living thing stone dead.

Cooking

Okay, so you've got your malt. Crush it up, grind it down, put it in hot water and stir. This porridgey gloop is called mash. Local water, untouched by aluminium hydroxide, fluoride or chlorine, but preferably nicely brown and peaty, should be used, again imparting its particular character. Do some distilleries just use tap water today? Is Paris a city? You drain off the resulting sugary liquid, and what you do now is brew. This sweet liquid, called wort, is put in big wooden tubs called washbacks, yeast is added, which immediately changes the liquid's name from wort to wash, and for three days, it bubbles and foams and becomes alcoholic.

(Because you're environmentally friendly, have an interest in ecology and want to make money, you sell the solids left from the mash to farmers. It is called draff. You feel pretty good about this.)

Nowadays, some distilleries use stainless steel or older cast-iron washbacks. They're easier to clean, but is there a secret in the larch or Oregon pine of traditional washbacks? The Findhorn New Age Community thinks so, anyway, because they buy the old ones to turn into houses. And perhaps bits of old yeast stick to the wood, or that mouse nest tucked away at the bottom, or the bird droppings and cat pee, add their own *je ne sais quoi* . . .

Some distillery workers will drink the wash, swearing it is a great hangover cure. As they are almost certainly hopeless alcoholics, this advice should be ignored. The wash, at about eight per cent alcohol, is stronger than Carlsberg Special. But you need to make it stronger still.

This is where the serious cooking comes in. You need a big copper kettle-like thing, wide at the bottom, less so at the top, with a narrow pipe leading in coils through a tank of cold water to a kind of catchment bowl at the bottom. This is called a pot-still. You heat the wash in the big copper kettle, and because alcohol boils at a lower temperature than water, the alcohol vaporises first. Up it goes to the top of the still, where it shoots down the coiled pipe, or worm, and condenses. Hey presto! – alcohol. The glutinous gunge left in the bottom of the still makes you happy, because you can sell it to those gullible farmers as well.

But the alcohol you've got is not pure; it's just not good enough. It's about 20, 25 per cent spirit, equivalent to a down-and-out's proprietary wine. This is an inherently inefficient system you're using, so you have to do the whole distillation again using the not-good-enough alcoholic mix, called low wines. The result is about 72 per cent pure alcohol.

There are a few problems here. When you're going around for the second time, you need to avoid the foreshots, the first lump of distillate which comes out of the still. This not only tastes horrid, it could be seriously poisonous, containing lower alcohols and esters. The same goes for the last bit of the distillate, the feints. All you want is the nice clean clear bit in the middle, the heart or middle cut. You don't want to go blind, do you?

How high and wide your still is will definitely affect the taste of the finished product. So will the angle of the pipe at the top which goes to the condenser. Some say the kind of fuel used to heat the stills will affect the final taste. Others say that even one dent in a still will change the ineffable character of the whisky. So will the removal of even a spider's web from the still-house. And there are these funny winged creatures at the bottom of the garden.

Now, doing this at home is almost indecently easy, if you have access to an old copper water tank, a braising torch and some copper central heating pipe. It is also totally illegal, because such spirit has to have tax paid on it. Illicit distillers nowadays tend to ignore the malting process, and use either bags of sugar in water or home brew kits to get their 'wort'. The resultant moonshine will normally taste like turps, will strip the lining out of your mouth unless diluted, and could result in a prison sentence if the customs and excise men catch you. If you fail to run off the nasty lower alcohols and things, it could also kill you.

Maturing

But say you've got a licence, and all's legal. The spirit that you've distilled is not whisky. It cannot legally be called Scotch whisky until it has been aged in Scotland in oak barrels for at least three years. Doing this will mean that, through evaporation and absorption, the spirit will begin to lose some of the nasty fieriness it had, and absorb the taste and colour of the wood and the air outside. So if you're next to an oil refinery, your whisky will taste of sulphur. If you're next to the smelliest, seaweediest beaches imaginable, your whisky will taste of that.

Other tastes can be added to the whisky, depending on what was in the barrel before you put in the spirit. Most people want old sherry casks, to add that deep amber colour and rich, sweet flavour. Others use second-hand casks from the American whisky industry, where bourbon is stored in oak barrels which have been charred on the inside. Others fake it, using new casks with grape juice painted on. And a few unscrupulous people, unable to get the right colour from mixing up casks from various years, will add a touch of spirit of caramel (perfectly legal it is too) to give the right romantic shade. This little trick is common in the producing of blends, using various malts to flavour cheap grain whisky, and not unknown in the vatting of malts. To get a consistent flavour and colour, barrels of differing ages and even of different types from the same distillery are used to produce a 'blend' of single malt. If it says ten years old on the label, that means the youngest whisky in there is ten years old. On the other hand, there are 'vatted pure malt' whiskies like Tobermory, which use a mixture only of malts from various distilleries.

Whisky snobs invest all aspects of the maturing process with a kind of ineffable, holy mystery. But here is a salutary note, and encouragement for all illicit distillers (traditionally called smugglers) should you decide (and we advise against it) to pursue such a lawless course.

The head stillsman at a certain Speyside distillery informs me that he and some friends, as an experiment, made some moonshine in their kitchen using a very basic home-made still and fermented sugar and water. They aged the result for twenty-four hours, added some caramelised sugar, a dab of Sanatogen Tonic Wine and water, and took the result to a local 'connoisseur' of fine whisky, claiming it was Old Bollocks 1962, recently discovered mouldering in an oloroso cask in a locked storeroom. It was pronounced by the 'expert' as the finest dram he had ever tasted.

Chapter Two

DEVIL'S ISLAND

There had been whisky in our house for as long as I can remember, hidden away in the bottom of a locked sideboard along with bottles of sherry and brandy, not one of them ever opened. My father, a dentist, tended to receive such spiritual gifts at Christmas and New Year, from grateful patients whose teeth he had religiously tended, whose abscesses he had drained, and whose dentures he had designed.

But our family did not drink at all, at least not until I was eleven and a caravan holiday in France seemed to open my parents' eyes and mouths to the possibilities of moderate imbibing. As members of an evangelical sect called the Christian Brethren, a Scottish equivalent of the furiously teetotal Plymouth Brethren, drink had been anathema. Mum and Dad's upbringing in this then-working-class sect, which was firmly rooted in the industrial wastelands of steel-and-coal producing Lanarkshire, instilled a fear of spirits. Even, as the 1960s became the 1970s, the relaxing influences of an annual fortnight of Mediterranean sun, an ever-increasing circle of friends and a professional lifestyle far removed from their working-class background did not extirpate that fear. A glass of wine was all right; a brandy after the meal was regarded with suspicion. 'All good things in moderation,' Dad would say.

The source of their fear was something I knew about too. Some of my earliest memories were of trips to Bellshill or Motherwell to see relatives, passing through the lurid, monstrous fires of Colville's now-dead steelworks at Cambuslang, and from the back seat of the family Morris Oxford glimpsing the shadowy, gas-lit horror of dead-drunk miners on a Bellshill Friday night, their wage packets turned to piss on the street, their families left to starve. It was from such backgrounds that people came to the Lord in spectacular conversions at the Gospel Hall, and bore witness to their salvation every Sunday for decades to come.

So the bottles in our sideboard remained firmly sealed, although I can remember one occasion when my sister and I opened the forbidden cupboard, and smelt a rich, sweet scent which seemed to hold all the excitement and evil of the flesh and the world we were being constantly warned against at Sunday school and blisteringly aggressive gospel services.

As myself and my two sisters grew, things changed. I can remember brandy being produced during a spectacularly awful ferry crossing from Southampton to Cherbourg, and teaspoonfuls administered to 'settle our stomachs'. To this day, brandy makes me feel sick, although I have a kind of hypnotic desire to drink it on board a ship. Whisky was occasionally used in the case of bad colds for weak, hot toddies, along with homoeopathic shock pills and something hideously minty called Life Drops.

At the age of twenty-five, I was the inheritor both of my parents' religion and their moderation. As a born-again, full-time evangelist of the street-credible, let's-capture-the-youth-of-today variety, I drank sparingly, and never spirits. Then my mother died, quite suddenly on the Spanish island of Majorca. After an awful, grief-defying stay there to help with the inevitably nightmarish logistics, Mum's body was flown home, and I found myself in my father's house, dry-eyed, wound up to a desperately high pitch and unable to sleep.

There was no beer, no wine. But in the successor to that childhood sideboard I found an unopened bottle of Old Antiquary, one of Dad's dental presents. I had no idea how to drink whisky, although I had a vague memory that you added water to it. I poured an inch or so into a glass, and knocked half of it back.

After the initial coughing, spluttering shock, the heat hit me and I began to feel better. Adding water seemed to me a travesty then, defusing and diluting so as to render the spirit tame, innocuous. Neat seemed best that night, although I think I only managed two large ones before I fell asleep on the sofa.

Three years passed before I began my drinking career in earnest, abandoning religion for an ageing adolescent fling through rock'n'roll journalism, drink, sex, night-clubbing and television work, not necessarily in that order. Drugs remained as spirits had been for my parents: a demon in the corner, not be messed around with. At least, not very much.

But drink for me was either a designer beer pose or a passport to oblivion. The taste hardly mattered. Pakora sauce and gin cocktails, Furstenberg (the strong beer drunk by German down-and-outs, and very popular among Glasgow hipsters in the mid-1980s) and vodka mixtures. Anything would do.

Then, whilst filming for some forgotten programme in Stornoway, I tasted Johnny Walker Black Label, and realised that it was different from other blended whiskies. Departing the hassles and heartbreak of Glasgow, I moved to the Shetland Islands, moderated and upgraded my drinking bit by bit, and encountered various malts: Glenmorangie, Talisker, Glenfiddich, Macallan. I read John Fowles' *Daniel Martin*, where the eponymous hero drinks only Laphroaig. I had to try it. Once the peaty, seaweedy power of Islay, that island taste, exploded on my palate, I knew my tastebuds had found a spiritual home. My maternal grandfather had come from Islay, I reasoned with the perfect clarity of two drams. Therefore I was genetically inclined to the sledgehammer attack of Lagavulin, the ozone kick of Laphroaig, the bigness of Caol Ila. As I drank less and less overall, I became a whisky drinker, one with a definite Islay bias.

Brief flirtations with transatlantic pretenders such as Wild Turkey, Jim Beam, Jack Daniels and trans-Irish Sea seductions from the likes of Paddy's aside, that is what I have remained. When Jimmy, the manager of Melven's bookshop in Inverness, suggested that I write a book about whisky, because any book about whisky sold at least a few copies, it seemed like a fine wheeze.

At the very least, I'd be able to claim, for the only time in my life, all my drink supplies as legitimate expenses against tax.

How to go about it, though? I liked whisky, sure, but I was hardly a connoisseur. I wasn't fat, old and bald with a face like a side of bacon, at least not every day, and I didn't come from Edinburgh or speak with a public-school drawl. So I couldn't be. I liked rock music, cars, guitars, cheap boats and trash films, not salmon fishing and deer murdering, the usual mythic accompaniments to a dram or twelve. Nobody would take me seriously if I began pontificating about the caramel, lemon-grass tobacco smelly socks meets mouldy armpits nose of some godawful fifty-year-old whisky from Glen Hell, least of all myself. So sure, write a book about whisky, but what kind of book?

The answer began to gel on Devil's Island in the late summer of 1991.

Well, one island and two causeways up from Devil's Island, to be precise, on Orkney's mainland. Burray lay between St Mary's, where I was staying with my family at the Commodore Motel, and the now-infamous isle of South Ronaldsay. Since February, I'd been virtually commuting to Orkney as one of the biggest stories of the year went from shock to shock, horror to horror, revelation to revelation. Lord Clyde's inquiry into the incarceration of nine South Ronaldsay children amid allegations of systematic, ritual sexual abuse had begun on 26 August, and, rather than leave my family for the fortnight's coverage I was ordered to give it, we booked into a self-catering chalet at the Commodore.

It was a bizarre, draining, distressing experience, reporting on the early stages of the inquiry. In some ways, having my wife and two children on Orkney was worrying: after all, the Commodore was stacked with social workers. 'One shout and they'll have them in care,' we joked nervously. On the other hand, what if there was something to the allegations? Were there weird people in Orkney preying on children? My wife was accosted by a stranger on an isolated beach, without, thankfully, any harm being done. It was a tense time.

The bike saved me. I'd hired a ten-speed pushbike from a Kirkwall shop, and every morning rode the eight miles to the inquiry at Kirkwall Town Hall from St Mary's. Every night I pedalled back, shedding some of the day's dirt along with a few centilitres of sweat and a few grammes of fat.

It was the first time I'd ridden a bicycle regularly over a reasonable distance for more than a decade. It was hard going at first, on the hilly, joyrider-prone A961. I'd be overtaken every morning by cars laden with social workers, parents, lawyers, speeding towards their daily confrontation while my muscles shrieked in protest.

But gradually I came to love those rides in the morning and early evening, just as an autumn chill was beginning to descend on Orkney. Strange movements in the grass beside the road, otters, voles, all kinds of birds . . . the smells of fresh fields in the morning, the beginnings of winter manure aromas, the eternally changing, enormous skies. And, warmed by the exertion of cycling, the soft Orkney drizzle ceased to be an enemy.

The great joy every morning was to reach the top of the long hill which sweeps down into Kirkwall itself, Holm Road. Over to the left, far below on the shores of Scapa Flow, lay the grey, squat mass of the Scapa Distillery, near the always-smoking Kirkwall incinerator. But next to the road, almost on the summit, was Highland Park, all pagoda chimneys, wrought iron and old stonework: the perfect image of a distillery.

As I swooped down, the bike whirring and chattering like some obscure plunging bird, the smells would hit me. Sometimes it was the acrid peat fumes from the malting kiln. Other days it was the sharp tang of carbon dioxide from the fermentation. On the occasional morning, I thought I caught a whiff of lower alcohols from the still room. But for the second week, all of these mingled with the overpowering scent of sherry and oak from a new delivery of used sherry casks. Where had I smelt that before, I asked myself for my five last bicycling days, as the autumn grew inexorably closer. Where?

I remembered eventually. It was the smell of that locked sideboard back in childhood. The scent of wine, spirit and wood, the child's image of the flesh-pleasing adult evils which even then we knew they feared because, secretly, they wanted to be seduced by them. And soon we would fear them too.

I was back in Orkney several times as autumn dragged into winter, and the Clyde Inquiry wended its interminable and hideously expensive way through the morass of the South Ronaldsay affair. Nothing became clearer. Christmas arrived, with strange lawyers' parties and journalists covering the inquiry appearing in a local pantomime. Then Hogmanay and Ne'erday were behind us, and it all began again.

I was in Kirkwall in February, for a children's panel hearing linked to the South Ronaldsay case, and found myself with an afternoon and the next morning to kill. It was cold, brutally cold, with flurries of snow skittering up the flagstoned streets of the town, battering at the magnificent red sandstone of St Magnus Cathedral. In the sea-worm-eaten wood interior of the Albert Hotel's Bothy Bar, I sipped a pint of locally brewed Dark Island beer, and pondered the idea of a whisky book. I ordered a Highland Park twelve-year-old to go with the last half of my pint, and what should have been blindingly obvious struck me: here I was in the home of Highland Park, Britain's most northerly distillery. Why not go and have a look at it?

At the very least, there might be a piece for the paper in it. I'd already interviewed the local tourist supremo, whose concern about the alleged widespread child sex abuse in Orkney matched most of his fellow islanders: how would it affect Orkney's hitherto unsullied image? He was glad to report that all the TV coverage, complete with scenic views of too-quaint-for-comfort St Margaret's Hope, had apparently brought an upsurge in tourist bookings. I hoped that no enterprising paedophile was secretly organising child abuse tours of Orkney.

I fancied just turning up at Highland Park anonymously, but when I telephoned to find out the opening times, it turned out the distillery was closed to visitors for the refurbishment of the reception centre. I asked to speak to the manager. 'Look,' I said. 'I'm a reporter, I'm in town, and I wondered if I could have a chat about a book I'm thinking of doing about whisky. Maybe you could tell me a bit about Highland Park.'

Within half an hour I was nursing an enormous dram in Jim Robertson's office, neither his youth nor his bluff, north of England accent quite what I had expected. What I received from Jim, though, was considerably more than a dram. It was a personal, more than somewhat biased foundation course in whisky-making.

To make whisky, what you need, basically, is barley, water and a fuel source, preferably peat. Malting the barley is mostly done at industrial maltings like Moray Firth Maltings in Inverness or Ord at Muir of Ord. But I knew that Highland Park malted its own barley in traditional floor malting barns, just the way it has since 1798. Pretty damn impressive, Jim, I ventured, wanting to display my knowledge.

'To be honest, we only do 20 per cent of our own malting. Hardly anybody does 100 per cent malting anymore and nobody does it with 100 per cent Scottish barley all the time. But from our point of view the 20 per cent we do is vital. The floor malting is very gentle on the malt, and we look after it individually.'

He illustrates this with a quick tour round the maltings. It's simply stunning, with the great quiet lakes of germinating barley spread out after their two or three days' soaking in the steep tanks. Old-fashioned wooden barrows, called chariots, are used to spread it out, and it is regularly turned by hand. Two cats patrol for any extraneous creatures, their names, whimsically enough, are Malt and Barley. 'They earn their keep,' says Jim.

But not as much as Billy does. Billy is a kilnsman, and we find him like some mythical firemaster, shovelling peat into the flames of the kiln. 'I've been here over thirty years,' he says, 'and my father before me. He's fine, by the way,' he tells Jim. 'But they won't let him have his dram in the hospital.' We all shake our heads over this woeful injustice.

'Some say they can taste heather in Highland Park,' says Jim, 'and there are stories of heather being thrown in with peat to give it that taste. Back when Barnard was touring the distilleries in the nineteenth century, there was supposedly a heather house, so maybe they burned heather then. Nowadays the peat we use is itself pretty heathery in its top section, but that's all. Some of it is black, some of it is heathery.'

'I've never seen heather being burned, anyway,' says Billy. 'Mind you, I've seen great lumps of heather-root being thrown in along with the peat, stuff the peat-cutting machine churns up. Never bothered too much about it. It just comes along with the peat.'

In fact, coke is the main fuel for Highland Park's kilns. 'Basically the peat's for flavour,' says Jim. 'We get the kiln up to temperature with coke and then we use peat for twelve hours. After that the peat reek doesn't stick to the grain anyway, so there's no point in doing it any longer. You're just wasting your time.'

Attempts have been made to imitate the Highland Park malt on a commercial scale off the islands, but all have failed, even when using the distillery's own Hobbister peat. So the distinctive pagoda-like chimneys of Highland Park are likely to survive for a while, and as more than a tourist attraction. It must be said that seeing Billy or one of his colleagues labouring in the flickering peat-light is an unforgettable experience. Like being given a guided tour of one of hell's more welcoming dungeons.

Highland Park, however, is not generally to be compared with Hades. It is an immaculate place. The old-fashioned maroon-painted iron of the Porteous malt-mill shines. The new Lauter mash-tun – 'the only bit of stainless steel in the place' – sits in machined splendour, ready to churn around the sugary mash of crushed malt and water. The huge larch washbacks have recovered from their role in the Second World War as baths for Canadian troops stationed at Scapa Flow, and now the wort ferments away without interference from bodily bacteria. The copper pot-stills gleam dully just as stills are supposed to; the spirit safe, the locked brass-and-glass box which prevents any unscrupulous person sampling the cratur before duty has been paid on it, glints in yellow perfection. There are two wash stills, where the eight per cent alcohol is distilled into 20 per cent low wines. Then there are two spirit stills, which produce the final magic.

'Everybody says you need soft water to make good whisky.' Jim Robertson likes to explode whisky myths. Trained as an industrial engineer, he is mostly a scientist, and only partly a reluctant alchemist. 'We've got very hard water, so there goes another piece of nonsense. I believe, however, that it's very hard to improve on traditional methods, on the whole.'

The casks I smelt on those freewheeling runs down the hill were indeed sherry casks, but Highland Park matures in used bourbon casks too. Charred on the inside, it used to be illegal in America, Jim tells me, to re-use the oak barrels, so they were sold cheaply to Scotland. Now they are like gold dust, and distilleries pull all sorts of barrelesque tricks: knocking together old bits of cask, wine treatment, or simply using new oak, which means the resultant whisky can be virtually colourless. How does your dram get that nice brown colour, then, if not from the cask? Amazing what you can do with a bit of caramelised sugar.

Not at Highland Park, though. 'We use a mixture of sherry and bourbon casks. Obviously they give different characters and flavours, but it's not just the whisky from one cask that goes into a bottle. There is a mixing. We mix different flavours, different colours to get the match for bottling a consistent product.'

So what makes Highland Park special? For Jim, it's everything in the process, although he admits that the maturing in the Orkney environment may be crucial.

'Ten, twelve, fourteen years in this kind of special climate must make a difference. It's different from Islay, from Speyside. It's even different from Scapa, just down the hill. And inevitably it's different from what it might have been fifty or a hundred years ago. Whisky is an organic product. It changes, just as the water, the peat, the air and the grain change with time.'

I'd tasted Highland Park twelve-year-old often, but that bitterly cold afternoon, drinking it at the distillery itself was something of a religious experience. As Neil Gunn says, and him an excise officer too, whisky is the warming spirit for the cold northern temperament. Everyone, cold and northern or not, should try it, preferably on an Orkney winter's day with the snow flurrying outside, and fresh from the sight of a roaring malting kiln being loaded with peat. You can taste the peat, all right. You can even taste the heather. After a few, you can taste just about anything you damn well like.

I told Jim about my idea for a book about whisky, maybe something a bit irreverent, a bit wild, a bit, well, down-market. Wasn't it about time the old buffers had such a precious commodity as malt wrested from them? Shouldn't a (slightly) younger generation get to wrap their lips around a bottle or two? Jim was pessimistic.

'I don't think we're particularly succeeding in attracting the younger drinker,' he said. 'The problem is that the younger palate doesn't quite appreciate the flavours. As you get older, you tend to appreciate less sweet drinks, like red wine as opposed to white. When I was younger I hated red wine. Whisky's a bit like that.'

Well, maybe. I took my leave from Jim still convinced that the market for malts was certain to open out to the less tweedy consumer. Malt whisky was just begging to become a mega-fashionable cult. Little did I know that in Continental Europe it had already done so.

Anyway, if proof were required of how masterworks like Highland Park knock everyday blends – those combinations of mostly cheap industrial grain whisky and dozens of young malts – into the proverbial urinal, it was on the wall of Jim Robertson's office. It was a letter from Troon, in Ayrshire, the town I was raised in. The address was Piersland Lodge, which is now a luxury hotel but which used to be a Christian guest house. Winston Churchill once stayed there, but that was when it was owned by the Walker family, not when it was a Christian guest house. The Walkers, that is, as in Johnny Walker. The Whisky Walkers of Kilmarnock and elsewhere. The letter, dated 1914, was from Allan Walker. This is what it said:

Many, many thanks for the two bottles of twenty-year-old Highland Park. I have duly sampled one, and am in the process of conversion to the idea that HP is the only whisky worth drinking, and Johnny Walker only fit for selling to deluded Sassenachs.

My point precisely. If only the stuff wasn't so bloody expensive.

Of course, in the days before 1798 when Highland Park became a licensed distillery, it was the site for Magnus Eunson's antics in 'smuggling', as illicit distilling was known. A United Presbyterian church officer, he was wont to hide his supplies under the pulpit of the kirk, and according to Alfred Barnard, in one of his less boring passages, 'was accustomed to give out the psalms in a more unctuous manner than usual if the excise officers were in the church, as he knew he was suspected.' Hearing, one day, that the church was to be searched, Eunson had all the kegs hidden under a clean, white cloth in his own house, a coffin lid added to complete the effect. When the customs officers arrived, having discovered nothing in the church, they found Eunson and his household kneeling solemnly around the 'body', weeping and wailing for all their worth. When the dread word 'smallpox' was whispered in the customs chief's ear, they hotfooted it out.

Religion, deception and the true spirit of Orkney come together nicely in what is almost certainly just a yarn. But it's a good yarn, and one that bears repetition, even if people sometimes repeat it about the wrong distillery, in the wrong part of Scotland, using names other than Eunson. But that's oral history for you.

The next morning, after by Orkney standards a spectacularly sober night at the Kirkwall Hotel, I took a taxi to Scapa's huddle of buildings just outside Kirkwall, overlooking Scapa Flow itself, tomb of the Kaiser's scuttled fleet and now a mecca for souvenir scavenging divers.

'We've got no secrets,' says Ronnie MacDonald, manager and possessor of a name well known in mountaineering circles. Tall, thin, very Scottish and, despite his protestations, seemingly a bit suspicious of me, he comes from a distilling background. He was brought up in the heart of Speyside, where his father was a distillery manager. But then, nearly everybody's is on Speyside. In fact, the previous day Jim Robertson had gleefully informed me that Ronnie's dad, on a trip to Orkney, had come for a tour of Highland Park and left after buying a bottle, uttering the words, 'this is a real distillery'. Ronnie won't confirm this tale, for some reason.

I'm writing a book about whisky, I say. Something a bit off the wall, not your normal tasting guide. In fact, I reveal, made expansive by a livener of salty, banana-and-coconut Scapa eight-year-old, at 10 a.m., I know nothing much about whisky. It'll be a sort of idiot's guide, I think. I do like Highland Park, though, I confide. Ronnie's face grows longer. I'm obviously not making a good job of this.

To tell the truth, I don't much like Scapa. I've tried hard, even including a crazed charge through every conceivable variety of the stuff held in the cellars of the Kirkwall Hotel, during one of the sex-abuse-scandal press binges which saw, among other things, an emotional and fortunately ill-fated attempt by a colleague to steal a bulldozer and drive it into the harbour. Even a 1963 mortgage-only dram didn't make much impact, possibly due to the lateness of the hour and the fact that I was lying on the floor at the time. Okay, it tastes of coconut and banana and you can detect the saltiness of Scapa Flow, but hell, who wants to drink salty coconut and banana liqueur? Where Highland Park is slightly sweet and peaty and muscular, Scapa is thin, unpeated and, matured in bourbon casks as it is, lacking the undoubted depth sherry barrels give a whisky over a decade or two. Then again, Scapa is not sold as a single malt, other than through independent bottlers like Elgin's wondrous Gordon and MacPhail or Campbeltown's cottage-bottlers, Cadenheads. So maybe Allied Distillers, which own Scapa, know a thing or two, piling 90 per cent of it off for blending.

That's what I think, anyway. I don't tell Ronnie though. He is explaining that he can't work out why, in 1885, J. T. Townshend should leave Balindalloch – his home town and curiously enough, Ronnie's too – to set up a distillery in Orkney. Thus Scapa was born. Not that too much is left of the original plant which was rebuilt in 1959. The Royal Navy was billeted at Scapa during the Second World War, illustrating what seems like a definite bias in Orkney towards housing soldiers and sailors in distilleries. Doubtless the RN had baths in the washbacks just like the Canadians did up at Highland Park.

There are no maltings at Scapa, and the malt brought in by sea from Kirkcaldy is pretty standard, according to Ronnie, although it is unpeated. It's a small two-still distillery, with an unusual wash still of the so-called Lomond design. This resembles an oversized, upside-down dustbin made of copper, or the expanded head of Dorothy's Tin Man. Instead of being boiled with heat applied from below, the Lomond still has steam pipes inside its jacket, thus giving, so it is said, a heavier, oilier result. Of course, at Scapa, a smaller, traditionally elegant pot-still comes up with the finished firewater, converting the low wines into higher things, but the use of the indisputably ugly Lomond still must have an effect. As will maturation in the scouring sea breezes of Orkney.

'It's a very fine malt,' says Ronnie. 'People say they can detect salt in it, and that must be from the maturation here.'

Outside, the snow is piling up, and I'm concerned about ordering a taxi to take me to the airport. 'Never worry abut that,' says Ronnie. 'I'll get someone to run you out.' And then from a locked filing cabinet, he produces four unmarked medicine bottles. Each contains a light yellow liquid, so it's either whisky or a complete set of urine samples.

He pours a little from each bottle into four small glass beakers, the kind school-children use in chemistry experiments. 'This is a ten-year-old,' he says, 'this is fifteen, this is twenty-five, and this is thirty.' And it's still only 10.30 in the morning. I knock back the ten-year-old. Ronnie nearly faints with horror.

'No, no! The idea is to nose it. Have you never nosed a whisky before?' My embarrassment knows no bounds. I explain that, as the idiot doing the idiot's guide, possibly, I had always tended to drink whisky rather than inhale it. The object of all my previous drinking exercises was to get, well, drunk. Ronnie is not appeased. He illustrates how it ought to be done, putting a drop of whisky on his palms and rubbing them together so it evaporates, leaving a pungent odour of sweat and booze. You then cup your hands over your face and sniff.

I try it, but the twenty-five-year-old Scapa now smells strongly of Paco Rabanne and Palmolive. I'm also aware that I'll be boarding the plane for Inverness scented not just by soap and aftershave but by slap-on whisky. Typical journalist, the stewardess will think.

I give up massaging booze into my hands and 'nose' the thirty-year-old, sticking my substantially broken proboscis into the requisite beaker. It smells like whisky, I tell Ronnie. I can tell he isn't impressed with me.

The snow is coming down in spadefuls as the distillery Ford Sierra cautiously slithers to the airport. Visitors are, according to Ronnie, welcome at Scapa, although there are absolutely no facilities for them, and aside from the curious Lomond still, there's not a great deal to see. Still, I've learned enough from my visit not to behave like a complete wally when asked to do a spot of nosing in future. My hands still stink of bananas and coconuts, though.

My flight is delayed until lunchtime, and when we finally take off, I nurse my miniature bag of British Ashtrays peanuts, sip a plastic miniature of Bells from a plastic cup, and it hits me: why not a trip around all the distilleries in Scotland, like this Barnard chappie? Why not write a book about that? And why not do it on a pushbike?

Outside, snow is battering off the fuselage of the Hawker Siddeley HS748 Budgie, but inside I am safe and warm and away, as they say, in a dwam: dreaming of the great whisky trek. I am pedalling, slightly downhill, into a glorious spring morning, my body bursting with fitness, my muscles hard, my stomach flat, my brain clear. I look wonderful. I feel great. And even better, I can't be done for being drunk in charge of a pushbike, because no such crime exists under Scots Law. I could be charged with breach of the peace involving a pushbike, or perhaps assault with a deadly pushbike, but they can't take away your licence to pedal, because such a thing does not exist.

By the time we land at Inverness, my course is set, and the book is all but written. All I have to do is get some time off from work, buy a pushbike and cycle around oh, what is it? A hundred or so distilleries? It'll be a breeze, I tell myself. It'll do me good, I mutter as I fight through a blizzard to the terminal building at Dalcross. And what's more, it'll be environmentally friendly. My yin will coalesce with my yang. My spokes will whirl like the wheel of life, my sprockets will whirr, my ballbearings spin silently. I will become one with the earth, feel her tensions and movements, move like a Flann O'Brien character, welded to the diamond frame of my bike, through the eternal landscape of my native land, discovering her deepest thoughts and feelings. My ride will be a metaphor for our society's existence, a journey of discovery, pain, joy, love and enlightenment . . .

Best of all, I tell myself happily, I'll be able to get pissed as a fart every night, and it'll all be tax-allowable. I decide to get my liver enzymes checked over, along with my stomach lining. It looked like there might be a lot of swallowing ahead, and there were preparations to be made. On the other hand, perhaps some practice might be in order. I tell the taxi driver to drop me at the Phoenix Bar.

Drinking Whisky the Easy Way

(1) *The glass.* Anything will do, but pretentious snobs prefer things like brandy balloons only thinner, so you can stick your nose in, swill the dram about and pretend to smell something interesting. Obviously, the size of the glass will vary with the nose. Do not, unless in an emergency, use paper, plastic or metal. Some cask-strength malts will eat straight through plastic. Only cheap rubbing whisky should be put in a hip flask, unless you're very rich or don't know any better. And now you do.

(2) *The bottle.* Choose your poison. It will not be cheap, but try and get it as cheaply as you can. Theft is very cheap, but can lead to embarrassing court appearances. The quest for bargains might also mean cultivating a wholesaler, hanging around distilleries (but be careful, distillery shops are sometimes rip-offs), buying duty-free or engaging in a little black importation from countries where whisky is sold cheaply because of low local wages. (This practice is very popular in Japan, where they get it from Malaysia.) Deep-sea fishermen are worth talking to, perhaps with a view to setting up a smuggling ring of some kind. If you're rich and stupid and have a lot of similar friends, you could always buy a cask and bottle your own. Come to think of it, maybe that's not such a bad idea . . . or you could join one of the clubs which do just that, like the Scottish Malt Whisky Society. Even if you don't intend buying anything, get on the Gordon and MacPhail and Cadenheads mailing lists. And dream.

Do not, on any account, be tempted to try and join ludicrous organisations like the Keepers of the Quaich, a cross between the Royal and Ancient Order of Buffaloes and Alcoholics Anonymous in reverse. They seemingly won't let you in unless you're a former movie actor and/or president of the USA, and/or have a very red nose, plus you have to wear cloaks, swear oaths and, it is said, not have sex after drinking. Avoid.

(3) *The water.* Optional, no matter what they say. Adding a little (and that means a little; literally a drop) does release the smell of the stuff, plus you can watch the little stringy swirl of the fusel-oils in the whisky as they mingle with the H_2O. This is fun to look at, especially when you're really pissed. But choose your water carefully. It's safer by far, if you're seriously trying to taste what you've paid vast quantities of cash for, to use bottled still spring water like Highland Spring, Caithness, Strathmore or Lovat. If you can get local spring water, hand-gathered, all the better. Why distilleries don't market their own water to purists, I don't know. It'd be money for old rope. Oh, and Glenlivet spring water is not the same as Glenlivet whisky, nor even the same water Glenlivet use.

Tap water might be all right, but is more probably full of aluminium hydroxide, which makes you demented, and chlorine and fluoride, which make you sick. If you're in the south of England, you've probably already drunk the tap water several times, not to mention had baths and other things in it. If you know this, don't use it. In fact, don't give it to your dog. If you're drunk, of course, none of this matters.

(4) *Ice*. Spoils the taste, but go ahead if you've been offered something horrible and you want to spoil the taste. Generally, whisky is a room-temperature drink.

(5) *Lemonade*. Out of the question, as are any of the following: Coca Cola, Irn Bru, tomato juice, Lucozade, Pakora juice, curry sauce, Gatorade, Angostura Bitters, Worcester Sauce, etc., etc. If you really want to add fruity, sugary things to a whisky, the only one designed for it is The Invergordon Single Grain. But if all you want to taste is the fruity, sugary thing in the first place, plus some alcoholic kick, why not just add a little methylated spirits to it? This will also make you go blind, meaning you won't have to look at what you're drinking, and you will possibly die in agony, which is possibly what you deserve.

(6) *Toddies*. Unless you're rich, foolish or blessed with abnormally sensitive tastebuds (and during the onslaught of a cold it seems unlikely that they'd be operating properly), use a blend, loads of it. Add hot water, lemon juice, sugar and/or honey. Repeat. This is also a good way of using up otherwise undrinkable sticky things, like Glayva and Drambuie.

(7) *Drugs*. Not advised, unless you're a biochemist with a hospital emergency unit (preferably in developed country, big city, National Health Service, not Fridays or Saturdays) nearby. Traditional drug used in rural Scottish communities in the past was psilocybin mushroom, picked on way home from pub if not enough drink had been consumed. Be warned. The wrong fungus can kill you, and psilocybin can mix very badly indeed with alcohol.

(8) *Technique*. Put glass on solid surface. Pour large measure of whisky into glass. Add minuscule amount of water, if any. Swirl glass. Hold to light (try not to move head along with liquid in glass, which can lead to accidents and accusations of overindulgence). Sniff. Drink. Order large one next time. Repeat.

(9) *Chasers*. Purists say no. But wait! There are avenues to be explored here, as in use of local beer to follow local malt. Raven or Dark Island goes very well with Highland Park. Beamish or Murphy's matches big Islay malts like Laphroaig. For some reason, Clynelish and Tennent's Gold Bier seems to work. This whole field is underexplored and worthy of considerable research.

Chapter Three

SETTING SAIL

So here I am, muffled in yellow plastic against a vindictive North Sea rain, astride not a pushbike but a motorcycle. And not just any old motorbike, either. B104 KSS is an MZ 250 ETZ, a product of the erstwhile German Democratic Republic's erstwhile nationalised motor industry, like that plastic pig of an almost car, the Trabant.

Unlike Trabants, however, MZs have always had a reputation for reliability. I am hoping it is deserved. This eight-year-old single cylinder two-stroke is as simple a machine as you can get. However, just to complicate matters, it has an appendage: a British-made Squire sidecar made of much-distressed fibreglass. Bike and sidecar are both what the anonymous person who sold the combination to me described as 'Vibroplant orange'. Truth to tell, the brutal functionality of an MZ, especially in its bright orange livery, would fit in well on the average building site. You'd have to watch you didn't mistake it for a cement mixer, though.

So I am sitting on the slipway at Cromarty in the Black Isle, on the southern shore of the Cromarty Firth, and I am waiting for the ferry which will launch me on my epic journey. The *Cromarty Rose* is a tiny, two-car vessel with a turntable deck so cars can get on and off without reversing, and she plies between Cromarty and Nigg, on the other side of the firth. I live in the Georgian conservation village of Cromarty, where not a few people use the ferry every day, commuting to the Highland Fabricators oil platform fabrication yard across the water in Nigg Bay. It's only the giant structures taking shape at Nigg, and the dozens of oil rigs which anchor in the firth awaiting repair, which alleviate Cromarty's whitewashed tweeness. Once the Highlands' main port, its eighteenth-century prettiness can be a bit too much to bear sometimes.

Whatever happened to the pushbike? To the environmentalist rhetoric? To the firmed-up thigh muscles and sun-bronzed visage? You may well ask. The first problem was the question of time off work. Three weeks was the maximum available, I was informed. No arguments. There are 107 malt whisky distilleries in Scotland. In a fast sports car, I might have managed a flying visit to each, but there would hardly have been time to shake hands with the janitor, let alone soak up the vibes and the umm, product, man. I would have to lower my sights, and reduce the number of distilleries to be graced with my presence. After all, who wanted to spend weeks trailing around Speyside, where most – okay, not all – of the area's fifty-odd single malts taste virtually the same, and the countryside is more boring than John Major's fashion sensibilities? Not me.

So, back to the bike, pedal-powered, that is. I took great pleasure in raising bicycle dealers' hopes that I was going to buy their top of the range, super-whizz-bang, carbon fibre-frame mega tourer. I counted the gears available to me: up to twenty-one, one for every slope from horizontal to the Matterhorn. I looked at lycra shorts and thought of shaving my legs to improve wind resistance. Then I examined my wobble-prone belly, realised I would have to cover at least sixty miles a day, and promptly decided I needed an engine. At thirty-six, it was too late to begin training to be a healthy, fit person, I wouldn't have looked good in lycra, and anyway, what this book needed was a bit of wild 'n' woolly character. A bit of street cred. A bit of burning rubber, a bit of exhaust smoke in the nostrils, a bit of risk . . .

But going by bus would take forever. I considered a classic car of sorts, say a Morris Marina or an Austin Allegro, but adventure might be difficult to come by in such a vehicle. After all, hadn't the manufacturer issued free 'I'm a boring bastard' badges with them when they were new?

'What about a motorbike?' my wife, a bikerette in her youth, suggested. 'I know a very good life insurance agent. We'd be well provided for if you went under a juggernaut.' Such kindness and consideration from one's significant other is, I always think, heartwarming.

The images flew before my inner eye: Marlon Brando in *The Wild One*, Peter Fonda and Dennis Hopper in *Easy Rider*, Mickey Rourke in *Rumblefish* . . . all those films about men with wee willies overcompensating by shoving something big and throbbing between their legs, something fast, dangerous and, even better, attractive to women.

'Great idea, my dear,' I said. 'The only problem being that I don't have a motorcycle licence.' As a car driver, I was able to ride a moped up to 50 cubic centimetres, or a bike up to 125cc if I avoided motorways and displayed L-plates. But big black shiny penis substitutes were out of my league.

'No problem,' said my wife. 'Get a bike and a sidecar. You can ride any size of bike on L-plates if it's got a sidecar. You can even carry passengers, and it'd be a lot safer. I was only joking about the insurance.' My heart swelled with affection. 'You have got some, though, haven't you, dear?'

I'd ridden a Honda 50 just after I left school, and had a brief, idyllic summer fling with a Honda 125 five years previously, so I thought I could handle a bike. The problem was how to find a motorbike and sidecar, cheaply.

The only bike-and-chair combinations available off the shelf, according to the rainforest of magazines I consulted, were Eastern European, and weird. MZ was now a privatised cog in the industrial wheel of Greater Germany, and a new, lean and thrusting British distributor informed me that combinations were no longer available. CZ, the Czechoslovakian company, still did dedicated combinations, but supplies were uncertain. Just my luck to be looking for the Communist Bloc's cheapest form of family transport as social and political change was upping everyone's ambitions for minimum mobility from three wheels to four.

'What about a Reliant Robin?' somebody suggested, but the thought of lurching from still to still in Great Britain's very own Trabant did not appeal. I mean, you'd hardly expect Brando to step out of a Reliant Robin flexing his leather-clad biceps and inspiring fear and lust, would you?

Then a brochure arrived from Neval Motorcycles Ltd of Hull. It was like stepping fifty years back in time. They specialised in motorbikes with sidecars, Russian ones with unashamedly communist names like Soviet Knight. They were enormous, glistening black and chrome affairs that looked for all the world like pre-war BMWs, right down to the military sidecars – which lacked only a machine-gun – and the 650cc horizontally-opposed flat-twin engine. Two thousand quid would buy me one, but it was mail order only, delivered direct to my door.

In fact, they *were* pre-war BMWs. When the Soviet Union defeated Germany in the Second World War, one of the spoils of victory was, lock, stock and cylinder barrels, a motorcycle factory, which was duly taken back through the Iron Curtain, assembled and put into production. Forty-seven years later, it was still turning out the same machines. The USSR did the same with cameras, appropriating the Leica design and churning out an appalling copy called a Zorki, one of which I actually owned. It did not work very well.

Still, I was tempted. A long leather coat and a coal scuttle helmet, and I would at least make an impression on a Neval Dnepr. And they were available. The only snag came in the form of cryptic comments in some of the less urbane motorcycle magazines, along the lines of 'don't on any account buy one of these unless you want to ride straight through Volvos and come out the other side unscathed, or unless you're very poor and stupid'. I seemed to fit all three categories, more or less.

Two things put me off. Miracle of miracles, a second-hand Dnepr came up for sale in Dingwall. Nine years old, it was vastly expensive at £900. It also lacked an MOT, tax or indeed any sign that it had ever moved an inch. Apart that is, from the 14,000 miles on the odometer.

'Even if it went, I couldn't pay more than £300,' I told the mysterious lady who was selling this monstrosity.

'Oh, I couldn't take less than £400,' she replied. You have to be suspicious of an immediate 52 per cent discount, I felt. I had no idea how to start the beast, but apparently the lady's son was coming home soon, and he would get it started for me. I went home, to be contacted a week later by the mysterious lady, asking if I was a mechanic, or had any friends who were.

'The thing you start it with, the kick thing, seems to be jammed.'

I said goodbye with no regrets.

Next day I telephoned Neval. Look, I said, just tell me if your bikes are reliable or not.

'Oh yes,' said yet another mysterious woman, 'they just need a bit of running in.' How much running in, I queried. 'About 2,000 miles,' she replied. 'You see, the pistons aren't machined, they're just cast, and they need to be bedded in carefully.'

Gulp. In other words, the engine did its own machining. The thought of changing the oil every five miles not appealing greatly, I regretfully passed on the idea of a Neval. The leather coat and Schmeisser machine pistol would have to wait.

I was saved, strange to say, by the Aberdeen *Press and Journal*. A classified advertisement beckoned: 'MZ 250 Combo', it read. 'Offers'. Back in the good old Stalinist days, MZ's then British distributor had tacked on a few Squire Torpedo sidecars to the DDR's most reliable export, selling, I'd been told, only about five or six in Scotland. Now one had surfaced, in the village of Balmedie, just outside Aberdeen.

I phoned. The seller had just bought a Laverda Jota, was leaving for an oil rig within the next few days. How much did he want? About two hundred quid. No, it wasn't MOT'd or taxed, but yeah, sure, it ran. Hold it until tomorrow afternoon, I pleaded. Sure.

Next day, myself and number three son raced through to Balmedie in a Luton van hired from Sharps Reliable Wrecks of Inverness, who may not be Avis but don't let it bother them. That was the first time I set eyes on the orange beast. It had covered 22,000 miles, which for a motorbike, especially a two-stroke 250, is quite a lot. 'The guy who had it before rode it all over the Highlands,' said the seller, 'with his girlfriend in the sidecar. He must have been mad.'

It seemed to go. It looked a bit rough, but hell, for £200 what did I expect. The anonymous seller was a very large leather-clad biker who was obviously, from the flapping net curtains on his perjink little private estate, regarded as the devil incarnate by his neighbours. He seemed pleasant, though, and did puzzles when not working offshore or twiddling with his three motorcyles. There were half-completed jigsaws all over the terraced house.

The MZ's registration document, it was explained to me, featured the previous owner's name, 'because I never got round to changing it'. We shook hands on £200 in cash, and a few hernias later, B104 KSS was in the van. I owned a motorbike.

'I want a shot, Daddy,' said number three son. Well, so did I.

It was three weeks before anyone had a shot. The mechanic at Finnies Motorcycles in Inverness looked at me like I was mad, when I drove the van into Inverness, proudly showed him the bike and asked him to fix it. Three days later, he phoned to ask if I was serious. It would cost £300 to get it roadworthy, including renewal of the entire rear suspension, chain, sprockets and just about everything else that moved. Or rather, in the case of B104 KSS, didn't. The engine, it appeared, was the only thing which functioned adequately. Just do it, I said. Even at £500, it seemed like a bargain.

My three weeks' off work was arranged. Four days before I was due to depart, I was told the bike was ready. I bought some clumpy motorcycle boots, a white, open-faced helmet, aviator's goggles and gloves, and prepared, for the first time, to ride a bike and sidecar.

'Be careful,' said the mechanic. 'It's not like riding an ordinary motorbike.' I shrugged. I had already stuck one self-adhesive L-plate on the back of the sidecar, but frankly doubted if I needed to display such signs of inexperience. This would be easy.

'Be careful,' said my wife. We had still not managed to insure my meagre life for anything substantial. 'I'll follow you down the road.' And so she did, and was thus witness to me riding the orange beast straight across an Inverness roundabout, to the astonished derision of pedestrians and car drivers alike. I stopped, sweating and palpitating. I just couldn't turn the bloody thing. Unlike any two-wheeled motorbike, it wouldn't lean, and that, in my experience, was how you got round bends on bikes. You didn't steer, you leaned. Gingerly, I conducted the MZ to a quiet housing estate, followed by my wife in her car and two much-amused sons.

'Just go away,' I shouted at my better half and offensive offspring. 'Go away and get some insurance sorted out. I'm obviously going to need it.'

It took an hour of practising to work out that a combination needs to be steered, often by brute force, using the handlebars in a way which would send you flying tarmacwards in seconds from a normal bike. Also, going left, you have to accelerate the bike around the bulk of the sidecar, which, if you miscalculate, will also lift that appendage disconcertingly above your head. Going right, you have to slow down to let the sidecar swing around the bike. Otherwise, you won't go right at all. You will go wrong, wrong, *wrong*!

I finally made it home, after numerous brushes with trees, a fence, and a near miss with a dung-laden tractor and trailer. I hated motorbikes, I decided. I hated sidecars. I hated whisky. Besides, the doctor had just warned me that I might have an ulcer, and here I was setting off on what promised to be a liver-busting, stomach-haemorrhaging, heart-attacking binge of a trip. Perhaps I should take up some normal activity instead, like table tennis. I could always write a book about Great Ping Pong Tables I Have Known: The Youth Club Years . . .

Now here I am, waiting on the *Cromarty Rose*. Wife and weans stand ready to wave me off. One or two friends have turned up to take some pictures and mock my battered oilskins, creased yellow veterans of piltock-fishing in the Shetland Islands, a lifetime ago.

I am the only passenger, the beast the only vehicle on board. I wave to my family as Cromarty recedes, not so pretty today in the greyness of a bad spring morning. Will I ever see the village again? My two sons, my wife, who told me just before I left that she'd forgotten to arrange the insurance?

Well, I certainly hope so. After all, I'm due back home in two days' time before tackling boring old Speyside. I may be an adventurer, but sometimes it's nice to know there's a microwave and an automatic washing machine waiting not too far down the road.

I had a hundred miles to go that day, up the A9 to Wick, site of Britain's most northerly mainland distillery, Pulteney. I'd plotted my route for the three weeks in a somewat casual fashion, leafing through a small library of whisky tomes such as Michael Brander's *Essential Guide to Scotch Whisky* (cheap and good but out of date), Michael Jackson's exhaustive and exhausting *Malt Whisky Companion* (expensive, more than a touch tainted with winesnobspeak, but useful) and Colin Bell's hilarious but again somewhat obsolete *Scotch Whisky, a Drambuster's Guide*. Best by far, though, was David Milsted's superb little *Bluff Your Way in Whisky*, which disguises the fact that it's brilliantly informative beneath a hail of witty one-liners. Alfred Barnard's 1887 *The Whisky Distilleries of the United Kingdom* has a few gems, but oh, the interminable boredom of his obsessive interest in the size and capacity of various pipes, tubes, stills, tanks and containers. Freud would have had a field day with him. The worst of it is, with such a golden opportunity to drink the product of all those stills, he barely refers to the taste or effect of the whisky at all. A strange man.

From Pulteney, I would head south, zigzag west then east back to Cromarty, head down-and-over to Speyside, then cross to the west coast and Skye. From there, I would head south again until I reached Campbeltown, once the world's 'whisky metropolis' with thirty-five stills, now with only two small distilleries. After that, I'd just have to see what time I had left, and what condition the bike and I were in.

But first I have to get to Wick. As we scrape on to the slipway at Nigg, the weather ceases threatening and starts getting physical, battering me with a mixture of rain and hail. I bump gingerly off the *Cromarty Rose* and sputter away into Ross-shire, trailing a cloud of blue smoke. The MZ needs filled with oil as often as it does petrol, because the engine cheerfully burns the stuff away as part of its simple *modus operandi*. So much for the ozone layer. I curse the vanity which made me buy an open-face helmet as the hail begins, it seems, to strip the skin from my chin. One hundred yards from the ferry, I stop, waiting until the brief hailstorm passes; for the rest of the trip, hail will be my main enemy, and my face will bear its attacks nearly every day, leaving me with a complexion worse than Stalin's.

But never mind, the bike seems to be going well, I've just about mastered the steering, and the only problem seems to be other motorists' impatience with my progress. Don't they realise that forty miles per hour on the beast feels like you're clinging on behind Nigel Mansell when he's in a bad mood with Nelson Piquet? I try to be nice, and wave them past when I can, but the fact is a combination takes up enough space to prevent easy overtaking, and queues can build up. Gradually, I learn to ignore the rude gestures being made out of back windows by children what have not been brung up right.

I cross the Dornoch Bridge, completed in 1991 and which knocks about forty-five minutes off the trip north. It's the subject of much justified complaining by that strange group of people who actually believe railways are a good idea. The train to Wick or Thurso now takes about forty minutes longer than the bus, as a planned joint road/rail bridge aross the Dornoch Firth was abandoned due to lack of Government funding. Now there are strong suspicions that the north rail line, which still follows a bizarre route dictated by the location of the Duke of Sutherland's isolated shooting lodges, could close due to lack of use. That, rasp the railwayites, could be what was intended all along by those conniving cost-cutters at British Rail. Oh, surely not? With privatisation on the way?

Beyond Dornoch, one of Scotland's great ignored championship golf courses, I enter the grim territory of the Sutherlands, the family which is infamous in Scottish history for what amounts to mass murder: the clearance of crofters from the land they had worked for generations to make way for sheep has inspired many books, songs and emotional rhetoric. The fact is, great, despicable crimes were committed by the likes of Patrick Sellar, the Duke and Duchess of Sutherland's factor. People died directly by fire and harassment during the evictions. Hundreds more did so during enforced emigration to the colonies and the model villages of Brora and Golspie and Helmsdale pay tribute to the vision which brought those crimes about: the vision of the remote, technocratic Victorian improvers, who despised the marginal crofting lifestyles of the people who still felt they owed their landlord's clan tribal allegiance, and determined to forcibly change things, no matter the human cost.

I am following the improvers' spoor as I battle north against the wind and the rain and the cold. The dispossessed crofters huddled beneath dykes on the coast; they froze in the grim weather, or tried to cultivate useless land. Over at Croik, you can still read the heartbreaking messages of those torn from their homes and destined for a terrifyingly uncertain future. Scrawled on the glass windows of the kirk, in the lee of which they sheltered, the injustices meted out to the cleared remain crystal clear to this day.

But the clearances are with us still, in the deserted straths and sheep-ruined former pasures of the Highlands. High above Golspie rears the hideously mocking memorial built by the Duke of Sutherland to himself, his forbears, his accomplishments, his crimes. Numerous half-serious plans have been hatched to blow this nasty excrescence to kingdom come, but nothing has as yet come of them. However, if I am spared, one day I may hire an explosives expert and, at dead of night, see the thing demolished in flame and smoke. Aye, and pigs might fly.

Dunrobin Castle, seat of the Sutherlands, lies partly hidden from the road, which is just as well. In plain view its fairytale, Disneyland, sugar-candy appearance would be likely either to paralyse sensitive motorists with shock and disbelief, causing needless accidents, or bring on severe mental illness, as was obviously the problem of whoever designed the monstrosity.

But on we go to Helmsdale, where the railway and a single-track road head off down the Strath of Kildonan, scene of some of the worst acts of the clearances but also once site of a Klondike-like gold rush. You can still pan for gold today in the Kildonan Burn, with licences and pans available from the farmhouse.

Anyone passing through Helmsdale must visit the wondrous La Mirage, 'as featured in the *Sunday Post*', one of the most bizarre restaurants in Scotland. Blazing in pink and neon, some may find it repellent. For others, though, its absolutely unconscious kitsch and accidental campness will be a hilarious shock, set as La Mirage (named, of course, for Alexis's bistro in *Dynasty*) is in this grey, orderly little fishing village.

The food's good in La Mirage, and cheap, and basic in the way that not just *Sunday Post* readers might appreciate. The large portions of home-made steak pie, fresh haddock, and steaks, all with lots of peas and chips, may be unsurprising. But the decor is unbelievable. Leaving aside the fish tanks, the straw parasols, the white wrought-iron tables, the massive Spanish-dancer dolls, the gold-sprayed statues, the ducks and cats, the internal neon signs, the plastic vegetation, and the life-size, silver-swathed figure of Alexis, there is Nancy Sinclair herself, the owner. Nancy is larger than a dozen lives.

Immaculately made up in the fashion of her heroine, Barbara Cartland – although she says the resemblance is accidental – Nancy's platinum-blonde hair glints in the neon glow of the restaurant she designed and built, she says, as 'a place where folk could kind of escape to, a wee bit of a fantasy'. She sits centre stage herself, at her own special table, smoking the Du Maurier cigarettes she favours, holding them between heavily be-ringed fingers, the nails of which are painted red with white spots.

Nancy's nice, and when you get her talking, she is very entertaining indeed. She'll tell you about Barbara, as in Cartland, who has a connection with the village through her nearby shooting lodge. Barbara often used to come in for a cup of tea and to share make-up tips with her, Nancy will say. Not that she's been much of an influence, of course. Of course not.

Outside La Mirage, Helmsdale seems suddenly even greyer, duller than before you entered. But a trip to Timespan, the award-winning 'visitor's experience' should liven up your senses. There, recreated in three dimensions, you will find Patrick Sellar and the clearances, the tragedy and the appalling acceptance of the people involved. And if you don't weep, you have no soul.

You'll laugh when you leave Timespan, though, because the final sight is a life-size model of dear old Barbara Cartland herself, in one of her pink and diamanté numbers. Buy the little booklet she wrote about herself and Helmsdale, if you're into patronising, love-me-I'm-an aristocrat nonsense. Then go for a cup of tea at La Mirage and meet the real thing, in the form of Nancy, who's much more interesting.

There are lots of toffs in and around Helmsdale, one of the best salmon rivers in Europe. Of a Sunday, some will be munching langoustines in the

Bunilidh, talking in braying voices over a chilled Muscadet whilst their Range Rover Vogue sits outside. One overheard conversation will turn your thoughts to dynamite, dukes and that insult in stone which overhangs Golspie.

The worst part of the trip to Wick, and the invisible border with Caithness, lies ahead. The Berriedale Braes leapt to national prominence when a freak spring blizzard stranded several cars there, and seven people died. It's a very high, mutant cliffscape, near the sea but still a trap for every ounce of snow going, and featuring a corkscrewing series of climbing and descending bends worthy of an Alpine pass.

Descending the steep brae going north, the escape roads and warning signs seem a mite too strident. Then, past the Caithness Spring bottling plant at the bottom, I cannot get the orange beast to go up the steep slope in second gear. Into first, as the hill gets steeper, and I stall the bike. Fortunately, there's no one behind me, and the weather has momentarily lifted. I stand on the footbrake to hold the bike, and desperately try to restart it. Succeeding, I over-rev on take-off, praying that I don't stall again, and the whole combination judders forward, a too-stressed chain pinging like a sonar. Somehow I make it to the top, just in time for the rain to begin. I hate motorcycling.

Dunbeath used to be as bad as Berriedale, until a new viaduct spanned what used to be a vicious, winding descent into a sea-level gorge. Now, you smoothly – or in my case, not so smoothly – pass Neil Gunn's birthplace, scene of the memorable battle between the boy and the giant salmon at the beginning of *Highland River*; the bit, in fact, everybody reads before giving up five pages further on.

At last, Wick appears, strangely sited on the coast below its Second World War airfield. Two vast hangars, once used to shelter bombers, still dominate the skyline, and the airfield – or airport, as Loganair likes to call it – is now used for short-hop passenger flights to Aberdeen and Orkney, as well as more sinister deliveries of spent nuclear fuel and waste, destined for reprocessing at the Dounreay plant not far away. There is, in fact, a public road right across the main runway, much used by that typical Caithness driver, the youngster constantly blipping the throttle of a gutless Escort 1300 with sub-Cosworth flared wheel arches, spoiler and a go-louder exhaust pipe. Macho jumping of the traffic lights when a plane is about to land is frequent, leading to some soiled Recaro seats and not a few fines at the sheriff court.

The Harbour Guest House is in Rose Street, just up from Wick's substantial harbour, which, on what suddenly turns into a sunny spring afternoon, lies almost empty. A few trawlers and derelict drifters like the once-lovely Eriskay boat *Rose of Sharon* sit motionless on the oily water, while fish float around them, dead and white and belly-up.

I switch off the beast outside the terraced house. Despite the weather, the road, and my ham-fisted-and-footed riding, we have made it: just over a hundred miles, the longest trip I've ever made on a bike. Olive Ross, the woman who, with her husband Ronnie, runs the Harbour Guest House, seems nervous. I put it down to bikeritis, until she mentions that they only took over the place a week ago, and I'm among their first guests. 'This is the first time we've ever done catering,' she says.

My room seems fine, and at £12.50 a night, who's complaining if the bedspread is of a lurid tiger-stripe material. The grime of the A9 relatively removed, I step out to see what Wick has to offer on a Sunday evening.

Not much, is the answer, save the strangely upright, prideful, decaying architecture of Pulteneytown, laid out as a model of early nineteenth-century planning as Wick expanded rapidly in the wake of the herring trade. Some of High Pulteneytown is extraordinary, all beautifully proportioned squares and gardens, with the widest streets imaginable. Even the most down-at-heel sections in Lower Pulteneytown near the harbour, have a seedy charm. And a giant barometer, fixed to a corner site on the slope up from the quay, adds an almost surrealist air.

Wick-stroke-Pulteneytown, now essentially the one place, is a curious amalgam of screamingly self-important buildings like its town hall and bank, and a jumble of seemingly unplanned modern estates, including one of almost Castlemilk proportions. Between the open thoroughfares of Pulteneytown's up-market section and this distinctly down-at-heel ghetto, lies the home of Old Pulteney, the Pulteney distillery itself. Of course, being a Sunday evening, it's shut.

Other places are not. I pass a Baptist church, where the sound of a few dozen tongues giving 'Oh For a Thousand Tongues To Sing' laldy reverberates out into the street. A couple of bars are open, and the desperately drunk are spilling out onto the pavement, including a couple of old men who look mummified. 'Is the Camps open?' one asks me, gripping my shoulder, Ramases the Second in a flat bunnet. 'Is the Camps open?' That's the name of the bar, exuding Karaoke Corries songs, which he has just fallen out of.

I decide to like Wick. It is clinging to a greater past, to the glories of the silver darlings, but it seems to have real character. The people are rude, barely moving a muscle to serve you if you do happen to find an open shop on a Sunday. There are hardly any restaurants, and the yoof, when they're not hanging about sullenly on street corners like yoof everywhere, are roaring around on small motorbikes or packed in sixes into bulbously customised Fords. But there's spark there, a distinctive pride which is totally absent from Thurso, just up the road. Thurso, swamped with incoming technocrat Dounreay Stakhanovites, is a lost soul of a place, famed for its surfing, in radioactive waters, and nowadays, for the fact that both Dounreay and the

US Navy base at Forss are being run down. For Thurso, both time and money are running out, and the locals appear to be resigned to it. Wick doesn't seem like that.

On the world's shortest street – oh, yeah? – the eight-foot-long Ebenezer Street, I find Mackay's Hotel. Well, actually, it's kind of hard to ignore it, because it's one of the biggest in Caithness. The lounge bar does an enormously filling lasagne in fast and friendly fashion, and then I decide to try an Old Pulteney. After all, that's what I'm here for.

The middle-aged, neatly dressed Wickian next to me at the bar coughs. 'Pardon me for saying this, but you're better off with a blend.'

Oh really?

'Absolutely. The grain alcohol in a blend is much purer than the stuff you get in a single malt. There's all kinds of chemicals and oils and nasty things in a malt, because they can't get it to the same level of purity as with grain whisky. Take it from me, I've been drinking nothing but Bells for twenty years, and look at me!'

I look at him. He is about five-foot-eight, overweight verging on fat, with broken veins from his balding forehead to his double-verging-on-triple chin. He grins. 'Joke, of course. Only joking. Too much beer spoils the effect.'

I point out that Bells does have at least some malt in it, and, flaunting my newly acquired book-learning, tell him that if he wants to drink patent or Coffey-still whisky only, he should go for Cameron Brig or The Invergordon, the only two readily available single grains. He shakes his head sadly.

'It's too late for that. Too late, I'm afraid. Much too late.' Then he looks at me angrily. 'What are you, anyway, a bloody whisky snob? A bloody expert? Don't bloody patronise me! I know all about bloody fusel oils and lower alcohols . . .'

He turns out not to be a Wickist at all. His name, he tells me, is Bob and he is on holiday. He is extremely drunk.

'Family here, of course, here a week, I pick up the accent. A natural mimic, me. I'm a chemist. Well, an amateur chemist. Actually I sell toilet requisites.' Abruptly, Bob slides off the bar stool, totters for a few seconds, then takes measured steps out of the door without bidding me farewell. Just another not-so-close encounter of the bar-stool kind.

But back to the Old Pulteney. It does have a coastal saltiness to it, but where Scapa is thin and rather weak to my tastebuds, Pulteney is substantial. Not heavy, but a bit like Wick – characterful, surprising, maybe a bit dour to begin with, definitely not be easily dismissed. However, something odd has caught my eye on the gantry. It's a bottle of eighteen-year-old Pulteney, specially bottled for an organisation called the Caithness Club. 'It's old. Old and pretty rare, I think,' says the barwoman. She doesn't know what the Caithness Club is.

At £1.75 a nip, I feel my research budget can stand the strain of a large one. With a dab of water, this dram goes down a treat, smooth as silk, hardly catching the throat, light, clean but malty and firm as well. It is only after I've finished it and try, full of bonhomie, to stand up so I can order another, that I realise how strong the stuff must have been. The world has assumed a kind of glowing warm clarity.

'Can . . . can I have another look at that . . . bottle?' I ask the barwoman. Sure enough, Caithness Club is 56.9 per cent alcohol. Far too strong for a mere boy like me, alone in a strange seaport on a Sunday night. If I have another, I might end up getting press-ganged, destined to sail the seas with some irascible Caithnessian fishing skipper, living off lard and Mars Bars. Worse, I might end up in the Baptist Church Youth Fellowship, arguing about predestination. My imagination is getting out of hand, so I stagger out into the still-sunlit evening, heading for the Harbour Guest House and another attempt on *Highland River*. I am in Neil Gunn territory and surely somebody, somewhere, once managed to finish the blasted book? If not, then I'll do it. I will be the first.

Chapter Four

BETWEEN THE LEY LINES

Next morning, Pulteney's telephone rang and rang without reply. I was a trifle disconcerted, but my idea for the trip was to arrange as little as possible, telephoning in advance for trips around distilleries, or simply turning up at the door. It would be an absolute last resort to mention that I was either a journalist or a would-be author. Some, but by no means all, had regular guided tours, but, because of my thorough and detailed research in preparation for the trip, I had absolutely no idea when these were.

Olive fed me bacon, eggs, black pudding and all the other high-cholesterol goodies involved with a British B&B. Worries about my possible ulcer gave me momentary pause for thought, but hell, this was supposed to be an adventure. The lining of my stomach would have to take its chance. Besides, I had a plentiful supply of Aludrox with me, the alkaline stand-by of a journalist acquaintance who had memorably told me: 'They said I had an ulcer, and I couldn't drink any more. I just took a bottle of this every evening before I started getting pissed, and I'm still as right as rain.'

Eventually I decided just to drive up to Pulteney and see what happened. I circled the low, stone buildings, which are typically blackened by the chemical reactions the angels cause as they extract their evaporating share from the maturing casks. All seemed deathly quiet. Behind the distillery itself, on the rough wasteland that separates it from a spectacularly shabby council housing scheme, a horse was roughly tethered, a certain sign in Ireland of gypsies, but something I'd rarely seen in Scotland. Nearby, an old man was raking through a rubbish pile for scrap wood. Suddenly, it seemed that Wick had a trifle too much 'character' to retain the image I'd constructed for it of being pleasantly run-down. The grubby children playing nearby, the old man, last night's public drunkenness – they were all signs of a poverty more desperate than I'd given myself time to notice.

I parked the orange beast in the long, empty street outside Pulteney's main entrance, walked into the courtyard and began shouting things like 'err . . . hello?'.

A surprised figure in a boiler suit popped out of a doorway. 'Can I help you at all?'

He could and he did. Bobby Clark was a service engineer, up with a team from Allied Distillers' Elgin service headquarters to give Pulteney its annual going-over. The manager had taken the day off, but yes, Bobby would be delighted to let me look around.

'I don't really know anything about the actual whisky-making,' he apologised. 'I'm mostly on the maintenance side.' In the still room, with its surprisingly small, classically shaped pot-stills, a figure garbed in what seemed like a diving suit was climbing out of the still's innards, for all the world like someone leaving an early submarine. 'Just cleaning up,' said Bobby.

Built in 1826 as part of the 'new town' of Pulteneytown, Old Pulteney is reputedly Scotland's fastest maturing malt. Its buildings huddle on the hill of

High Pulteneytown, turning their backs on the sea, but the North Sea's frequent lashing gales must contribute to the dram's coastal taste. Much of the distillery is original, including the cast-iron innards of the mash tun, but Pulteney did not strike me as the most desirable tourist destination. Still, it is the most northerly mainland source of malt whisky, and it's worth a look, as you try to decide exactly what is wrong with Wick. Bobby was quite upset that I wasn't getting a proper tour, and sorrowfully informed me that Balblair, just outside Tain and also an Allied distillery, was having its spring-clean as well. Never mind, I said, as I left him and his colleagues to sand, brush, clean and paint. All I had to face was the A9, the Berriedale Braes again, and even more bad weather.

The weather began a schizophrenic cycle of hail, rain, sun and at one point snow as I struggled south. The A9 coastal route from Wick can be spectacular, with the oil platforms of the tiny Beatrice Field just discernible on the watery horizon. All I had eyes for that day was the road immediately in front of me, and sometimes, when the hail was at its worst and I couldn't stop, not even that. The early lambs sheltered beneath their mother's woolly flanks, and even the prospect of ending up as someone's roast dinner couldn't prevent me wishing I could join them.

On a motorbike, you quickly develop a weather eye, like a sailor. You watch the sky, searching for breaks in the cloud, scanning the horizon for storms sweeping in from unexpected quarters. Sitting on a bike at, say, 50 mph in a heavy rain is like having a fire-hose turned on you at close quarters inside a refrigerator. There is nothing pleasant about it. And as heavy lorries swept by me heading north, the awesome power of their slipstreams, often twenty or thirty feet behind them and twice as broad as their loads, would hit me like fists, releasing handfuls of dirt, mud and spray as they did so.

I barely noticed the Berriedale Braes, and at Brora I stopped for a coffee, almost sobbing with relief. As I stopped, so did the rain; God was having fun with me.

I telephoned Clynelish, the next distillery down from Pulteney, and begged a guided tour, even though I'd missed the regular morning jaunt by half an hour. I was particularly keen to see Clynelish, and not just because it's supposedly Jeremy Paxman's favourite drink. Who cares what Jeremy Paxman's favourite drink is?

No, Clynelish is the distillery built by the Marquess of Stafford in 1819, before he became the Duke of Sutherland through marriage. Having conceived, according to an old Distillers Company Ltd booklet, 'a scheme of economic improvement that entailed moving the inhabitants from the interior to the seaboard', the distillery was built partly to make use of the coal he was intent on extracting nearby, partly to give employment to the crofters he'd had run off their lands for sheep, and partly to provide a legal market for the barley being produced by the tenant-crofters who had been forced to try to scrabble for a living on useless coastal sites. Most crofters would otherwise have been selling mainly to illicit distillers, in a desperate attempt to make some money. Either that or making the hard stuff themselves. This, according to the marquess's lands commissioner James Lochs, had 'nursed the people in every species of deceit, idleness and dissipation'.

Well, the coal from Brora's Ross Pit was not of the highest quality, and had to be supplemented with Lowland fuel until 1966, when the distillery was converted to oil-firing. Distilleries traditionally employing about two men and three cats, employment was not massive, and the tragic crofters forced to struggle for survival on the coastal strips were hardly able to feed themselves, let alone the gaping maw of a distillery. Many left for, or were forcibly sent to Canada and America.

But Clynelish prospered. In 1896, it attracted the highest price of any Scottish malt, and it became, as it still is, one of the favourites of the connoisseur.

For a while there were two distilleries, Clynelish itself, completely rebuilt by DCL in 1968 in the standard 1960s, glass-fronted-still-house mode, and the original nineteenth-century Clynelish buildings, renamed Brora.

I rolled up at the immaculate visitors' carpark; and was hardly off the bike before Liz was welcoming me. 'You must be Mr Morton,' she said, bubbling with genuine enthusiasm. 'If you come this way I'll get you a dram.' What more could one ask for?

While not really geared up for visitors, Clynelish has Liz working part-time as a guide in the spring and summer, and Brora's increasing popularity as a holiday resort brings thousands of tourists in every year. In a tiny office, she poured me a generous measure of fourteen-year-old Clynelish, which comes in United Distillers' wooden-boxed flora-and-fauna series of classic malts, with a nice illustration of a wildcat.

Clynelish, however, isn't fierce at all. Peaty, smoky, reminiscent of a lighter Islay like Bunnahabhain, it's a subtle malt, substantial but delicate. After the morning I'd had, believe me, it went down a treat.

The modern distillery, with its line of big copper stills, didn't interest me as much as the old one, which has been in mothballs since the early 1980s. Liz took me down to see the filling shed, which is still in one of the old buildings, and we peered through the windows of the disused Brora still-house. It was a melancholy, slightly creepy sight; the copper pot-stills stood, shrouded in darkness and dust, with crumbling plaster and all kinds of debris around them. There were, Liz told me, thoughts of converting the whole thing into a visitor centre. I only hope the roots of Clynelish's existence in the blood of dispossessed crofters are detailed, if UD ever decide to build such a thing. A stone bearing the coats of arms of the Marquess of Stafford and the Duchess of Sutherland, along with the date 1821, remains. It is ironic that such a lovely dram should have such a dodgy history. Still, as Colin Bell memorably puts it, 'you might profitably drink to the perdition of Highland landlords and their factors': I bought a bottle of fourteen-year-old from Liz – at least £6.00 cheaper than off-licence prices – and determined to do just that.

Tain beckoned. I telephoned Balblair, and got no answer. On phoning the supposedly ever-welcoming Glenmorangie, Scotland's favourite malt, I was told in no uncertain terms that they couldn't show me around, no way, until one of the regular visits, and that wouldn't be for two days. However, at Tain I had contacts, and besides, weird things always happened in Tain. It was something to do with the ley lines intersecting, somebody had once told me. I was not downcast. At least not until I got back on the beast, my bottle of Clynelish safely packed away in the sidecar, and the big black cloud that had pursued me from Wick released its load of rain and occasional hail upon me, all the way across the Dornoch Bridge and then as I navigated along the old A9 towards Balblair.

At first, it's difficult to see how you reach Balblair Distillery, which sits between the north rail-line and the Dornoch Firth at Edderton, pretty in old stone. People have been making whisky here for almost 250 years. The weather broke horribly as I finally reached the gates, but as Bobby Clark had warned, there was little sign of life. I peered through the battering rain for a stray maintenance man, but the old buildings, most of them dating from 1870, remained silent, apart from the rattle of huge, globular raindrops.

Next door, at the Balblair Hotel, I ordered a restorative local ten-year-old in the public bar, as water dripped on to the floor and my boots steamed gently. It was a fruity dram, slightly sticky, somehow, compared to the Clynelish which had proved so restorative in Brora. Like Pulteney and Scapa, Balblair tends to end up in the Ballantine blends. Even on its home ground, applied to a shiveringly wet motorcyclist, it didn't particularly impress in its own right.

I tried a 1964 Balblair, which seemed even more sweet, more intensely sticky. I ordered soup and lasagne as the conversation between the barman and his one other customer reached some form of appeasement over a vague incident which had taken place the previous night.

'I have to apologise, I really must, if I was out of order, I really do apologise.'

The barman is smiling in forgiveness. 'Och, no bother, don't you worry, all water under the bridge . . .'

'Just a pint of lager shandy for me, not after last night. My God, I was drunk. I'm really sorry, you know, I don't know what came over me.'

'No bother at all, everybody goes over the score once in a while . . .'

The talk switches to employment at the Nigg oil platform yard, and fears of redundancy. This man is off work at the moment, nursing a bad back and his pint of lager shandy. 'See, the Spanish, the Spanish and all these ones can undercut us, the Government copped out, all this Europe shite. It means all these two-bit yards in Spain and Africa and God knows where can compete for our contracts. I mean, the North Sea is our sea, right? What the fuck has it got to do with the Spanish?'

He doesn't look at me, and the barman, an Englishman, has perfected that Highland flick of the head, that non-committal 'right enough'. Am I on holiday, the barman asks. Sort of, I explain. I'm on a tour of distilleries, and unfortunately Balblair next door seems to be deserted.

'Aye, they're cleaning it up and servicing it at the moment,' he says. Then he reaches below the bar. 'Ever seen this?' And come like a ghost to haunt me is that old bore Barnard, this time in the form of a fairly rare 1960s hardback edition of his mammoth tour. Yes, Alfred and I have met before, I tell the rather crestfallen barman, but out of politeness I have a swift browse.

'As the internal arrangements and vessels are like the other distilleries in the district, it is not worth while to recapitulate them,' says Arthur about Balblair. Well, quite, but that didn't stop you describing every other pipe and cross-weld from Orkney to Cardiff, did it, Art? Apparently, though, Edderton was known as the 'parish of the peats' due to the inexhaustible source of fuel nearby, and was 'the scene of many a struggle between the revenue officers and smugglers'.

I leave Balblair and Edderton and Barnard in the same soaking weather that I arrived in. My idea had been to visit Glenmorangie, then spend the night in Tain before heading home along the north shores of the Cromarty Firth, taking in what stills there were to see on the way. Glenmorangie having slammed their door in my face, however, I must see whether I can find one of the sixteen men of Tain to tell me about Scotland's favourite malt. It is simply a question of the ley lines. I know it.

I pass the entrance to Glenmorangie, with its famously irrelevant stone commemorating Sir Walter Scott now on the opposite side of the new Dornoch Firth Bridge approach road from the distillery gates. Separated from the sea by the same railway which runs past Balblair (is that a hint of diesel oil you can detect in the nose of both whiskies?), it's a bonny spot, although not as pretty as the ludicrously romanticised advertising in which those sixteen saintly sepia-stained men of Tain constantly feature, ever ready to die for the purity of the Glenmorangie (and that's pronounced as in orangey, by the way) spirit.

I know Tain, and have a very soft spot for the douce wee town, whose main street is a classic of Scottish architecture: wide, straight, and with some really impressive buildings like the full-stop Royal Hotel at one end of the street. But Tain is also more than slightly weird, full of refugees from the Summer of Love, people who dropped one too many tabs of acid, small-minded local politicians who ought to drop a couple of tabs of acid, aristocratic, staunchly liberal cheesemakers, craftsmen and women, ugly little vandals and some very nice folk indeed. There's an RAF bombing range nearby, which adds to the strange atmosphere, with the distant thump of high explosive an interesting sonic backdrop. And there are some brilliant pubs.

What about the ley lines, though? Well, Tain has a fairly cosmic history. As the burial site of St Duthac, Tain was a place of pilgrimage for the Stewart kings of Scotland, and for some, St Duthac's Chapel remains a bit more than just another a sacred spot. Attempts to revive it as a place of pilgrimage are underway. It is also generally recognised, by those into such things, that Tain is a place where all the mystical vibes inherent in ley lines (those supposedly powerful earth-energy veins) converge. There is some dispute as to whether the lines converge at St Duthac's Chapel, or in the lounge bar of the St Duthac Hotel.

What can I say? I like the place. In my days as an amateur rock musician I played several times at the St Duthac Hotel (The Saint) or the St Duthac Centre, courtesy of local promoters Rob Ellen and Jimmy Sutherland, and lo! who should I see wandering down the street but the bold Jimmy himself, bald, wiry, grinning and shedding surplus energy like sparks as usual. He's in search of cigarettes.

'What the hell are you doing on a wreck like this?' Jimmy, sports car and bike *aficionado*, is not impressed with the orange beast, which, it has to be said, has behaved impeccably despite the vindictive weather thrown at it over the past two days. I explain my mission, to boldly drink where few have drunk before. 'I certainly think I can help you out in Tain,' grins Jimmy. 'I know a few people who might have some interesting things to say. And you'll stay at my house – save wasting your money on a bed and breakfast.'

Truth to tell, I have arrived in the midst of a crisis. The record shop Jimmy runs with Rob, along with their concert promotion business, has been broken into, and hundreds of tickets for imminent gigs ripped off.

'The truth is, the shop's not going well,' says Jimmy, shrugging. 'But what the hell, we did the Ralph McTell tour the other day, and what a gentleman! A hero of mine from the old days, and he couldn't have been nicer. Even did *Streets of London*. In the end, the crack makes up for everything, Tom.' Crack, in this context, not being microwaved cocaine, but conversation, discussion, interfacing, networking, social mixing. Tain is a good place for the crack.

'It's all pish against a wall in the end.' The speaker does not wish to be identified, but is one sixteenth of the sixteen men of Tain, the makers of Glenmorangie. According to a typically precious brochure, these persons – and in actual fact there are more than sixteen, including at least one woman – 'contribute their experience, intuition and skill with quietude and modesty, confident that time, wood, location and ingredients will, ever and again, work their own magic . . .'. Will somebody please shoot that copywriter.

Jimmy has inveigled our man down ostensibly to discuss the comparitive merits of my bottle of fourteen-year-old Clynelish. 'It's all right,' says our man. 'Bit too peaty for me. I prefer that lovely vanilla flavour you get out of Glenmorangie.' So he actually likes it? 'Yes, absolutely. It's clean, and I'm not biased, but it's really well made, not like some others I could mention.' Oh? Like what, for example? 'Well, like some of those Islay malts. They're just disgusting, full of all the shit that we would get rid of when we were distilling. I don't know how they get away with it, honestly. It's nothing but feints disguised as whisky.'

Feints is the impure stuff which the stillsman is supposed to avoid including in the pure 'middle cut' of spirit which he chooses to run from the still. According to our man, at Glenmorangie the stillsmen will take hours pouring off the middle cut 'as slowly as if it was syrup'.

The official line on Glenmorangie trips easily off our man's tongue. The stills are the tallest in Scotland, thus providing, so they say, Glenmorangie's smooth, clean, light, frankly Lowland taste. Only small, former American bourbon casks are used for maturation, thus avoiding the Macallanesque taint of sherry which the sixteen men sneer at so disdainfully. Maybe they really are like the advertisements, these guardians of their employer's good name.

So there's no scandal about Glenmorangie, then? No outrageous behaviour? Well, apart from the workforce being generally amused at their outrageous fictional appearances in the company's advertising brochure ('what a load of bollocks that is'); people are nowadays very well behaved.

'Ach, the old days, when the dramming was still going on, when you could actually drink on the job, so to speak, quite legally . . . that's when all the fun was. All the dunking and dooking – but that's all over now.'

A word of explanation. 'Dramming' was the whisky industry's equivalent to a tot of naval rum on the poop deck. Workers were entitled to three or four drams each day, usually of the plain, unaged, 70 per cent alcohol coming straight out of the stills. Special tasks undertaken for the manager, or dirty jobs, would carry payments of extra drams. This amazing tradition was finally scuppered by the Health and Safety Executive. One doctor friend told me that dramming was a cynical ploy used by the whisky industry to ensure that their employees became job-dependent alcoholics and thus could not leave. It also militated against union activism (hence the strong left-wing bent towards the Temperance Movement in late nineteenth and early twentieth-century industrial Scotland), basically because everyone was half-cut the whole time. But I think that doctor pal might be a communist or something, actually.

'Dooking' or 'dunking' is, or was, quite another matter. 'Dunkin' jars' were usually home-made from copper or some other soft metal, and could be easily concealed about one's clothing. Long, and just wide enough to fit into the bung-hole of a whisky cask, they were used to extract, illegally, the maturing, duty-free spirit either for instant consumption or for removal from the premises.

'It just doesn't happen any more,' said our man. 'It's not worth it. Look at us. It may be a fucking boring job, but it's a good job. Frankly, I don't have any idea why people want to visit distilleries on a hot day when we're all boiling and desperate to get out, but it's a good secure job. We're well paid, we work for a private company and we can get shares if we want. There's a good pension scheme, a free bottle a month and for some people a tied house. What more could you ask for in this day and age? People won't take the risk of losing their jobs just for a few drams.'

Not at Glenmorangie, perhaps. But it sure as hell still goes on elsewhere, if some of the rumours I heard before setting out on this trip are even halfway true. And all those lemonade bottles full of firewater you buy for a fiver must come from somewhere . . .

Our man leaves. Clynelish, he concludes, comes in a nice wooden box, and that's about the best he can say about it. 'Must add about a fiver to the price, that box.' Well, quite. The whole upsurge in highly priced 'premium' malts is the distilling industry's attempt to come up with a value-added product they can charge enormous prices for. Nobody except the taxman can make much money charging £8.00 for a bottle of supermarket blend. But something taxed at the same rate, because it's the same alcoholic strength, which you can charge nearly £30 for is a different story. And if a wee wooden box can add a fiver, well and good. Okay, the malts linger in casks for years and years and years, evaporating and using up cashflow like nobody's business. But the fact remains, everyone's getting into malts because the profit margins are much, much higher than they are in the realms of rubbing whisky.

Of course, if you really want to make some money, the best thing to do is come up with ludicrously expensive 'limited edition' bottlings of either really ancient or really strong whisky. There will always be an idiot prepared to pay £50, or £80, or even £500 for a bottle of smoke so strong it'll dissolve your teeth, or so old that all it tastes of is wood.

Glenmorangie, in the most coyly packaged and marketed way, of course, have a couple of 'supermalts' – a single-cask, 57.6 per cent alcohol ten-year-old which goes under the entirely stupid name of The Native Ross-shire (all Glenmorangie is native to Ross-shire) and an eighteen-year-old.

Jim Robertson back in Orkney, whose own company, Highland Park, had just started marketing, at vast expense, an eighteen-year-old encased in polished black wood, had been typically dismissive of the cultish, modern obsessions with age and strength.

'You can never tell where the marketing people are going to lead you,' he'd said. 'They're the ones who drive the decisions based on what they think they can sell, and on that basis I think the industry is doing quite well. But this notion that just because it's old and because it's strong it must be good, I can't necessarily agree with.

'There's this image that if you do everything in a sherry cask and say it's strong and old it must be good, and that's anything but the truth. People have this perception that if it's eighteen years old it must be good, if it's twenty-eight it must be brilliant, but I don't subscribe to that. There is extremely good old whisky, but it's not necessarily the case.'

No problems with the sherry obsession in Glenmorangie's case, anyway, because they only use bourbon casks. Jimmy and I decided that we would conduct an experimental tasting of all three Glenmorangies on their native Tain turf, and after a pretty superior bar supper in the Mansfield House Hotel, we headed for the Star Bar.

The Star is a Tain institution, unrefurbished late Victorian and quite splendid. Primed by a few Budweisers with dinner, Jimmy and I are keen to try the Native Ross-shire, which our man inside Glenmorangie had assured us was not chill filtered, as most malts are to remove any of the stray gunge called charl and also, they say, a good bit of character. The numbered bottles you get through the mail from certain whisky clubs tend to be straight from the cask, complete with bits of old oak and dead mice floating about in them, as do many of the specialist bottlings available from the likes of Gordon and MacPhail, Cadenheads and Signatory. The Native Ross-shire was, we were told, hand-filtered, a concept which fair boggled the mind. Whose hands had they used?

But there it was atop the Star's gantry, still in its box. 'Two Native Ross-shires, please,' I said. There was a dead silence.

'Two whats?'

'Two Native Ross-shires, darling,' said Jimmy, pointing to the bottle in question.

'Oh, you can't have that,' said the barmaid. 'We're keeping that for a special occasion.'

No amount of pleading would move her, and in absence of any eighteen-year-old either, in the end we had to settle for a couple of bog-standard ten-year-olds.

'Not bad,' said Jimmy, a former bar manager with a family background in the spirit trade. 'Not bad, but maybe a wee bit bland.'

Yes, perhaps Glenmorangie is a wee bit bland, a wee bit innocuous. It's awfully drinkable, though, gluggable almost, a Liebfraumilch amongst malts. It's awfully . . . nice. Let's face it, if it wasn't fairly bland it wouldn't be the top-selling malt in Scotland, where Lambrusco and Fry's Chocolate Cream are, after all, popular delicacies.

I once was in a position to glug almost unlimited Glenmorangie at the pre-match, half-time and post-game receptions associated with the Glenmorangie-sponsored Camanachd Cup shinty final, shinty being well known as the game where the hospitality begins long before the two teams start their apparently enjoyable task of seriously injuring each other. I was also celebrating the birth of my fourth son, so restraint was not the order of the day. All I can say is that the whisky went down a treat, and yes, it was gluggable. And I don't remember much about the game, or even if I saw it, or who was playing, or where it was.

The critics, that lucky band of folk who get paid to find strange scents in drinks, have always waxed lyrical about Glenmorangie, from Professor David Daiches, master of spiritous hyperbole which would undoubtedly sound better slurred, to the slightly more restrained but far too nice Michael Jackson. It's funny that out of all the books on whisky, nobody has a bad word to say about any particular brand. Some are very good, of course, but none is identified as downright innocuous or plain boring, for example. Then, they all get you drunk, I suppose, and that is the prime aim of whisky. Isn't it?

Jackson detects cinnamon, walnut, sandalwood, the sea and a touch of peat in Glenmorangie, while apparently a French perfumery found twenty-six fragrances in its golden depths. Jimmy and me, well, we quite liked it. But it's bland. Nice, clean and creamy, but bland.

Our man inside had also informed us that it was not quite true, as was sometimes claimed, that no Glenmorangie went for blending. Highland Queen contains a wee drop of the Tain cratur, although the word is that Glenmorangie 'doesn't mix well with grain'. Jimmy and I had a couple of Highland Queens, if you'll pardon the expression, and pronounced our-selves reasonably impressed.

But it was essential that we encountered the big, bad Native Ross-shire, so off we marched from the Star's cosy atmosphere of red-nosed comfort to the cocktail bar of the Royal Hotel. And there, at some ridiculous price per nip, we tasted it. And it was just like Glenmorangie, only more so. Stronger, yes, but with a kind of intensified blandness. So we had a couple of eighteen-year-olds, and from what I can remember, the eighteen-year-old was just like Glenmorangie, only more so. Except I'd be lying if I said I could remember exactly what that 'more so' consisted of. And because by this time, our ability to detect the subtle differences between the old, the not so old, the strong and the not quite so strong was, shall we say, diminished, we decided to revert to American beer, which doesn't taste of anything.

'You know, I've seen the tinks down at Balblair, sometimes,' said Jimmy. 'And do you know what they do? They sneak in for the empty barrels of a night, get a kettle of boiling water, pour it in and run that barrel around for half an hour or so. Then they empty it out and drink it, and apparently it's all right, not bad at all. They seem to get pissed okay on it.'

'Don't listen to him,' interrupted a Glaswegian accent. 'He's just talking rubbish.' And there was Doug Scott, grinning in the 1970s' tawdriness of the

Royal's chrome and velvet bar. I'd heard of Doug before, but never met him. A silversmith, his own company, Tain Silvercraft, now produces jewellery to his own and Celtic designs for outlets all over the world.

'I just got into it through necessity, basically,' he says. 'I was a sheet-metal worker at the Invergordon smelter, and when it closed and I was made redundant, I just decided to go for it. I never had any training in silversmithing as such, but, well, I was a sheet-metal worker, and I suppose there are similarities.'

Doug's brother-in-law, Alan, is with him. Alan, from Glasgow, is up staying with Doug and good grief, he is not impressed with Tain. 'Is this all there is?' he asks. 'Where do the young folk go in Tain? Where's the designer beers? Where's the happening bars?'

Alan, it seems, works for Scottish and Newcastle Breweries, where he is a kind of roving pub trouble-shooter. His pride and joy, he tells me, is a mammoth fun palace in Cumbernauld where punters have to pay to get in. 'First pub in Scotland with an entry fee,' he says proudly. 'We provide live music, karaoke, whatever. It's packed, absolutely packed. They don't mind paying. They get value for money, a good time. It's a good, lively atmosphere.'

'The Tories have been good to me, I can't deny it,' Alan goes on. 'I mean, the way I look at it, it's simply a question of the contents of your wallet, and there's just no doubt that I'm better off because of them.' Doug looks at him, shakes his head. A socialist and a nationalist, he explains, the Conservatives' 1992 election victory has plunged him into a depression which he doubts he'll ever recover from.

'Vote for the man, not the party, that's what I say,' says Jimmy. 'I suppose I've got liberal sympathies, but Charlie Kennedy's a good guy, and that's why I voted for him. Good old Charlie.'

All eyes turn to me. Political sympathies have been paraded, and it's my turn. But all I say is something like, 'Hey, isn't it amazing? Four people, four different political viewpoints.' That election result, so inevitable, is part of the reason I'm on this trip. But I'm not looking for answers. I'm looking for a drink. And I don't really want to talk about politics.

I suggest a visit to The Saint, the Saint Duthac Hotel, once the only place to go of a Highland Sunday afternoon, where dodgy rock bands could be guaranteed to provide a soundtrack to some serious boozing until it was time for the evening service. There is general assent.

'Is this where the young folk go?' asks Alan. 'Actually, I'm working. Wherever I go, I've got to check out the pubs and clubs in the area, and frankly, I have to say, I'm not impressed so far. No way.' And someone gets paid for doing that. I ask him if he has any vacancies, but apparently I don't spend enough time in Cumbernauld.

The Saint is an amazing place. The public bar presents a line of determinedly hunched backs, displaying fashion statements ranging from army surplus anorak to Oxfam non-chic. Robert, the manager, his red spectacles blazing, asks us what we'd like.

'What we'd like, Robert, is a game of pool,' says Jimmy, who more and more resembles Para Handy under full sail, Bruttish Spurits having taken. Jimmy used to be the manager at The Saint, in days of yore, and, he confides, Robert used to be his brother-in-law. Everyone nods.

Having a game of pool entails the lounge bar being specially opened for us, the heating switched on, together with electricity circuits which don't seem to have been used for decades brought into sizzling operation. Alan, it appears, is a bit of a hustler, but we decide to play simply for pleasure. It quickly becomes apparent that none of us are in a fit state to sink anything but – well, maybe, okay, if you insist – another weak American beer, and we repair to the back lounge bar, a snug little alcove tucked away in the oldest part of what is a very old building indeed.

Now, there is something odd about this bar. A gigantic, raw stone fireplace dominates one wall. There is a tiny counter made of polished wood, and a few stools. Yet you immediately feel at ease in it. It is a bar for long conversations, for settling the affairs of Tain and the world, for Keeping Bad Things Out There. It draws you in and will not let you go.

Robert joins us, and I begin idly tracing my fingers along the huge fireplace. Cut into the headstone, sharp and clear as the day they were carved, are two sets of initials, a date, and a heart. The heart, in the middle of the stone, is surmounted by the date 1730, and the initials JM and MMG are carved at either end.

'I remember the day we found those.' Jimmy leans against the opposite wall, a faraway look in his eyes. 'We were tearing out an old tile fireplace, renovating the bar, back just after I took over this pub. I shoved a crowbar in, and the whole fucking lot came roaring down. I was covered in dust, man. And then I saw that heart, and we just cleared the whole lot away, built up the back of the chimney, and that's it, exactly as we found it.'

Everyone falls silent. It's as if a spell has been cast over the dimly lit little bar. 'They say it was a marriage stone,' Jimmy continues, dreamily. 'We searched and searched through the records to see if we could find who it was, but we never did. But this is an old, old building, man, and maybe it was a couple setting up home here for the first time or something.'

'Any malts, Robert?' I feel curiously emotional after Jimmy's tale, and decide to take my mind of such esoterica by continuing my research. All The Saint has to offer is a very old bottle of Ord, made in Muir of Ord and a distillery on my list for visiting the next day. I can remember thinking it was a great dram, a dram drenched in history, but not a lot else about it. All my notebook says, in big scrawled letters, is 'Ord . . . marriage stone . . . history.'

71

Suddenly, the sound of very loud singing reverberates from along the corridor. 'Hello, there,' comes a voice which sounds happier than anyone has any right to be. 'Pleased to meet you! I'm a hippy!'

Ripped, stoned, on another planet . . . well maybe not, but in walks a man whose joy is uncontained and probably not of this world. 'I am a Gaelic hippy,' he announces. 'Do you want to hear a Gaelic Highland hippy song, straight from the horse's mouth?' We are all too surprised to say anything. At the top of his voice, Keith, as I shall call him, begins to bellow:

> Oh, a heederum a hoderum a heederum a ha
> A heederum a hoderum a heederum a hiiiii
> A teuchter teuchter hoderum a heederum a a coo
> Hari Hari Hari, Krishna Krishna noo.

We applaud, buy Keith a drink, and he bursts into a furious rendition of *Rattlin' Roarin' Willie* by way of gratitude. I run my fingers once more around the heart on the wedding stone, and I could swear I feel a tingling sensation. It could, on the other hand, be circulation problems associated with the consumption of strong drink.

'Hey, man,' says Keith. 'Got to watch this place. Ley lines, man. Tain is absolutely fucking full of them, man, and where you're standing there's probably fuckin' *hundreds*! Between here and St Duthac's Chapel, man. That's why Tain's a place where things happen. Tain is just an amazing place.'

It's late. Leaving the intersecting ley lines, the marriage stone, the empty bottle of Ord, and Robert to lock up, I bid goodnight to Doug and Alan, who keeps muttering, 'I just don't believe these toilets,' and head back with Jimmy to his house.

It takes an hour for us, jointly, to make up the spare bed, feeding a duvet into its cover in an advanced state of inebriation not being one of the easiest tasks in the world. By the time I collapse, exhausted, into said bed, Jimmy is sound asleep on the living-room floor, back against a couch, a can of Export in his hand. I fall asleep thinking about JM and MMG, dreaming about the solid, cut-in-stone legacy they have left us to wonder about, and about the strangely welcoming, warm atmosphere in that corner of The Saint, very possibly the greatest pub in the known universe. It must be the ley lines.

Chapter Five

AGAINST THE GRAIN

I was awakened by an enormous, throbbing, humming, buzzing noise, like a mutant vibrator from hell. According to my watch it was 6.30 a.m., and in that incredible state of aural and visual sensitivity induced by only the very worst hangovers, the whole house seemed to be vibrating in waves along with the huge racket.

I climbed out of bed, noticing that the duvet cover had been put on inside out, and searched for the source of the noise. Jimmy was still sound asleep in the lounge, but in what was obviously his bedroom a stereo system appeared ready to explode; it was loudly droning noise of a vomit-flecked, greyish-green colour, through not two, but four massive loudspeakers. I was certain it would take half the street with it when the blast came, so, after failing to master the touch-sensitive digital control, I ripped every wire I could see out of whatever it was connected to. The brain-liquidising noise stopped, and I crawled back to bed.

Three hours later Jimmy and I were breakfasting, almost capably, on All-Bran, vast quantities of sugar and Camomile tea. 'Great crack last night,' said Jimmy. 'Great. It's a long time since I've gone out and stayed so sober.' I knew then that I was not of sufficient calibre to survive the Tain experience for longer than an evening. One more sober night like that and I'd have Kattomeat for brains.

The morning, what was left of it, was dry but dull as I revved away from Jimmy's house. Something seemed wrong with the bike, though. There was a dragging, scraping noise from the front wheel, and I realised I hadn't unlocked the security chain, which had wrapped itself securely around the front forks and mudguard. It was not an auspicious start. As usual, though, the forcible application of fast-moving oxygen revived me as I headed for the gigantic grain distillery belonging to Invergordon Distillers of, yes, Invergordon.

The beautiful shores of the Cromarty Firth have always been ravaged by industrial and military complexes taking advantage of the deep, sheltered water. Invergordon was for over a century one of the main bases for the Royal Navy, and it is still dominated by the dirty-grey oil tanks which once held fuel for some of the biggest battleships of the line. Efforts are being made to dismantle these eyesores, as the Navy no longer has any use for them, and since they have recently put their shore base, occupied for over a century, on the open market.

Then there was the Invergordon aluminium smelter, one of the great hopes for Highland regeneration, which remains mothballed, a mute reminder of moronic economic policies and the unemployment and social disarray which still afflicts this area. Many moved from central Scotland to the Highlands, living in hastily built houses at Alness and Invergordon, to work at the smelter. When the unwieldy, expensive plant closed in 1983, some, like Doug Scott, switched careers successfully. Other did not, and the resulting social problems make this piece of the Highlands sometimes seem more like the run-down heartland of industrial Lanarkshire than anything else.

The rig repair bases are flourishing, attracting the great spidery structures in their dozens to the firth, but adding to Invergordon's unremitting ugliness. The enormous Invergordon grain distilling complex too is determinedly unattractive, all grey steel and endless pipework, looking more like a gas processing plant than a source of *uisge beatha*.

Invergordon do not court visitors. There is nothing picturesque about a continuous, grain whisky still, and since the brutal, ultimately successful battle to avoid takeover by Whyte and Mackay, the press has not been exactly *persona grata* either.

I'd met the manager, Bill Scott, at a function in Inverness. Invergordon had provided each table with a bottle of their youth-and-woman-targeted The Invergordon single grain whisky, and one of Isle of Jura, the bizarrely light, characterless spirit produced on the Hebridean island next to Islay, without even the slightest whiff of that isle's famous stuff-seaweed-and-peat-up-your-nose whisky personality. Funnily enough, Bruichladdich, actually made on Islay and also owned by Invergordon, is another bland, smooth, urbane drink. However, you can detect hints of geographical character in it if you persevere, and use your imagination.

Be that as it may, I'd telephoned Bill from Jimmy's the previous day, when I was still relatively untainted by Tain, to see if a visit to Invergordon was possible. It was, he replied, 'so long as it's not journalism'. It's for a book, I'd said, thinking I'd better be honest. Rather reluctantly, I thought, Bill agreed I could come along.

So here I was swinging into the carpark of what was definitely the busiest distillery I'd seen so far. Tankers and trucks roared in and out of the gates, steam and smoke belched urgently from chimneys, and everyone appeared to be in a hurry. The workers seemed a fairly contented lot. Mind you, if some of the stories about the enormous profits Invergordon employees had made through selling their personal shares in the company to Whyte and Mackay during the takeover attempt were true, you could understand them looking happy. Company loyalty, don't you just love it? A share-owning democracy is a wonderful thing.

Mike Jenner, assistant chief chemical engineer, had been detailed to explain the mysteries of continuous distillation to me. The very image of a chemist, small and intense, Mike cheerfully admitted that he didn't drink whisky himself. 'The occasional can of lager suits me fine.' In truth, at Invergordon there is none of the emotional attachment to the making of whisky you might find at malt distilleries.

Aeneas Coffey, a former Inspector General of Excise in Ireland, developed the patent or continuous still in 1831 – three years after the Scot

Robert Stein had produced a more cumbersome version. The system used by Invergordon is basically a very large, developed version of Coffey's invention, with computerised controls and the capability of producing alcohol of virtually any strength up to almost 100 per cent.

How does it work? Well, it involves two 60-foot-high columns, one called the rectifier, one the analyser, linked up by a pipe. A lot of steam goes into the bottom of the analyser and this directly boils the beery, not very alcoholic wash. Steam and alcoholic vapour shoot to the top of the column, and is then brought to the bottom of the rectifier column. At the top of that, the alcohol condenses.

Simple, isn't it? Well, not as simple as the production of malt, which is basically just large-scale cooking. The beauty of the continuous process is, first of all, that it is continuous. It can run twenty-four hours a days as long as there's wash available. Secondly, the fact that you can produce almost pure, neutral alcohol means that the variety of drinks you can concoct is almost infinite. And not just drinks.

From a continuous still comes the root of vodka (add concentrated bitter orange juice and water) and gin (add juniper berries and cardamom). And the wonderful thing is – compared to whisky – that those spirits don't have to age for at least three years in oak before they can be legally marketed. They give instant profitability.

Grain alcohol can be produced to virtually any strength at the touch of a button, and some of the industrial grade stuff goes for, well, industrial uses, including perfume manufacture. I'd heard that Invergordon actually supplied Chanel in Paris with raw spirit, but nobody could confirm this.

The first thing you need, of course, is grain from which to make the alcohol. 'Almost any starch source will do,' said Mike Jenner. 'In the past we mostly used maize, but recently it's been all wheat, due to European overproduction.' The fact is, because the system is so efficient, you won't get any taste of the original starch source in the finished product, so even old rags would do as a starch source, theoretically.

However, the production of anything which will carry the name Scotch Whisky is governed by The Scotch Whisky Act of 1988, which asserts that Scotch Whisky must 'be produced at a distillery in Scotland from water and malted barley (to which only whole grains of other cereals may be added)'.

In practice, what that means is that grain whisky, whether for blending (nearly all of it) or bottling as a single grain like Cameron Brig or The Invergordon, has to have some malt in it. It needn't be that much, but there is a legal requirement for some to be in there. It also cannot be distilled to a strength beyond 94.8 per cent alcohol by volume, 'so that the distillate has an aroma and taste derived from the raw materials used in, and the method of, its production'.

In reality, the strength of the spirit would be carefully tweaked below that figure – about 22 per cent higher than the maximum alcohol content you can get out of a pot-still – but whether or not you can get a huge amount of character from a grain whisky *per se* remains a moot point. The kind of casks they mature in will almost certainly provide both colour and taste, although the law explicitly allows spirit of caramel to be used as a colouring agent. Both Cameron Brig and The Invergordon remain resolutely – and in the case of the latter, deliberately, in a misjudged effort to attract 'new whisky drinkers' – bland. It must be said, though, that The Invergordon is also ferociously drinkable.

But the main destination of grain whisky is blended whisky, where it will make up between 40 and 85 per cent of your average bottle, depending on its name and price. The rest will be a marriage of various malts. When you see a bottle of 'twelve-year-old blend', it means that the youngest whisky – including the grain – must be twelve years old, although other, older whiskies, could also be used. The same is true of single malts, which are often mixtures of various casks from a variety of vintages. As far as your actual Own Label Old Cheapskate Real Scotch Supermarket Crap Whisky (thankfully, no longer available legally at under strength, 37.5 per cent alcohol, due to the great god Europe), that will be three years old max. It'll get you drunk, but not pleasantly.

The whole idea of blending began in Edinburgh in 1853 when Andrew Usher, an agent for The Glenlivet, began mixing grain and malt. Significantly, it was blended whisky which gripped the tastebuds and livers of England and the rest of the world, basically because of its blandness. It's sad but true that malt whisky was, and to some extent still is, considered by those of lesser sensibilities to be just too strong a taste. Or as the Scotch Whisky Association's otherwise admirable little booklet *Scotch Whisky: Questions and Answers* puts it:

> Pot-Still Malt Whisky is inclined to be too strongly flavoured for everyday drinking, especially by people in sedentary occupations and warm climates. The demand for a whisky that is milder in flavour and more suited to the conditions of modern life can be met only by mixing Malt Whisky with Grain Whisky that has less pronounced characteristics.

'More suited for the conditions of modern life . . .' Aw, come on. This is plainly nonsense, and a mere sop to the multi-million-pound trade in blended whisky. The time has come for the true spirits of Scotland to be given their just recognition, not hidden away in the murky depths of some blend calculated to appeal to the passive palates of Essex Man or any other unacceptable racial and cultural stereotype. There are well over a hundred Scottish malt whiskies, and they range from the icy clarity of, say, Tamnavulin, to the smoothness of Lowland malts like Bladnoch, through the peaty textures of Longrow and Clynelish to the big, bad Islay medicinals.

Some will suit different climates, different temperaments, different occupations, sedentary or not. But most have distinctive characters, and the whisky industry has tried to bury that in the past, attempting to produce cheap, supermarket tat for what was thought to be the money-spinning mass market.

Only now is it being realised that there is money in good taste, that people, ordinary people, can appreciate natural, organic, regional quality and are prepared to pay for it. That national and regional character is now a marketable commodity, and the wonderful range of characterful malt whiskies available is a tremendous resource, already finding a ready market amongst the young and cool in Spain, Italy and France.

My manifesto, 'The conditions of modern life', calls for the breadth of character and distinctiveness in the various forms of our national drink to be celebrated and publicised. It is happening already. Malts are going to be the cult of the early twenty-first century, from Alaska to Australia. And can I recommend, just as a start, a Lagavulin for Alaska and a Dalwhinnie for Australia? Just a thought. Another suggestion is this: get some of The Invergordon and a selection of malt miniatures, and start making up your own blends. The 'master blenders' will tell you that some malts just don't go together – producing, they say, 'fire' or 'water' in unacceptable proportions – but wouldn't it be great fun finding out? And here's my patented idea, O great whisky-makers: market a blending kit, with instructions, glasses, grain and malt whisky, for home use. And remember where you first read about it.

'I'm quite proud of our process,' said Mike, 'in that nothing is wasted.' We spent, it seemed to me, a quite inordinate amount of time examining the machinery which produces animal feed pellets from the used draff, the grain which has been fermented to make the wash. In malt distilleries, this is simply loaded on to trucks as animal food; at Invergordon, it is turned into proper pellets. I made impressed noises.

What *was* impressive were the twenty-two washbacks, containing a veritable ocean of wash. Where, I asked, was Ben Wyvis, the little malt distillery Invergordon has on site? 'Oh, that hasn't run for years,' said Mike. 'Most of the bits have gone. It's been cannibalised, I'm afraid. I don't think we could get it running even if we wanted to.'

Oh, I don't know. I feel sure that Mike, a technocrat if ever there was one, could get Ben Wyvis back into operation if he wanted to. Meanwhile, I'm peckish, with the drouthy hunger of the previous night's excesses, and it's time to move on.

I lunch in the smelter suburb of Alness, in the seated area of a fish and chip shop which serves packet soup and a very dodgy variety of cheeseburger, rather pink and slimy in the middle and obviously straight out of the deep-freeze via a microwave. I have a problem with cheeseburgers. No matter the risk, no matter the dingy, mouldering decay of the hamburger van, the grease stall, the caff, I will go for a cheeseburger. It's like the Japanese habit of eating filleted blowfish, in the sure and certain knowledge that somewhere along the line is one where the poison has not been properly removed; one that'll kill you. With me it's cheeseburgers and mad cow disease.

Two neatly besuited young men sit nearby, also eating cheeseburgers. They have open bibles in front of them, and are discussing the moral implications of St Paul's teaching on the place of women in the church. 'It's plainly wrong for a woman to have authority over a man,' says one, 'both practically and spiritually.' The other nods.

Brethren, I guess, of a fairly narrow sort, endlessly debating the kind of bankrupt fundamentalist theology I was raised to believe was more important than life itself. In our gospel hall, a girl once got up without a hat (St Paul says women must have their heads covered 'because of the angels', whatever that means), and preached to the assembled congregation. Four people were taken seriously ill.

The two young men, no more than boys really, pay their bill and leave, bibles clutched like talismen under their oxters. Free Kirk, possibly, bent by culture and family into the shapes of their elders. The suits hint at that, all dark and shiny. Not Mormons, anyway. I munch raw cow's brains and drink chicory-spiked coffee, nursing a late hangover headache as they make their evangelical way down the street. There but for fortune . . .

Teaninich had been described to me as a particularly bonny distillery, but truth to tell, the recently reopened United Distillers plant down by a weir on the River Alness looked just like Clynelish: modern, with six stills visible behind plate glass. It appeared quite nice in a late 1960s sort of way (although apparently the building was put up in 1970), and it had a field in front of it with horses. However, that was about it. I was not, as Barnard was, struck by the plethora of 'verdant meadows in which cattle were placidly grazing', but it was certainly a pleasant contrast to the brutal practicality of the Invergordon complex. I'd tasted Teaninich (which is fairly obscure) in the past, and as far as I can remember I enjoyed it without feeling in the least inclined to order up a case or buy the distillery. At any rate, without the time to spend hassling the management into a tour and a free nip, I headed for Dalmore, back a short distance towards Invergordon.

Dalmore, I have to say, is a delight. Apart from being a really interesting, beefy but under-recognised malt, the distillery itself is beautifully situated right on the shores of the Cromarty Firth, and its buildings, some of them very old indeed, have recently been tastefully renovated. There is no reception centre as such, but even casual visitors, which is how I presented myself initially, are welcomed not by guides, but by the folk who actually make the whisky.

I parked the bike literally a foot or so from the sea, dismounted and walked into the stunning offices, lined with wooden panelling dismantled from a now-demolished country house on the Black Isle opposite. It was like being in an old-fashioned bank, a church, or a film set for *Brideshead Revisited*. The effect of the aged oak was quite overpowering. It made you want to whisper.

Andrew Sinclair, the brewer and, in effect, the assistant manager, did not turn a hair when he saw my biker's garb. I'd left the yellow oilskins on the beast's rack, but even in fairly dry weather – the rain had still not materialised – I made for intimidating viewing, six-foot-two of black leather and stained cord trousers, hair plastered sweatily to my skull by helmet pressure.

'Not a bad day,' he said, dressed in a pressed blue cotton coat, hair immaculate in a now conservative style which had its roots in original Elvis. Andrew was of that era.

'Not bad at all,' I affirmed.

'Do you know much about Dalmore?'

'Err . . . not a great deal, no – but I know how the basic process of distilling works. I've, eh, been round one or two other distilleries, you know.' I was fairly anxious to show that I wasn't a complete ignoramus. The fact that I hadn't even tasted Dalmore was not a good beginning.

But Andrew's tour managed to be detailed without being patronising in the slightest. From the loading hatch where Dalmore's lightly peated malt arrives in truckloads, he took me past the peaty spring running down from the snow-capped heights of Ben Wyvis through the exquisitely modernised plant, which manages to combine the brand new with the best of the traditional – like an original 1874 copper pot-still, identifiable among its seven more modern neighbours by the old-fashioned dovetail welds. Andrew ran his finger down that weld with real pride.

A great deal of money has been spent at Dalmore, doubtless stemming from Whyte and Mackay's place in the American Brands scheme of things, the folk who brought you, among other things, Jim Beam. You'd think that would imply a ready supply of nice, charred, bourbon casks for maturing the whisky, but Dalmore sticks to sherry and wine-treated casks, many of them remade, or reconstructed from cask-kits, bits and pieces of broken-up barrel.

As ever, most of the production goes for blending, and doubtless you'll find Dalmore in Whyte and Mackay itself. The duty-free, bonded warehouses are right on the shore, and Andrew let me drink in the atmosphere of those great, gloomy whisky cathedrals. There is something thrilling about those huge warehouses, knowing that the casks may be in there for decades or already have been, smelling that heartily uplifting smell of wood and alcohol and sherry and the sea.

Aye, it fair brings on a thirst and, having recovered my equilibrium after the previous evening's adventures, I followed Andrew back to those fabulous offices for a dram. I was ushered into the manager's own inner sanctum, and came face to face with John MacDonald, forty-two years at Dalmore and the very image of what you hope a distillery manager might look like. Long, wispy white hair surrounded a cherubic, impish face, with a huge briar pipe a permanent fixture.

The amazing thing about all this was that as far as Andrew and John were concerned, I was just a mad biker who had turned up out of the blue and asked for a guided tour. This was Highland hospitality at its best, and an example of the pride whisky-makers used to take in displaying their craft to visitors, the kind of pride which does shine through Barnard's book, and which to some extent has been destroyed by the glossy Disneyworld extravagances to be found on the Speyside Whisky Trail and elsewhere.

John poured me a dram of the twelve-year-old Dalmore, a small one at my own request. It's a fine whisky, big and hearty and powerful, without much peatiness, but benefiting from the sherry-cask ageing and the nearness of the sea. I make loud appreciative noises.

'Aye,' says John, who looks as though he ought to be in an advertisement. 'Well, here we have the mountains, with Ben Wyvis behind us, and we have the sea, so I suppose we take a little character from both.'

Andrew and John ask if I'm on holiday, and I decide to come clean about my mission. Am I the Tom Morton who works for the *Scotsman*? I am. And Magnus Linklater is the editor, is he not? He is.

'Oh well,' says John. 'Give your editor my regards. I was his sergeant-major in the Territorial Army when the Linklaters lived around at Nigg there. Tell him I'm very glad he decided to pursue a career outside the military.' (Second-Lieutenant Linklater of the 11th Battalion Seaforth Highlanders was later to claim a 'brief but glorious' sojourn with the Territorials, 'in which I had at least a Field-Marshal's baton in my knapsack. They had stopped supplying knapsacks when I was there, but there was no doubting the baton.')

John tells me a bit about this most scenically situated of distilleries: how the old stone jetty jutting into the firth outside is known as 'The Yankee Pier', because the distillery, which used to have its own railway siding, was taken over by the American Navy during the First World War, and used as a mine factory; how it was damaged by fire in the Second World War.

He and Andrew reminisce about the great days, the dramming years. 'I can remember when you'd have your three official drams,' says Andrew, 'and your dram for a dirty job, for cold work or hot work, and your dram for a favour done for the manager. Those were great days, days when there was tremendous crack in the trade . . .' However, he doesn't miss it. 'No, that was many years ago now, and when it stopped, I didn't bother. It didn't bother me at all.'

I ask about the infamous habits of dookin' and dunkin'. John goes to a cupboard. Out of it he takes a copper tube, about two feet long and an inch and a half wide. It is sealed at one end and has a leather thong at the other.

'There you are,' he says. 'A dooker, one I confiscated many years ago from a workman here. That's something else we just don't get any trouble with any more. People are more responsible nowadays.' I take his word for it. 'Have a look at this,' he says, taking something else from the cupboard. It is a small, corked medicine bottle, with only about an inch of thick, golden liquid in it. John uncorks it and hands it to me. I sniff something incredibly rich and heavy.

'Well,' I say, 'this is undoubtedly whisky!'

'Fifty years old,' says John. 'Distilled well before the war.'

'Ach, let the boy have a wee taste of it, just a dribble,' says Andrew, and so a tiny sliver of the glutinous fifty-year-old Dalmore trickles into my glass. Both Andrew and John watch intently as I raise the glass to my lips. It seems crazy to add water. I don't.

'Amazing,' I murmur. 'Astonishing.' What does it taste of? A war, fifty years of world strife, the depletion of the ozone layer, the end of communism in Eastern Europe? No, not really. It tastes old, old and golden and honey-like, but mostly old. I feel duly privileged to have had the experience, but was it four times better than the twelve-year-old? No. It wasn't a truly drinkable whisky at all. A religious experience? Not that either. It was actually a bit salutary, tasting that malt. It was a whisky from which youth had departed, leaving only memories. There was something sad about that taste.

I promised to give my editor John's regards, and left the wooden womb of that glorious office for the orange beast, which sat, grimy and down-at-heel, but with a dry saddle for once. The weather, unbelievably, was still holding; it had been a good day, in lots of ways.

Hurtling along through Dingwall, where the now-closed Ferintosh Distillery has been uneasily converted into a 'business centre', I tried not to remember the dreadful behaviour of myself and other members of the press corps during the 1991 National Mod, the celebration of all things Gaelic, traditional, musical, poetic and liquid. It was no good, though. I caught a glimpse of the Dingwall British Legion, press base for the event's duration and it all came flooding back: the unwelcome attempt to participate in a children's rugby game by the cream of Her Majesty's Journalists; the furious verbal assault on a friend for daring to remain sober; the two hours it took to type one paragraph on a lap-top computer which seemed to be moving about the room of its own volition; the banning of one reporter from the Legion for vocally supporting the opposition during the screening of one of Scotland's doomed international football matches . . . ah, the demon drink. I had remained teetotal for a month following that little extravaganza, which by all accounts had been a tame affair. Previous mods, featuring, as they did, alcohol-fuelled press conferences, had become known to the Fourth Estate as 'the Whisky Olympics'. Dingwall was more of a school sports day, hardened modites informed me. Kids' stuff.

Just outside Muir of Ord, the tall tower of the Ord maltings, source of various specifications of malted barley for many of the Highland outposts of United Distillers, rears above the road. The Ord, or Glen Ord, or Glenordie (a typical eastern Highland familiarisation, by the way, used of people and places, as in Inversneckie for Inverness, or Cullicuddenie for Cullicudden, or Jimmie for Jim) Distillery proper is a hundred yards up a road beside the maltings.

It is, officially, now Glen Ord. The Ord back in Tain was very old, although a lot of that ageing had been done in the bottle, and thus would have had no effect on the contents, so they say. I'm not entirely convinced of this, though, especially if the bottle is half empty and is corked rather than capped. The trapped air and/or evaporation must surely have some effect.

Anyway, here I was, about to enter for the first time the realms of the custom-built reception centre, uniformed guides and multinational bus parties. I tried to make myself look as much like a tourist as my grimy motorcycling gear allowed, and walked towards my fate.

'Hello. Are you English?' I was disconcerted, to say the least, but Lorraine, the name-tagged guide, had a nice smile.

'No,' I replied, somewhat shortly. 'Scottish, British or perhaps European, but certainly not English.'

'Glad to hear it,' replied the lovely Lorraine, who looked like she was practising to be a minor-league television personality. 'That means I don't have to translate.'

Already in the raw-wood and old-implements reception centre was a fair representation of the United Nations, presumably from the motley collection of cars and minibuses I'd parked beside. Japanese, Dutch, German, French and Spanish all sounded as if they were being spoken simultaneously.

'Can you all understand English?' asked Lorraine. There was a multinational murmur of assent, and we were off, a jolly group of twenty, one or two families, one minibus party from what seemed to be a youth camp, and one couple whose ambition seemed to be sexual congress atop any non-vertical surface.

Lorraine was very good, having learned her lines well. The difficulty is, I suppose, how much complexity a non-specialist visiting group can take in. What we got was a simplified, slightly romanticised version of how Ord is made. For example: 'We get our barley from local farms. If it's not good enough, then we travel around the country to get the best.' Well, yes, and possibly out of the country too. Lorraine also asserted that the barley was malted 'over burning peat', but redeemed herself by pointing out that while in Islay and Skye a lot of peat was used to produce smoky malts, at Ord 'we don't use too much. There's just a hint of peat and smokiness in our whisky.'

Everybody stuck their heads in the mash tun, gasping from the blast of carbon dioxide they duly received. We got splashed with foam from the washbacks. Lorraine described, accurately and simply, what happens in the distillation process, while most people seemed slightly awed by the sight of six big copper pot-stills, evidently boiling hot, and the rush of white, middle-cut spirit, neither foreshots nor feints, through the polished brass spirit safe. We followed the black, always highly visible pipe which carries the spirit to the filling house, and there Lorraine told us about the three different types of cask Glen Ord use: the 110-gallon butt; the 60-gallon hogshead or hog, and the American 40-gallon barrel.

They let you into a warehouse at Glen Ord, where it is possible to see the name 'Drambuie' stencilled on some of the casks of maturing whisky. Drambuie is a sweet whisky liqueur, supposedly made according to a secret recipe given by 'Bonny' Prince Charlie to one Flora Macdonald, out of gratitude for her engineering of his escape (allegedly dressed as a woman) over the sea to Skye and finally a drunken, brandy-soused death in Italy. *Mincin' wi' Chairlie*, as Michael Marra's superb song refers to the inglorious '45's whole sorry mess.

Does this mean that Prince Charlie specified Glen Ord in the recipe? Well no, as there was no official distillery there at the time. However, I suppose he could have known about the illicit product from the Beauly and Muir of Ord area, couldn't he? Okay, so it's just a load of tartan codswallop, but never mind. The tourists love it.

Actually, there is an ever-burgeoning range of these whisky liqueurs springing up, as distillers – and in fact, just about anyone – realises that a funny-shaped bottle, plenty of sugar and a couthy name will sell like Perrier in the Sahara to the sweetness-obsessed Scots and, sad to say, lots of other folk who ought to know better.

Lorraine reveals that Drambuie insist on the Glen Ord they use being more than twenty-two years old, which seems just a tad extreme for something you can actually find inside chocolates. I can just imagine, post-Christmas dinner, biting into a chocolate Drambuie liqueur ('Just half for you children,' says Mum, 'we don't want to get you drunk') and with a blinding flash of inspiration identifying a twenty-two-year-old Glen Ord as one of the significant components. How do you nose a chocolate, anyway?

I begin to realise that Lorraine is actually very well informed about the whole process, and some of the details she comes up with are the kind of things distillery managers often fight shy of making public. Both wine-treated and sherry casks are used for maturing Glen Ord, she says, but the wine-treated barrels are used for the 97 per cent of production which go for blending. The 3 per cent of spirit which is to be matured for bottling under the Glen Ord label at twelve years old is matured exclusively in genuine ex-sherry casks. Hmmm . . . interesting. She also reveals that you can find Glen Ord lurking in blends like Haig, Johnny Walker and Vat 69, if you really feel inclined to do some extensive and abstruse research.

Back we all go, chattering in our Babel of tongues, to the reception centre to actually taste this whisky of the gods, which Lorraine assures us 'is in competition with brandy, because it's reckoned to be so smooth'. And it is, too. Smooth, that is, and clean; as far as I can remember the Ord I tasted in Tain had a big, peaty wallop to it which this just doesn't have. It's nice, though pleasantly innocuous. After what has been a pretty enjoyable tour of an immaculately kept and interesting distillery – and after all they do get all their own malt from their own maltings next door – it's a wee bit disappointing.

Glen Ord has a whiff of Speyside about it, and that provokes concern in me that my bias against Speyside malts may be a baleful influence on my whole approach to whisky, to the trip, to my whole life, in fact. And Speyside is where I am bound next, after an overnight stay back in the bosom of my family in the Black Isle. Surely all Speyside malts cannot be light and bland and creamy and (yawn) smooth? Or have I been forever damaged by overindulgence in Laphroaig and chicken vindaloo?

I am pondering this, making odd squiggles in a notebook, when one of Lorraine's fellow woman guides spies that there is a chiel amang them taking notes. She is upset. 'If you're writing anything about being here, don't quote anything we say! Speak to our supervisor in the office!'

I mumble something placatory, and stuff my notebook inside my leather jacket. Should I buy a miniature of Glen Ord? A tea towel? No. Should I talk to the supervisor? No. I think I'll go home and have my tea instead. Will quoting Lorraine land her up to her ears in pot ale and draff? I doubt it. Not only was she doing a good job, but she's bound to be doing the weather on Sky Television soon.

Chapter Six

INTO THE HEART OF BLANDNESS

I can't believe it. Ashers Bakery in Nairn, one of the great tea-rooms of all time, a nostalgic throwback to the 1950s, won't give me anything to eat.

'Teas only, son.' Well, at least I'm being called 'son', a flattery increasingly rare and valued. 'This is half-day closing. We're nearly shut.' It's still only twenty to two.

I shuffle noisily downstairs, annoyed. The trip from Cromarty, cursed as ever with rain and hail so bad I have had to stop three times, has been made bearable only by dreams of home-made broth and a couple of Ashers pies in the amazing wood-veneer and wrought-iron restaurant above the Nairn shop. These goodies have been dashed from my lips, and I am all undone.

The A96 does that to a motorcyclist. It undoes you, frazzles the nerves, leaves you with the certainty that all truck-drivers hate anything with two wheels, that lorry designers deliberately build in those ferocious slipstreams which hit you thirty seconds after the juggernaut has swept by. In fact, so bad is the reputation of the 'killer' Aberdeen to Inverness road, I am somewhat surprised to have survived at all. However, I am gradually getting used to the vulnerability inherent in motorcycling, and Elgin is still a good twenty-two miles away. Fatalism is always helpful in such situations.

Food is required, though, and I wander through the charming, slightly raffish streets of Nairn looking for sustenance. Once one of the giant Scottish holiday resorts and a favourite retreat of one Charles Chaplin, Nairn still boasts superb golf courses and relatively clean beaches, but looks a bit run-down, a bit out of time. Me, I like the place a lot. Perhaps we resemble each other.

In Poppies, a weird cross between tea-shop and wine bar, I eventually find the possibility of lunch. I am shown to a corner table, and watch the waitress bring a steaming bowl of what seems like sawdust to the table opposite, where an elderly couple and a huge Alsatian dog wait expectantly. The waitress smiles over at me. 'Special biker's food,' she says, putting the bowl on the floor for the dog, who wolfs the contents in seconds. We all laugh at the waitress's levity.

'It's a good job I'm not sensitive,' I say. It's also a good job I'm so hungry, or I'd be out of the door in high dudgeon at her remark. I feel like stripping off all my road-soiled bikerclothes, standing on the table and shouting, 'Look at me! Can you not see I am a sensitive, educated human being without tattoos or any permament disfigurement from knife battles or strange sexual relationships with farm animals? Am I not clean, and smelling strangely of Drakkar Noir deodorant?'

But I don't, and content myself with a cappuccino and a tuna-filled baked potato. I even tip the waitress because, let's face it, I'm such a nice guy. I don't even spit on the floor as I leave. I do give the Alsatian a very nasty look, though, and I can tell he's frightened.

Elgin is approaching through the rain and mud and spray, and I decide to have a look at Miltonduff, the first distillery I'll have seen on what could loosely be termed Speyside. And loose is a good description of Speyside, as it covers areas quite distant from said river. A triangle formed with Elgin, Huntly and Grantown-on-Spey as its pointy bits would include most of the whisky-producing outposts, such as the infamous glen of Glenlivet, which is only six miles long but which, due to the enormous reputation accrued by J. and G. Smith's The Glenlivet, has had its name affixed to whiskies made as far away as Pitlochry.

Miltonduff is near Pluscarden Priory, where the monks will take you in for meditation or drying out. I file that possibility away for the end of the trip. No Visitors Allowed is the message at the distillery, although it looks quite nice. I've never tasted its product, although I aim to put this right at Elgin, home of the whisky-drinker's heaven, Gordon and MacPhail's wondrous licensed grocery.

Elgin is a bustling sort of place, giving every evidence of prosperity, and it has not suffered the architectural indignities inflicted upon Inverness by the morons of 1960s' planning. Big buildings, wide thoroughfares, the remains of the sacked cathedral and loads of parkland make it an attractive place. But it's hardly Highland. I am well into Morayshire now, and a certain self-conscious Aberdonian dignity is evident in the buildings and some of the folk. They seem to think a lot of themselves in Elgin.

The people who run Gordon and MacPhail probably have every right to think highly of themselves. The Urquharts who still run this family firm are direct descendants of the John Urquhart who joined Mr Gordon and Mr MacPhail in 1895, the year they founded the company, initially just a licensed grocer.

Things have changed. The grocer's shop is still there, but Gordon and MacPhail have become the biggest specialist wine and spirit wholesalers in Scotland, and, as well as bottling weird and wonderful whiskies of all ages and varieties, in miniature and full-size bottles, the firm has many other strings to its bow, some of them a bit strange.

There is, for example, 'Van Der Hum, the world-famous tangerine and brandy liqueur' advertised by Gordon and MacPhail to the wholesale trade with the subtle little slogan, 'Have a Hum-dinger of a tourist season'. This stuff, with which I have no personal acquaintance, comes from South Africa. G&M are Scottish agents for a company called Edward Cavendish and Sons Ltd who, according to a G&M brochure, 'control the importation and distribution of KWV South African Wines, Brandies and Liqueurs and Santa Carolina Chilean wines'.

Maybe I'm just an old hippy at heart, but it leaves me a little uneasy to find what certainly used to be two of the world's most repressive régimes suddenly having their products pushed cheerfully into pubs. Perhaps, to make the marketing job easier to sensitive souls like myself, the South African stuff should carry special labels stating, for example, 'We as a company do not and never have exploited anyone on the grounds of race'. And the Chilean wines should bear a slogan like: 'We, of course, had nothing to do with the massacre at the Santiago Football Stadium, and always thought General Pinochet a bit extreme. We didn't like to say anything at the time, of course, and we're sure you understand. Forget your moral sensibilities and get pissed.'

I'm sure that would help.

Gordon and MacPhail's Licensed Grocery is, quite simply, paradise, tempered only by the hellish realisation (in most cases) that you cannot possibly afford everything you'd like to buy. At first, on leaving the actual grocery part of the store and entering the off-licence, you think well, this isn't very big. Then the floor-to-ceiling whisky displays hit you, the island racks of wine and liqueurs, the thousands of miniatures. The staff's knowledge is encyclopaedic, they will put you on a free mailing list, there is always a bottle on the counter for free tasting. You can have your own blend made up with your own personalised label, although believe me (I know someone who had this done), it isn't cheap.

I am browsing amid the astonishing array of miniatures, many not malts at all but oddly named blends aimed squarely at the collector. Miniature-hoarding is fairly common, and particularly rare, unopened examples can sell for hundreds of pounds.

Here, prices range from about £1.60 upwards to £2.70 for five centilitres, from 'Fisherman's Friend' and 'Drover's Dram' to really obscure things like the three Inverness whiskies, all from long closed distilleries. There's something rather odd about seeing a 1966 Millburn for sale as part of G&M's Connoisseur's Choice series, knowing that the distillery has been converted into a truly awful steakhouse and bar complex. Or finding Glen Mhor and Glen Albyn peeking out at you like ghosts, with not a stone remaining of either distillery back in the Highland capital.

There are whiskies for minority groups, including Cyclist's Dram, and geographical nostalgia likee Glasgow Mist. There is also George Morton's, a Dundee blend which bears my father's name.

I gather a basketful of miniatures to fill in a few gaps in my tasting experience, and am thoughtfully regarding the shelves of full-size bottles, when two thoroughly disreputable-looking young men in their early twenties enter. They have long, straggly hair, incipient beards and are wearing odd clothes with large woolly hats. They look like they've slept in a hedge. Gesturing at the shelves of whisky, the duo jabber away in a language I have difficulty recognising. Is it Spanish? Portuguese?

'Hello. You have fifty grade whisky? Macallan fifty grade?'

The woman behind the counter looks quizzically at the two foreigners. 'You want fifty-year-old Macallan?'

'No, fifty strong. *Strong*! Excuse, we are Barcelona.'

So, are these Catalan members of another national and cultural minority visiting their Scottish comrades in repression, post-election? Or are they international whisky thieves? I look more closely at their rumpled clothes and realise my mistake. What at first appeared to be rumpled and ill-fitting is gradually revealed as unstructured, bank-breakingly expensive designer wear. They are offered the strongest whisky G&M stock, a 64 per cent alcohol cask-strength (some cask) Bruichladdich at £46. They take it. They also take a twenty-four-year-old Macallan, two eighteen-year-old Macallans, and a half-bottle of ordinary Macallan. The shop is filling up, so I miss the extraneous bottles and miniatures they purchase as well, but the bill comes to £352. They pay in cash.

'We are for collecting, in Barcelona,' they say, taking pictures of each other with an expensive miniature camera. 'And for drinking too.'

I am reminded of a Faroese yacht crew who spent £600 on drink in the space of ten minutes at the Wine Shop in Lerwick, Shetland. Of course, the value for smuggled drink in the near-prohibitionist Faroe Islands is so vast that you could probably live for a year on the income from that little lot. But these young, cool and rich Catalans are collecting and drinking specific malt whiskies, and the question is, how many more are there back in Barcelona doing the same? Or in Madrid, or Milan, or Paris, or Rome? Is all this stuff about young palates not being mature enough for strong, heavy tastes just a load of balls? I mean, twenty-four-year-old Macallan?

I go to Crawford's for a cup of tea, clutching a jingly bag of miniatures. I can tell my purchasing power did not impress the G&M assistant, as she did not offer me a free taste of Glentauchers 1979, as she did the two Catalans. I asked for one anyway, and got a small glass of ignorable Speysidish malt. Objectivity, Tom, objectivity.

As I sit in the formica-topped modernity of Crawford's cafeteria, the heavens open outside. An old lady sitting opposite says to me, 'You'll need that helmet.' She follows this with: 'Are you on a motorbike?'

Yes, I reply.

'Can I have a lift home? I've no one to take me home.' She is parchment-skinned, at least seventy-five, and clutches both a heavy walking-stick and a shopping trolley. Feeling terrible, I mutter something about doing some shopping myself first, pay for my tea and leave her sitting there, like a date who's been stood up one time too many.

Guiltily, I start the beast and head for my chosen bed and breakfast, courtesy of the Scottish Tourist Board B&B book. The Lodge, run by Orcadian Marilyn Spence, is an enormous and immaculate detached house in the well-heeled Victorian part of Elgin. She eyes my attire nervously, and I am aware that I smell distinctly of burnt two-stroke oil. 'It's okay,' I tell her. 'I promise not write on the walls.' She seems reassured.

That night I eat dreadfully in a Chinese restaurant, and encounter Elgin's night-time role as a military town. The RAF base at Lossiemouth is nearby, and small, relatively well-behaved herds of short-haired young men roam the quaint old alleys and wide streets. Women seem in short supply. I have a Rolling Rock beer in a pub converted from a church, run by a sunlamped man called Roger in a floral shirt and heavy gold jewellery who could have stepped straight out of *Miami Vice*. The pub, which would like to be up-market but doesn't quite make it, is called High Spirits.

'This used to be a furniture store,' he says defensively when I ask if there were many problems getting the building deconsecrated. 'It hasn't been a church for sixty years.'

The White Horse has no pretensions to being anything but an ordinary pub. However, they do have Aberlour ten-year-old, at £1.25, which to my surprise goes down very well indeed, big and meaty and spicy and full of, yes, character! And from Speyside, too! This despite the fact that, when I ask for a drop of water, my glass is briskly given a douse of soda from the taps beneath the bar. Oops. I head back to the Lodge, passing Thunderton House, a young-and-happening bar complex converted from an eighteenth-century townhouse. It's full of RAF types, all chatting up about three women. The men drink heavy beer, the women Diamond White cider. Back at the Lodge I sample one or two of my miniatures while watching TV in the small but perfectly formed room, which smells of fabric conditioner and carpet shampoo. Miltonduff seems all the usual Speyside things, clean and bright and smooth, but I enjoy it. What's happening to me? Am I being seduced by my surroundings? I try a Mortlach twelve-year-old, and have to admit that it's really good, deep, dry and smoky. Only the smell of the sea is lacking. Maybe Speyside won't be so bad after all.

Next day, after a hearty and heart-damaging breakfast, I dug the orange beast out of the foot-deep gravel which covers the Lodge's drive, and headed for Keith along the next section of the 'killer' A96. My destination was Strathisla, my first stop along the 'official' Speyside Whisky Trail, as enshrined in a Tourist Board booklet and map. Eight distilleries, all offering visiting facilities you don't have to book in advance, are officially on the trail: Strathisla at Keith; Glenfiddich at Dufftown; Tamnavulin and The Glenlivet in the six-mile stretch that really is Glenlivet; Glenfarclas near Ballindalloch; Tamdhu and Cardhu, and Glen Grant at Rothes. It's a round trip of seventy miles, the whisky trail, and we are talking serious tourist tat here. Never has so much tartan bullshit been added to whisky and, believe me, the taste is much worse than a John Collins.

Strathisla's okay, actually, although I arrived about 9.30 in the morning and was given a complete tour to myself by a guide called Audrey who knew her stuff, if by rote. The distillery, owned by Seagrams along with the massive Keith bonding complex nearby, is impossibly pretty, which is quite an accomplishment because Keith certainly isn't. Strathisla lies just across the River Isla from its gloomy sister Glen Keith, also owned by Seagrams. Both it and Strathisla can be discerned, if you've got psychic tastebuds, in the much-exported luxury blend, Chivas Regal.

And it's the popularity of Chivas Regal which brings North Americans by the truckload to Strathisla, 'the heart of the Chivas blend', and probably the oldest extant distillery on Speyside, dating production back to at least 1786. The distillery is supplied by a spring in the immaculate Victorian park across the road, while the beautifully kept distillery buildings, despite being blackened by the escaping angels' share during the maturation of millions of gallons of whisky, looks just the way a distillery ought to.

Inside, the wooden-beamed still-house is pretty and very, very couthy, and the whole place is immaculate. There is an awful introductory video, worth avoiding, but the reception centre itself, all dark wood and old photographs, is pleasant enough. The pictures are interesting, showing how peat was cut in the old days for Strathisla's own maltings. Inevitably, that's not done anymore.

As a morning malt, Strathisla is just fine. They'll offer you either the twelve-year-old single or a Chivas Regal as your post-tour dram, and it's worth trying the undemanding Strathisla, if only because it's difficult to find elsewhere. Having tasted it, though, I was happy enough to move on, much deeper into the heart of tartanry.

The weather remained dull but dry, thank God, as I took the B9014 out of Keith for Dufftown and Glenfiddich. The countryside is resolutely pleasant, fertile farmland and rolling hills: hardly Highland. Then I hit Dufftown, with its legendary 'seven stills' (Glenfiddich, Glendullan, Pittyvaich, Kinninvie, Mortlach, Balvenie and Dufftown *per se*), and found myself in Disneyworld.

I suppose you can't blame Glenfiddich. It's a populist malt, easy to drink, easy to like if you've been reared on the lighter blends. It doesn't even specify its age, except when you get into its more expensive ranges, which in this day and age is a bit contemptuous of the public. I just think Glenfiddich's a waste of time, really, and I particularly hate the way they've taken what is essentially a minor-league whisky, a kind of white Lambrusco of the spirit world, and surrounded it in all this stupid, poncy, overpriced packaging, all this Spode and Wedgwood and silver and crystal. You want to buy me a present? A case of Longrow, soon as you like, and forget the labels. Don't even think about a limited edition Edinburgh crystal decanter with silver stag's head stopper, containing Glenfiddich thirty-year-old, which I have no wish to taste anyway. And this excuse that the Japanese (get this) *prefer* to pay more for their whisky, especially if it's packaged in platinum, cuts no ice. How come, if that's true, that the Malaysians do such a roaring trade in cut-price 'grey' whisky which they ship to Japan, undercutting the official imports?

It is said that Glenfiddich introduces people to the wunnerful world of malt whisky. Maybe, but for some, this is where malt whisky begins and ends, with the skirl of synthesised pipes, a piece of pottery for the mantelpiece which is never opened and a souvenir Glenfiddich ashtray. People will also say that without Glenfiddich, who pioneered the aggressive marketing of single malts in England and abroad, malts generally would be in decline, a mere localised sideline to the mass-merchandising of mongrel blends. I'm afraid that's no excuse for Spode decanters, even if it is true, which frankly I doubt.

There is a snag with all this righteous rage, and it is called Balvenie. Balvenie is next door to Glenfiddich, and owned by the same people, William Grant and Sons. It's very good, and even someone like me, with bluntly hooliganesque tastes in whisky, can appreciate that. It's big, sweetish but very serious indeed in its ten-year-old 'Founder's Reserve' form. The Balvenie Classic is even better, although again, no age statement, which is pathetic even if the stuff is vatted from various different ages and casks.

But to Glenfiddich, the tourist experience. Actually, considering it's all free, and that at the end you get either a dram or (and this is a nice touch) a miniature if you're driving, it's a bargain. Glenfiddich has a gigantic carpark and even its own tourist accommodation office; you just park, then wander down into the huge complex of buildings and abandon yourself to the Grants. This is still very much a family affair, Glenfiddich having remained in the hands of the Grant family since its foundation in 1886. The Grants pop up in the excellent audio-visual presentation (available in six languages) and their military heritage is much-displayed around the massive visitors' centre.

The malt barns at Glenfiddich may have been converted to the cause of tourism, but interestingly, Glenfiddich malts its own barley next door at Balvenie. With its own bottling line, the whole whisky-making process is kept in-house, on-site, unique outside of Campbeltown. What a pity the whisky itself is so boring.

Carol guides me and a dozen or so others of all nationalities around the distillery and the bottling plant. It's very impressive, from the thirteen traditionally coal-fired stills to the automated bottling line, where those hideous labels are stuck on the triangular bottles of the rubbing Glenfiddich. And no, the triangular bottles were not devised so that extras could be squeezed into a case. It just seemed like a good idea at the time.

Glenfiddich is matured in a mixture of sherry, bourbon and plain oak casks, with the usual vatting procedure to even out the taste and colouring. At the end of the tour, you're asked to fill in a card with your name and address, with the promise of free entry in a prize draw and, no doubt, entry too on some marketing firm's database. But hell, as a free day out, with a drink thrown in, it could hardly be beaten. And you've got to be impressed with the whole set-up, which is organised like an American football team: huge, glamorous and glossy, while taking no prisoners in the drive for marketing supremacy.

If only the actual whisky was more of a mouthful. In the Glenfiddich shop, which is like a cross between Next, Oddbins, Harrods and Robertson's Rainwear, all the horrid expensive containers are available. But then, so is The Balvenie, and for that very nice dram I could almost forgive Glenfiddich everything. Almost, but not quite.

It was cold, as out of Dufftown the B9009 grew more exposed and the countryside changed into something altogether rougher, more elemental. Four miles down the road, on the lower slopes of the 2,755-foot Ben Rinnes, lies the best-looking modern distillery there is. Stunningly located, Seagrams made every effort when building Allt-A-Bhainne (the Milk Burn) in 1975 to merge the distillery with the stark surrounding countryside. It is a total success. Unfortunately, I've no idea what the product tastes like, all of Allt-A-Bhainne's whisky, to my knowledge, having gone for blending. It's said to be 'smooth and clean', but isn't everything from this neck of the woods?

I stopped for lunch at the Croft Inn, a real find near the Hill of Achmore. Small, exquisitely but simply decorated, the Croft is a well-run pub (by Englishpersons, but don't let that put you off) with some of the best bar food in the Highlands. Home-made lentil and vegetable soup, home-cured ham with real chips and fresh salad. Add an LA lager, and the bill was less than a fiver.

A middle-aged man in the corner was telling his wife and the barman about non-polluting cars. 'You go to Salt Lake City, and you'll find 80 per cent of the cars there run on hydrogen. That technology's been available for donkey's years, but the car manufacturers don't want it, because the engines don't wear.'

I hoped he didn't see the clouds of oily smoke the orange beast was wont to spout, especially when cold. At first I'd been worried by this, before realising that it was one of the essentials of two-stroke running. At least it used unleaded petrol. I finished with a coffee, then walked outside just as the middle-aged couple, who spoke with strong Merseyside accents, were leaving.

'Lovely bike,' said the man, the first positive comment anyone had made on the beast since the trip's beginning. 'British, is she?' No, I replied. German, East German to be exact. Pre-reunification. But the sidecar's British. He didn't seem to notice. 'Conventional. A big thumper, eh?' Well, more of 250cc buzzer and rasper, actually. 'Eh, go on forever, that will. Conventional.' Maybe he thought the sidecar was full of hydrogen. His wife smiled politely. 'Lots of fresh air on that, I'd think.' I agreed. There was lots of fresh air to be had on the orange beast. 'Must be good for the complexion.' There was a silence, then I laughed, and they laughed, and I started the beast in absolute clouds of blue smoke, moving jerkily out of the carpark as the engine gave out its velcro screech and the couple smiled and waved, smiled and waved.

As I arrived at Tamnavulin, near the hamlet of Tomnavoulin (different spelling, same name, like Cardhu and Cardow, Gaelic spelling being notoriously inconsistent), the sun broke through, bathing by far the nicest visitors' centre on Speyside in a weak but rosy light. The former Tamnavulin carding mill, where wool from local sheep was once brought for cleaning and processing, is now a truly spectacular reception centre, down below the rather ugly distillery in a little glen, next to the mill stream and a picnic area.

This is an Invergordon distillery, and continues the group's apparent liking for light, clean whiskies. Yawn, I thought, as I waited for our small group of tourists to assemble. Two couples I'd already seen at Glenfiddich, and from their expensive winter clothing and sun-lamp tans, I assumed they were snow-starved skiers, trying to distract themselves from the lack of snow at the Lecht or in the Cairngorms. But the tour was interesting. Tamnavulin is so clean it glitters, and everything, except for the copper stills and the exclusively bourbon casks, seems to be made of stainless steel. The whole place is high up as well, and the cold winters must have an effect.

'That's why there's so much space for malt,' said Betty, our guide. 'In the past, we used to get snowed-in quite frequently, and there needed to be plenty of supplies on-site.' This piece of information did nothing to cheer up the snowless skiers.

Back at the old mill, we were served with our choice of either Glayva, Invergordon's pitch at the medieval Celtic mists-of-time, twilight-of-the-gods liqueur market, of which Tamnavulin is a component, and Tamnavulin ten-year-old itself. I don't like Glayva, although I know a lot of people who swear by it for flesh wounds, so I went for the local nip. And what a surprise. Maybe it's because we were in Glenlivet proper, in the very heart of the whisky heartland, but the stuff tasted great. At last, the cleanness, the crisp, dry white-winey flavour people rave about made sense, leaping cold and clear from the glass after a little water had been added.

Thus cheered, I wandered around the old mill, which features a restored waterwheel and all sorts of goodies from the smuggling days, including flat copper flasks which fitted invisibly under tunics next to the skin. The centre was opened in 1985 by the then Scottish Tourist Board chairman, Alan Devereux, who took the opportunity to write a speech which delivered a swingeing blow against the marketing conservatism of the Scotch whisky industry. Unfortunately, the best paragraph of that speech was never reported, being deleted instead at the last minute, although reporters there at the time had it in their typed copies, to be, as always, 'checked against delivery'. Nobody will mind, I'm sure, if I resurrect that lost chunk of ferocious prose: 'Much of the whisky industry,' the STB chairman did not say,

plus, it must be added, hundreds of other indigenous manufacturers of branded Scottish products, have the same attitude to trading possibilities as the shopkeepers of Stornoway on a wet Sunday afternoon in mid-January. Millions of pounds of sales and job opportunities have been lost and we are wasting invaluable opportunities for building brand loyalty throughout the world.

Malts are now, at last, being seen as a moneyspinner and given the push recommended way back in 1985. But there's still a long way to go. Scotland has some of the most astonishing drinks known to man hiding in its hills, in warehouses, in the depths of dismal blends. They should be dug out and allowed to stand on their own, perhaps on a regional *appelation controlée* basis, much as the French do their wines. And what about some new, small, craft farmhouse distilleries like, again, the French armagnac and *eau-de-vie* producers? The tourists would love them, and some fascinating new malts could result. Okay, we'd have to wait a decade or so before we knew what the new wee whiskies would be like, but what the hell, the craft distillers could always market some mysterious handed-down recipe liqueurs, possibly featuring home-grown magic mushrooms, in the interim.

Minutes away from Tamnavulin is the place of pilgrimage for many whisky lovers. The Glenlivet, home of . . . The Glenlivet. I have to say I was tired, saddle-sore, and I'd just about had enough of stills and washbacks and legends about former moonshiners who went legit in 1824 and had to carry a brace of pistols to defend themselves against their naturally very upset former colleagues.

Still, there's a good video at Glenlivet which tells the tale of George 'Smith', whose real name, according to David Milsted, was almost certainly Gow, which was Gaelic for Smith as in blacksmith. George Smith's grandfather, Thomas Gow, a refugee, it is thought, from the '45, apparently changed his name so that none of the nasty Hanoverians would say 'there goes that bastard Gow' and have him hanged, drawn and quartered before you could say 'have a drink, chaps'.

Thomas was an illicit distiller, as would become his son and grandson, George. Ironically, the Hanoverian King George IV, a real mess of a monarch, set the seal of success on George Smith, and indeed the patina of respectability on whisky as a whole, by loudly and drunkenly insisting on nothing but illegal Glenlivet during an infamous visit to Edinburgh in 1822.

In 1823 the Act of Parliament bringing in licences for distillers became law. A year later, George Smith became the first man to apply for one, hence the guns, to ward off his outraged erstwhile comrades. Glenlivet became so famous that everyone wanted to call their whisky by that name, so legal action was eventually required, limiting the definite article to the Smiths' product, whereas everyone else had to be content with a hyphen, as in Dufftown-Glenlivet, Macallan-Glenlivet and Nothing-Like-Glenlivet.

Okay, okay. I'd tasted Glenlivet before, and frankly it was one of the causes of my anti-Speyside feelings. Sure there was sherry in there, maybe even a touch of peat, but I couldn't see, smell or taste much to get excited about, and all the talk about floweriness didn't convince me. Who wants a flowery whisky, really? Well, loads of people, seeing as The Glenlivet is the world's number two malt in the moving-of-units stakes.

So I turned up at the distillery, and David, a kilted guide, took myself and a few others around, cracking jokes about how he had to be careful where he stood on the still-room grids as people could look from below and see what he did nor did not wear underneath the kilt. The distillery looked . . . well, it looked just fine, with little very exciting about the pipes and pots and safes and stills. The malt was brought in 'to their own specifications'; the casks were mostly bourbon, but with a few scarce sherry casks supplied by Sandemans, Seagram's sherry arm. The most exciting aspect of the trip was the removal of a child who was bored beyond endurance. I had a certain sympathy with the wean.

Back at the reception centre, we were served with the twelve-year-old. It tasted good, but not magical. It didn't taste of history. It tasted, in my case of tiredness and fed-upness, and brought the bad bias against all things Speysidian flooding back. It had been a long day, and I still had a good fourteen miles to go before the orange beast would be still for the night. I left the legend of The Glenlivet, the earth having failed to move.

I had decided to spend a couple of nights at Grantown-on-Spey, mainly because it was the nearest community of any size to the bottom bit of the whisky trail. On arrival, it seemed pretty, laid out in the classic Victorian model town way, with a wide main street, grassy gardens, trees and loads and loads of hotels. Grantown used to be on a main rail link, and all the mouldering signs of Victorian huntin', shootin' and fishin' prosperity are there. There are plans afoot to rebuild the rail link from Boat of Garten, as part of the private Strathspey Steam Railway which operates from Aviemore and is possibly the only good thing in that misbegotten concrete excrescence.

True, Grantown looked grey and quiet, and there was disturbing evidence of men in funny trousers with rods and guns, but I thought I'd manage to survive. The Bank House B&B seemed fine, and I checked in just as the heavens opened for the first time that day. I felt that was a good sign. Two hours later I was jittery, nervous for no reason, uneasy. I phoned home, checked that all was well. It was. My life insurance had finally come through. I had a dismal bar supper in a deserted hotel, then wandered the street of Grantown. It was a strange experience.

Dominating Grantown is a massive nursing home in what obviously used to be a gigantic hotel, a legacy of the railway days. Now the Grandview probably holds hundreds of elderly folk, whiling away their twilight days in what, it suddenly struck me, was a twilight town. I peered through the Grandview doors. Bent, stick-like figures slumped in those high, forbidding chairs they put old people in so they can be removed easily if they fall unconscious or die. Shadowy, static shapes waited by the lift, their walking-sticks making them look like weird statues or pieces of furniture. Out of the doors leaked the smell of impending and inevitable death.

At a hotel just up the street, other old people, not quite so elderly, not so weak, abandoned, unloved, were emerging for an evening constitutional. Midlands-accented, they were part of a bus party, their silver coach parked outside the hotel, gleaming in the rain and street-lights. Transient and temporary, they walked past the last terminus of other old people, the Grandview, peering in curiously. I wondered if they felt a chill. Some of them certainly seemed to pick up their pace as they walked past.

There is only one public bar, as opposed to hotel bar, in Grantown, and it obviously used to be part of the Grandview when that establishment was a hotel. I walked into the Claymore, which thankfully contained a majority of youngish locals.

Sharon, behind the bar, told me that the Grandview had once been the Palace Hotel, and indeed the Claymore had been one of its bars. Just then, one of the bus-party couples, all Birmingham bonhomie, eye-blanching clothes and cheery red faces, entered. They ordered drinks, and immediately began talking to the entire bar: 'Can't go wrong up north,' they begin, in the seamless style of a long-married double act. 'Quiet, really, isn't it? Lovely spot. You local? Lucky to live here, you are. Housing here's so cheap. You'd never look at these prices where we come from.'

A long-haired, edgy youth at the bar turns to them. 'Aye sure, Grantown's okay. But not for young folk like me. I can't even get a council house. No offence meant, but it's white settlers coming up here from England buying up property that's stopping us finding places to live.'

The couple grin happily. 'Oh no, surely not,' they say, their accents round and fat amidst these hard, thin local voices. 'We looked at a bungalow today, two bedrooms, thirty thou. I mean, thirty thou! What could you get for that down south?'

'*Thirty thousand pounds*!' shouts the youth. '*Thirty thousand*! Fuck *off*! I couldn't even afford seventy-four quid a month for a council house. And I know a boy who's paying rent of a hundred pounds a week. Fuck off wi' yer thirty thou.'

The couple smile, nod, but do, after a short space of time, quietly fuck off. But the youth hasn't finished. He turns to Sharon behind the bar. 'No offence meant, but see women. They just get pregnant, and they get a council house it would take me fourteen years to get the points for. And all the furniture.'

Sharon regards him icily. 'I'm a single parent, and yes, I've got a house. But I got nothing else, not a stick of furniture. If you want a house, why don't you get a kid and see how you like it?'

I am drinking soda water and lime, pretending, as ever, that I'm not listening.

'I'm no' married,' says the youth. 'Give us a loan of yours.'

'Aye,' laughs Sharon. 'Forty-eight hours of that would sort you out . . .'

'Anyway,' the boy is swaying slightly. 'I haven't eaten for two days. I'm off to Canada next month, and believe me, I won't be coming back.'

I order a Tormore, and drink it as I watch the boy leave, cannoning off the chairs the old English couple have vacated. I couldn't tell you what the whisky tasted like.

In the morning the rain is coming down in hogsheads, butts, oceans. My goggles steam up, and the rain is seeping down through my oilskins, down the salopettes and settling in a warm pool around my bottom. My dip-chilled fingers, inside leather gauntlets and special mountaineering inner gloves, have long since disappeared from whatever perceptions I have left.

I won't be going back to Grantown.

I told Mrs Hunter, after a breakfast of stunning wonderfulness and a million calories, that I liked her B&B, but I'd been called away by urgent family business. I don't think she believed me, but I didn't really care. Shyness, as they teach young reporters, is a conceit. Five minutes after saying what you don't want to say, after asking that question, you won't remember feeling nervous. Do it and then forget it. My problem is I never can forget it. But I pretend I'm going to.

The rain is unbelievable. I'm chafed and chattering, and I've no clear idea what I'm doing, where I'm going. It's too wet even to look at a map. All I want to do is leave Grantown-on-Spey behind me. Maybe, like the boy in the bar last night, leave the whole bloody country behind me too.

I'm past the entrance to Glenfarclas before I notice, and have to force myself to go back. At the door of the visitor centre, I strip off my filthy oilskins, leaving them with my helmet in an untidy heap on the floor. The staff eye me curiously, but by this time I just don't give a shit.

I do the tour, squelching, my hands gradually recovering some sensation. It's just another distillery, isn't it, I tell myself grimly. Just another source of temporary anaesthetic for the masses. The guide has an umbrella. I covet that umbrella. The young, rich family doing the tour with me, and eyeing me with some suspicion, have a Vauxhall Calibra. I covet that too.

'Glenfarclas' means 'valley of the green grass', but I don't care. It is owned entirely by the Grant family, who are related neither to the Grants of Glenfiddich nor the Grants of Glen Grant. I don't care about that either. Their stills are the biggest on Speyside and frankly, I don't give a damn.

But the after-tour dram of Glenfarclas ten-year-old sends warmth and well-being surging through me. This is a big, be-muscled, smoky malt, and I am impressed. I remark that it seems just the thing for the weather, and the guide says I should try the Glenfarclas 105 cask strength. I fall in love with her and buy a bottle.

I do notice one thing about Glenfarclas. The old wood panelling on the walls of the reception centre's Ships Room, where the drams are served, comes, our guide proudly says, from the Canadian Pacific Liner *Empress of Australia*. It is, in fact, very lovely wood panelling, dating back to 1913 when the ship was built. But I discover a plaque which reveals where Glenfarclas really got the panelling from. After the shipbreakers removed it from the German-built *Empress*, the wood graced the walls of that esteemed institution, the Rosyth British Legion Club. It was from there that Glenfarclas obtained it.

Outside, it's still teeming down, and the bike won't start. After half an hour of sobbing effort, it finally stutters to life, and I decide I've had enough of whisky, enough of motorbikes, and most definitely enough of Speyside. I decide to make a charge for home, where at least I can get properly dry, and find a hire car or a helicopter to do the rest of the trip in. Or perhaps just abandon the journey and write about politics instead; do something serious.

So I rampage north to Elgin through the foul weather, ignoring Cardhu and Glen Grant and Tamdhu, the last three distilleries on the official whisky trail. I turn left at Elgin, my mind now emptying of all thoughts save getting home and getting a bath and never going out on a motorbike again. I am leaving Speyside, together with about fifty distilleries I haven't seen round, not to mention about twenty drams I've never tasted. But all the distilleries are the bloody same anyway, so who cares, I tell myself savagely, as Forres looms, and the bike begins to hesitate.

I turn off the main A96 kill-all-bikers trunk-road as the orange beast at last begins to display its unhappiness with the weather. Down Forres main street I go, gritting my teeth as the engine alternately dies and spits, the throttle wide open so the bike surges dangerously or slows to a crawl.

I'm leaving Forres on a very upset motorcycle when I see a signpost for Dallas Dhu Distillery. It's news to me that there is a distillery in Forres, and I have a dim recollection of Dallas Dhu being out of production. Maybe a break would let the orange beast recover, my waterlogged mind surmises, and so I wearily follow the signs to yet another boring whisky palace.

But Dallas Dhu is no ordinary distillery.

I parked the bike in the massive, empty carpark, confused by the Historic Scotland signs. It wasn't until I reached the glass doors to reception that it hit me: this quiet, picturesque place was a museum. This distillery was, in fact, dead, or at the very least in suspended animation. Everything seemed intact, but the figures of workmen were full-size models. The fires were out, the stills were silent, and I was the only person there.

Apart from Len Sutherland, that is. Len it was who told me I'd have to pay two pounds to visit this particular distillery, although that included a free dram. It seemed ironic that I was paying to see around a dead plant when I'd been able to visit any number of working ones for nothing. But I gave him the money anyway.

Dallas Dhu was closed by what was then the Distillers Company Ltd in 1983, and handed over lock, stock and several hundred barrels to the Secretary of State for Scotland. Now it's the Government's only distillery, operated, with taped interpretation soundtracks, models and displays, by Historic Scotland, with considerable imagination. But little spirit.

I was cold and wet, but Dallas Dhu is actually impressive; dead good, so to speak, if undeniably creepy. It has an original floor maltings complete with kiln, and absolutely everything looks to be in working order. In no other distillery are you able to crawl all over the still-room, or actually work the spirit still.

The rain stopped. Fascinated by the surrealism of the whole place, I went back to reception to claim my included-in-the-price dram and watch what turned out to be a genuinely informative, if occasionally hammed-up video, courtesy of the excellent Derek Cooper. The dram was interesting, too, being the only official British Government whisky I've ever tasted. Because there are still stocks of Dallas Dhu maturing, it's being bottled for sale at the museum shop, courtesy of the Secretary of State. Not only that, but a celebrated blend, Roderick Dubh, has been recreated by Historic Scotland using Dallas Dhu and other malts. So the Government actually pays itself duty on its own whisky.

Dallas Dhu is a fine, strong, peaty malt. For me it was a final reminder that there's more to 'Speyside' (and this was nowhere near the Spey) than creamy, bland, clean, boring whiskies. Although let's face it, some are.

'Roderick Dubh is a fine blend,' said Len Sutherland, his Historic Scotland uniform resting, I thought, rather uncomfortably on him. 'There's more malt in that blend than almost any other I can think of.' Len, moving to the tail-end of middle age, looked as if he might have been at Dallas Dhu when it was functioning, I guessed. I was right.

'Yes, I worked in the mashroom,' he told me, 'for over twenty years. It was a sad day when the place closed, but I'm happy to have this job, and let me tell you, with a bit of oil and the raw materials and about a day's work, I could have this place working again. I go round it every day, and everything's perfect. It's in perfect working order, just like it was the day it shut.'

Not only that, it's more modern than many a functioning distillery, with steam-heated stills refurbished in the 1970s. The thought of the Government actually running a working distillery is an interesting one. It could be a wonderful political experiment, run according to the prevailing party philosophy of the day. A microcosm of the country, veering, from election to election, through free-market management dynamism and co-operative worker control. Assuming, that is, that future elections in Britain do see any change in government.

Meanwhile, Dallas Dhu is fascinating. It is also a corpse. It is part of the burgeoning heritage industry, where dead trades become titillation for tourists, where skilled workmen and women cannot produce, but only explain and illustrate. Where the past is packaged into a comfortable, comforting, clean 'experience', to be conveniently filed away and forgotten: people used to work here. Weren't they quaint?

Of course, Dallas Dhu could be made to work, could be made profitable, especially combining its tourism function with actual production of whisky. But does the Government have the vision to realise that, to take heritage into the present day and make it live?

'I remember we were once taken down to a blending plant,' said Len, 'and . . .' but a party of visitors had come in, and he had to work. When he returned, he was looking thoughtful.

'Is that your motorbike and sidecar?' he asked. I nodded. 'I used to have one too, a 1936 BSA V-twin. It was a wonderful machine, although the engine sounded like a tractor's.' He smiled. 'I wish I'd kept it, kept it going. It'd be priceless now.'

A timid sun was coming out. The orange beast started at the first kick, and I revved out of the carpark, wondering if the engine sounded like a tractor to Len. It still sounded like tearing cloth to me. I pulled on to the A96, unable to believe the lack of rain. In an hour and a half I'd be home. And maybe for good, the way I was feeling.

Chapter Seven

WESTWARD

There are Speyside voices I can neither identify nor give precise geographical locations for; there may no longer be excisemen stationed at every distillery, but their ears – and arms – are long. There was, for example, the distillery I had an introduction to by way of an old friend who knew the manager. There, in direct contravention of the law, I was taken into a dark and dingy bonded warehouse by the manager, who grinned a secret grin.

'You've never tasted whisky,' he said, 'until you've had it out of a warehouse cask.' Then he called to one of the warehousemen, who were obviously used to this sort of thing: 'Any loose bungs, Jimmy?'

Down a dusty, dank alley we went, stopping finally before a cask on which the white stencilled date 1975 was almost obscured by grime. The oak bung, sealed in place with hessian,was with a bit of wrestling removed, and I was told to cup my hands below the bung-hole while the cask was cautiously rocked back and forth, back and forth, the iron hoops scraping on the stone floor. The icy splash of whisky on my hands came at last, and I supped the liquid like a nervous communicant.

In the Brethren, communion was only open to those who had publicly professed their conversion, been baptised by immersion, again publicly, and then been accepted into the church. I had been converted at the age of eleven after seeing a ludicrously manipulative Billy Graham film about death, illness, religion and, I think, cowboys. With my parents, I had prayed for God to forgive my sin, and received a glass of orange juice and a biscuit afterwards. At sixteen, in the worn old tank beneath the gospel hall's speaking platform, I was baptised by one of the church elders, who was dressed for the occasion in full fishing waterproofs and thigh-length waders. As I emerged, gasping and blinking from my watery symbolic tomb, the congregation burst into song: 'Up from the grace He arose, with a mighty triumph o'er his foes . . . Hallelujah, Christ arose.'

Communion was celebrated every Sunday morning, in a service without official structure or leader. Any male member of the congregation could suggest a hymn, preach, pray or read from the Bible. All the women wore hats or headscarves because of the angels, and sat mutely, rising only to sing, sometimes at terrifying volume, one of the hymns their menfolk had given out.

The communion wine was contained in large silver goblets which were passed from hand to hand, until all the celebrants had drunk. As a child, I was fascinated by the occasional glimpse of this thick, pungent liquid as it passed by me, and by the sweet smell which filled the whole building when the goblets were uncovered. Our locked, secret sideboard and its full, glinting bottles flickered in the back of my mind. Once, with some of the other children, I had been raking through the church dustbins, when we came across the bottles the 'communion wine' had come in. They were labelled Fine Old Tawny Extra Strong British Wine, an up-market version of the

ferocious proprietary wines made from imported South African grape juice
that fuelled much of central Scotland's alcoholism.

For a church steeped in teetotalism, it was an irony few noticed or
commented on. I remember someone saying that the communion wine had
to be alcoholic to prevent the transmission of disease. Some communicants
never tasted drink any other time but on a Sunday morning, and while many
hardly let the liquid, which was probably about 20 per cent alcohol, moisten
their lips, others took notable pleasure in allowing a great draught to go
down. If you'd had an early breakfast, I discovered when I began to take
communion, it could go right to your head.

In the anonymous distillery warehouse, the whole secretive atmosphere
was intoxicating, let alone the 60 per cent alcohol dribbling through my
fingers. I drank the cold liquid, which in the fluorescent half-light was a
mixture of blackness and pale blue, and it tasted . . . well, it tasted of wood
and dust, because my hands weren't too clean after navigating through the
dingy warehouse and leaning against the barrel.

'What do you make of that?' asked the manager, panting slightly as he
rolled the cask back and fixed in the conveniently loose bung. I let out a sigh,
a gasp if you like, meant to signify transcendent amazement. But I couldn't
get the bitter tang of wood and dirt out of my mouth and nose, and not even
the burning sensation in my gullet from the fiery spirit could compensate. I'd
enjoyed my first taste of communion wine better, I reflected.

Near another distillery I met a head stillsman, who regaled me with tales
of dookin' and dunkin' calculated to give an exciseman a coronary. 'Let's face
it,' he said. 'Wherever you get alcohol made and stored, people are going to
try and get at it. That's the whole idea of the customs locks on the spirit safe,
to prevent the stillsman actually getting access to the stuff.' There were ways
round those locks, though. 'I knew one stillsman who got the maintenance
man at the distillery to modify the spirit safe with a hidden hinge of some
kind . . . and he used to take the middle cut home with him. What he didn't
drink he used to light the fire.'

The scams to remove drink from warehouses were frequently minor
league, he insisted, giving a few extra pounds to someone who might supply
his friends with a couple of illicit bottles a week. But there were other, large-
scale frauds worth tens of thousands of pounds going on at warehouses, and
these often, he claimed, involved the participation of bent customs officers.

'Not that they're all that bad. When I was younger I remember one
excise guy, a really good guy that I knew socially, saying to me, look, nobody
minds you taking a wee bit out a week, we all know what's going on. I take a
wee bit too. Just don't make it obvious. Anyway, years later, and I might
have been pissed, I mentioned that story to someone I thought I could trust,
and it got back to the customs, and they began snooping around asking about
this guy, who was fuckin' retired, man! You've got to watch your mouth in
this industry.'

Other stories sounded more apocryphal. 'Tradesmen in warehouses, man, like painters; they're the worst. They see all the barrels and go fuckin' loopy. They don't even try and cover their tracks.' One had improvised a fairly imaginative approach, however. 'Remember when you used to get milk at school, and everyone'd get a straw from a big box the teacher had? And how you could get a whole pile of straws and join them together in one enormous one? Well, there was this painter who remembered that, and he was working in a warehouse. So he joined up enough straws to go about ten feet, from a cask on an upper rack to a window. That night, he spent about five hours sucking on this huge straw, until he finally got a syphon effect going, and began filling bottles. That's true!'

Then there was the coppersmith who specialised in hollowed-out, moulded copper breastplates, with one tiny stopper and virtually undetectable beneath a boiler suit. I believed this, actually, because the eighteenth-century smugglers used similar methods to move their spirit. But that straw. . . and what about the firebuckets?

'Those firebuckets full of sand. One distillery I was told about, that sand covered a polystyrene floater to a depth of about half an inch. The rest of the bucket was chock full of whisky.'

It was all a lot more fun in the dramming days, my informant told me. 'Sometimes we'd just leave the stills running and all go for a pint.' Nowadays, jobs were scarce, and responsibility had taken hold. To an extent. 'I'm telling you, the scams do go on, though, and at the really big warehouses down in central Scotland, it's serious shit, man. Don't go poking your nose around down there too much.' I promised not to.

Regrets, I had a few about Speyside. One was not being able to visit Macallan, where casual tourists are not encouraged and where relationships between myself and the heid bummer, Willie Phillips, have not been just 100 per cent since I had, he claimed, quoted him out of context in a story about one of his other business interests. A pity, because, even in the depths of my anti-Speyside bias, I'd always enjoyed the classic ten-year-old Macallan, with its kick-ass, no-holds-barred sherry character. Plus, their advertising and marketing has always been a cut above the cretinous herd, as one might expect considering the presence as chairman of the firm of the co-author of such screenplays as *Don't Look Now*, *The Witches*, and other Nicholas Roeg extravaganzas, Macallan family member Allan Shiach. Still, as I made my sodden flight from Moray, I did pass through Craigellachie, home of The Macallan sherry-flavoured spirit empire (maybe I just happen to like sherry), and metaphorically tipped my helmet to the place, for a micro-second. Out of context indeed.

When I did get home, chilled, rain-marinaded, lorry-shocked and generally not a happy camper, I poured myself a Glenfarclas rocket fuel 105 and spent half an hour thawing out in the bath. Only then did I seriously consider my options. Outside the house was a perfectly good Ford Escort Popular 1300, mine for the exclusive use of. In my mentally and physically drenched state, that car, that undeniably unromantic repmobile, took on all the romance and attractiveness of a Lamborghini P400 Miura. Imagine, I fantasised, being dry, being comfortable, having the radio on, not staring death in the face every time you see a bus coming towards you . . . Then it occurred to me that I could just stop the trip, right there and then, order every available whisky from Gordon and MacPhail and simply taste my way round the country, from the comfort of my own home. From the comfort of my own bath, even.

The Glenfarclas was going down a treat. I felt my eyes closing, and my head, resting as it was on a froth of Safeway fake Wash and Go shampoo bubbles, slipped down the end of the bath towards the water.

But the accident insurance didn't cover drowning under the influence in my own home, so I pulled myself together. It was Good Friday. I'd wait until Sunday, and see if resurrection was a concept, myth or reality which could reverberate into my own lassitude and generally get me moving again. Despite the large glass of super-strong water of life lurking amidst the suds, I felt like death.

On Sunday the sun fuelled a warm, blustery wind, and, hardly able to believe it, I waited until wife and weans were away rolling painted hard-boiled eggs down on to the Links, loaded the sidecar with clean clothes and headed for Kyle of Lochalsh.

I took the the narrow, winding road through Strath Bran and Glen Carron, going high up to Achnasheen beside the railway, a trip which in good weather and sometimes (in a car) even in bad can be a delight. It was that Sunday. For seventy-odd glorious miles, past the shadowed Lochs Luichart, a'Chuillin and Bran Achanalt, the orange beast performed with panache. I contemplated a name change for the bike, something to honour its so far unfailing performance. But what? Some shamefully sexist, racist appellation like, for example, Helga? I had considered calling the combination after Father John Cor, the mysterious figure mentioned in the Scottish Exchequer Roll of 1494 as having acquired 'eight bolls of malt . . . wherewith to make aqua vitae' but it all seemed a bit precious and twee and besides, the orange beast seemed to me quite sexless. The fact that there was a motorbike and a sidecar prompted the possibility of 'Mr and Mrs Honecker' in tribute to the MZ's origins under German Stalinism, but then I remembered the sidecar was actually British. 'Thatcher and Honecker'? No.

So it was on the orange beast that I continued through Attadale and along the A890 beside Loch Carron, braving the ever-present risk of landslides and rockfalls until the giddy climb past Stromeferry took me past Beinn Raimh, and over on to the main A87.

I parked the bike next to Kyle's amazing privatised public toilets, where for twenty pence you get perfection in a pan, as long as you like plastic flowers and tiled walls decorated with postcards while you pee. It was past two p.m., and on a Sunday too, but the Islander Bar was offering lunch and liquid refreshment. Sticking to the LA, I participated, appropriating the bar's motley collection of Sunday newspapers to accompany my ingestion of solids and fluids.

The peaceful murmur of conversation and passing wind was broken, quite suddenly, by an unearthly electronic noise. I looked at the one-armed bandit in the corner, and wondered how its digital doings had been programmed to come up with Scottish jigs and reels in the form of bleeps and bloops, like Waldo De Los Rios gone native, or Jean-Michel Jarre joining Runrig. The noise grew louder and louder, until finally an exasperated customer shouted, 'For God's sake, Duncan, turn it down!' Only then did I notice a young man, perched on a bar stool and playing what amounted to an electric bagpipe chanter, than which no more horrific concept can be imagined. Actually no, because at least it's possible to remove the batteries and thus stop such an evil being perpetrated, if only temporarily. Bagpipes should stick to their proper function, which is scaring the trousers off any army the Scots happen to be ranged against; hopefully terrifying them so much they run away and no actually physical warfare has to be engaged in. I've always postulated that some kind of worldwide bagpipe broadcasting network would be enough of a threat to keep the world at peace forever. MAAD: Mutually Assured Aural Destruction.

I left about three o'clock, amazed that it was possible, on a Highland Sunday afternoon, to obtain cheeseburgers, chips and beer. But times have changed, and the smile of servility provoked by prospective tourist bucks has become ever more present in the north. I mean, soon they'll be washing your windscreen in petrol stations and saying 'have a nice day'. Next, the food will actually be edible.

True, a new note of sophistication is sweeping the Scots. Horrid extensions out of a box are sprouting on houses everywhere, along with lurid signs proclaiming 'B&B. Dinner. Own facilities. En Suite'. Tourism, what some cynically call 'the fourth of our three traditional industries', has meant that French may not be understood, but when it comes to private bathrooms, she sure is spoke.

When I got back to the beast, the saddle was warm from the sun. People in shirt-sleeves gazed over Loch Alsh at the Cuillins shimmering in the distance. Could my meteorological luck be about to turn? Had God given me an Easter break?

I should co-co. The short trip to Kyleakin on the giant Calmac ferry *Loch Dunvegan* took hardly any time at all, but the time my tyres touched Skye there was, I swear, a chill in the air. Maybe it was the mountains. Or maybe Easter was drawing to a close, and my divine luck, such as it had been, was running out. Soon going over the sea to Skye will only be possible between Mallaig and Armadale and, in the summer, from the amazing lost paradise valley of Glenelg over to Kylerhea. Instead of Mr Macbrayne's new and efficient ships, a vastly expensive toll bridge will rip one of the great views in the world to shreds and tie Skye forever to the mainland by reinforced concrete. Skye the island will, romantics say, become Skye the peninsula, but the main objection from island folk is the cost per crossing: the same as the ferry fare for twenty-five years, or until the bill for building the bridge is paid off.

Past the wonderful Skye Serpentarium, the private reptile zoo where the snake-fearing public is encouraged to cure any aversion to scaly slitherers by actually handling them, I rattled into Broadford, home of the main Skye hospital and the last radical newspaper in Scotland, the *West Highland Free Press*, scourge of plans for a toll bridge to Skye, useful source of thick, white, shiny paper for lining drawers, and repository of the greatest column in Scottish journalism, Aimsir Eachain and his 'View From the North Lochs'.

Sunday as it was, I knew there would be editorial activity at the *WHFP*'s offices, so I dropped in to scavenge a coffee. Editor Ian McCormack and thrusting young newspup Jason Allerdyce handled this interruption with great forbearance, although Mr Allerdyce disconcerted me by announcing that his mother had, in the dim and distant past, bought a copy of my first (and only) single, a religious paean to the delights of conversion called *Born Again*. I made my excuses and left.

First, though, I obtained a few more details about the last great crackdown on illicit distilling which took place in the West Highlands – or in the whole of Scotland, in fact – as exclusively reported at the time in the *Free Press*.

People will tell you that illicit distilling doesn't go on any more. Rubbish. It may not be rampant, but it is widespread, and in fact on Speyside in recent years a retired coppersmith has, I was reliably informed, been making mini-stills to order for anyone who wants one to fit into their garden shed. On Skye, you can still see the burn marks around a telephone pole, the result of someone's ill-fated attempt to bend red-hot copper pipe into a condensing worm. Because the pole had, as one might expect, the top twenty feet covered in wire and the bottom sunk into the ground, removing the cooled 'worm' proved impossible without a hacksaw.

Most of the 'smuggling' is now little more than a bit of 'fun', involving the ham-fisted distillation of rough alcohol, frequently containing poisonous esters, and using just one still. It is often just bags of white sugar dissolved in water which is fermented and then distilled, and the results can be erratic, to say the least. I once suffered from double vision for twenty-four hours after a brush with home-made moonshine, and I swore never to touch it again. There are, however, stills around to this day, from Shetland through Orkney to Skye and definitely Glasgow. And the customs men, when they're not allowing billions of pounds' worth of cocaine to slip through their fingers and ashore all up the west coast, take the 'problem' seriously.

So seriously, in fact, that quite recently a team of them arrived at a small private museum in Onich and deliberately smashed a copper still that was on display 'as it could have been used'. But the Melvaig raids were something else again.

It happened on 9 December 1987. At 8 a.m., fourteen customs and excise officers arrived on the remote Wester Ross peninsula with three local policemen, and proceeded to raid seven houses and out-buildings which included, according to Torcuil Crichton's report in the *FP*, 'digging up floorboards and searching babies' cribs'.

A Mr Kenneth MacKenzie of North Erradale was detained for four hours and questioned about the half-bottle of home-made spirit discovered in his house, which he claimed was a sentimental reminder of long-abandoned activities. 'It might have been an embarrassment for the customs officers to find only one half-bottle but it was a bigger embarrassment for the people whose homes were raided,' said Mr MacKenzie. 'People around here are generally law-abiding – the way the customs officers behaved you would think we were making whisky wholesale and exporting it worldwide. We don't make a habit of drinking whisky here. I've still got the bottle from last New Year in the cupboard.'

The customs officers were unrepentant. 'Clearly something is going on,' said Brian Scott, an Aberdeen customs official. 'We acted on suspicion of illegal distillation and a quantity of spirit was found.'

And it was. There was more than just Mr MacKenzie's half-bottle. One and half litres in total, although in the end the whole incident was allowed to pass into oblivion without charges being brought or the raids repeated. Perhaps the phantom distillers went quietly underground. Or perhaps they never existed. Fifty-one years previously, though, they most certainly had. In 1936 six Melvaig men were sent to prison for illicit distilling, and one of them was Mr MacKenzie's grandfather.

This was all reported in the Christmas Day 1987 edition of the *Free Press*. The following week's paper had to carry an apology to a Mr Kenneth MacKenzie of Gairloch, whose telephone number was one digit removed from the North Erradale Kenneth Mackenzie and who had been inadvertently credited by the paper as being the man with the illicit half-bottle.

'He has been inundated with telephone calls requesting New Year orders of the famous dram,' read a paragraph. 'We apologise for the inconvenience caused, Mr MacKenzie: *bliadhna mhath ur* [happy new year] to you both!'

By the time I reached Portree, the Skye sky was darkening down to a typical Morton motorcycling shade of purply black. I slotted the beast into a space opposite the Royal Hotel, overlooking the too-pretty-by-half harbour, unpacked my Chinese Joy Bag hold-all and briefcase, and contemplated Portree's perjink villageyness. Skye is jam-packed with white settlers, and the grievances aired in the Claymore at Grantown are even more deeply felt across the Kyleakin Narrows: high house prices, overbearing arrogance in English and even mainland Scottish accents, the prettification and touristification of what was once wilderness. Having said that, I like Portree. It's a kind of halfway-house between Highland 'civilisation' and the Hebrides, containing the acceptable and unacceptable aspects of both.

'Hello please,' said a voice. I turned from my ruminative gazing to find a diminutive young hiker smiling at me, a stuffed rabbit peeking from his front parka pocket. 'Hello! You drive MZ?' I assured him that I did. 'MZ is made in Germany, where I am from,' he said proudly. 'In Eastern Germany, near my house. Very good strong machines, even if old.'

I was delighted to have this young post-reunification tourist applaud my choice of transport, but his next words were saddening.

'Now, they seek to close factory down, of course. Since the one Germany, they say, must make money, and they say, not enough people want MZ. It is old, you must kick it to start, very few equipment, but tool kit is good, no? Now the workers must fight to keep factory open, and this they are doing now.'

My conversation with the hiker, whose name was Rolf, began to crumble then, faced with his poor English and my non-existent German. I wished him good luck, and he wished me 'God's speed'. A good omen, I thought, shouldering my stuff to the Tongadale Hotel.

The next day, the steering on the bike came to bits, and a bird hit me in the face.

Bob, the real biker, roared off the MV *Iona* into the drizzle and fishguts smell of Mallaig. A busy harbour and the colourful jumble of fishing boats could not disguise a town offering, it seemed to me, little in the way of creature comforts save a chip van, so I decided to take my life and dodgy steering in both hands and head for Fort William.

The forty-eight miles between Mallaig and Fort William is one of the legendary journeys, particularly the single-track sixteen miles between Lochailort and Morar, the last piece of single-track trunk-road in the British Isles. Spectacular isn't in it. The stunning Sands of Morar, where the beach scenes for Bill Forsyth's masterwork *Local Hero* were filmed (not the village; that's Pennan, 180 miles away near Banff); the rugged hills, with Moidart looming to the west; the beached, near-derelict boat with smoke seeping from a crooked chimney; the lochs, the sky, the sea and, more than anything else, the bloody road itself. It's a nightmare. As if it wasn't bad enough to have corkscrewing single-track bends, dozens of them, often at impossible cambers and one after the other, the road is used by fleets of articulated fish lorries, racing Mallaig catches south to the cities. These drivers are very competent indeed, know the road and do not take risks, but for unsuspecting tourists or people on orange beasts, they quickly assume the image of the driverless truck in Stephen Spielberg's first film, *Duel*: out to to crush all cars.

It's the road's fault, or more to the point, the fault of various governments over the past sixty years, who have signally failed to keep promises that the road would be improved. Now, at last, there is hope that something's about to be done.

As it is, I approach Fort William with nowhere booked to stay the night, at just before 5 p.m., and I quickly realise that the town is crammed with Easter tourists. They are there because of Fort William's convenience and location, in the shadow of Ben Nevis, Britain's highest and most dangerous peak, killing as it does on average a dozen climbers a year. Road and rail links from the south are excellent, and the horrors of the Mallaig road can be avoided if you let the wonderful train take the strain, especially if you're lucky enough to hop aboard one of the summer steam excursions, where you can get cinders in your eyes as you hang out giddily over Concrete Bob MacAlpine's splendid Glenfinnan viaduct.

But as for Fort William itself . . . it's a disaster. Not as bad as it once was, admittedly, especially since the Nevis Range ski development took the whole place slightly up-market. But its greatest asset, the spectacular waterscape of Loch Linnhe, is divided from the town by a fast sweep of bypassing road, calculated to leave pedestrians legless. Years ago, the false hopes of industrial success offered by the huge aluminium smelter and pulp mill saw planning considerations sacrificed for economic convenience. Now what could have been one of the great tourist beauty spots, in probably Scotland's most spectacular location, is a rag-tag mess of roads and streets and bypasses and 1960s' shopping malls. It's a real pity.

With five minutes to go before closing time, though, the tourist office ladies are perfection, obtaining for a booking fee of £1.00 a bed in a £12.00 a night B&B within walking distance of the town, on one of the hills sloping steeply to the east. This service, available at all Scottish tourist offices, was a godsend to me and deserves the highest possible praise. I'll even forgive the explosion of 'en suite' signs at the side of Highland roads. At Abrach House, a crisp, clean and modern establishment, I am greeted enthusiastically by Mrs Moore, whose dad used to ride a motorbike and sidecar.

'I used to love going out in that sidecar,' she says. 'But maybe this isn't really the weather to get the best out of it.' I agree, fervently.

That night, I decide to treat myself. Finlay Finlayson's Crannog restaurant has been converted from the old Caledonian Macbrayne buildings, set on their own private pier sticking out into Loch Linnhe. There you can eat fresh prawns caught by the boat Finlay (who comes from Plockton) has always dreamed of owning; you can eat smoked salmon, mussels and, indeed, just about anything smokable, produced in the smokehouse that economics told Finlay he had to set up if fishing wasn't to become the dead-end debt-ridden misadventure it has for many west coast owners. And you eat in the Crannog, the last link in Finlay's ownership of the entire chain of production, right through to consumption. (There is now a second Crannog in Glasgow, and I can't recommend it too highly.) It's the second-best thing in Fort William, after Ben Nevis. And that overgrown hillock isn't actually in the town, so much as above it.

I go for the langoustines and the *plat brûlé*, which comprises about fifteen different kinds of smoked seafood, complete with salad and tatties. I have a couple of glasses of Sauvignon and finish with a Talisker, replete and just about recovered from the wrenching stresses and strains of the Mallaig road.

As I saunter through Fort William on my way back to Mrs Moore's, I encounter the kind of visitors which feature in every tourist officer's worst nightmare. Two cars, crammed with beefy males of indeterminate Scottish origin, race through the town, windows and sunroofs open. The back windows of one, a Ford Escort XR3i, are occupied by the hairy cheeks of two unappetising arses. Out of the sunroofs, torsos extend, and voices compete with the exhaust roar to scream obscenities at any female in the vicinity.

I feel I should run up to some of the obvious tourists and explain that this is a rare sight, one of the oldest ceremonies of welcome in Gaeldom, and that they, in this *anus mirabilis*, so to speak, are priviliged to see a special ceremony which has been organised by Lochaber District Council using professional bottom-barers, at great expense . . .

But I don't.

Chapter Eight

BODILY FUNCTIONS

Jocky the Grey African Parrot enlivened things at breakfast. Unless you know there's a parrot in the house, the sound of someone or something going 'hello' insistently in an empty room is, to say the least, disconcerting. The young French couple, completely fazed by the invisible speaker, whose cage was draped with what appeared to be a piece of carpet, kept freezing in mid-Weetabix and gabbling at each other in a frenzied fashion.

Eventually the golf-bronzed Mr Moore revealed Jocky for us all to see. He and Jocky were not, it appeared, on the best of terms. 'It's not ours,' he told me gloomily. 'It belongs to my mother-in-law, who has been looking after this place while we were on holiday. Now she has announced that she is going on a long trip to the USA to see her son. And we have been landed with parrot-sitting.'

'Who's a pretty boy then?' squeaked Jocky. I could see Mr Moore's point. The re-enactment of Monty Python's famous sketch seemed a distinct possibility ('I'm sorry, maw-in-law, but yours is now an ex-parrot'.)

I dropped in, bright and early, to see the man through whom Fort William channels all of its newsworthy events to the outside world: journalist, humorist, literary gent and dealer in rare books, Iain Abernethy of the West Highland News Agency. He was engaged in a verbal battle with the leaders of the Lochaber Labour Party which involved the constant use of telephones and a fax machine, so I paid my respects and departed for the Ben Nevis Distillery.

Ben Nevis is interesting not just because it's Japanese-owned – Tomatin, south of Inverness, Scotland's largest malt distillery with an incredible twenty-three stills, has been in the hands of the Rising Sun for years – but because of who Takeshi Taketsuru, company chairman, is. Chairman of Nikka, one of Japan's top distilling companies, he is the nephew and adopted son of Masataka Taketsuru, the 'father of Japanese whisky', who built that country's first successful whisky distillery in 1935 and is recognised as the man who brought the techniques, skills and traditions of Scottish distilling to the Orient.

Masataka Taketsuru had been sent to Scotland just after the First World War by his then employers, Osaka, to study the art of whisky-making, at Glasgow University. He fell in love with the country, and with all the lore and magic of Scotch whisky production. He also fell in love with a girl called Rita (Jesse Roberta) Cowan, of Kirkintilloch. Looking at old photographs of Rita, which was the pet name her family used, it's easy to understand how Masataka fell for her. She was stunningly beautiful, in a delicate, tubercular kind of way. The couple met when the young Masataka came to the Cowan household to teach her brother Ramsay the elements of ju-jitsu. An epic love-story, crossing racial, continental and eventually wartime barriers, was about to begin.

In Japan, the tale of the 'father and mother of Japanese whisky' has become a folk legend, and Nikka have booklets and a memorial museum at their Hokkaido headquarters recounting what happened. How, on an icy January day in 1920, the couple – he twenty-six and she just twenty-one – were married at Calton Registry Office in Glasgow, forced by absolute disapproval from both families to seek strangers as witnesses. After ten months living in Campbeltown, where Taketsuru worked at the Hazelburn Distillery to gain practical experience of his chosen trade, the couple left for Japan. Rita would never see her parents or Scotland again.

In Japan, Osaka's plans for a whisky distillery had been shelved, and a frustrated Taketsuru left the Settsu Shuzo-based firm in 1922. Rita supported the family by teaching English, until Taketsuru was head-hunted by a company called Kotobukiya to oversee the construction of a whisky distillery at Kyoto, the Yamazaki, Japan's first. Kotobukiya would later become the biggest of all Japanese whisky names, Suntory. (Not a bad dram, either, the Suntory premium blend, which may not be too surprising as it contains many Scottish malts, notably Laphroaig.)

But there were problems at Kotobukiya, and concern over the long wait until mature whisky would be ready for sale prompted Taketsuru to leave in 1934. He set up Nippon Kaju KK, which would become Nikka, and began producing apple juice as a short-term source of cash. Then in 1935 his first pot-still arrived, and spirit production started, using just the one still: Taketsuru could not afford a second one.

In 1939 the first whisky was vatted, along with Nikka's other distillate, brandy, and a year later the first consignments left the distillery for sale, exactly twenty years since Taketsuru and Rita had returned from Scotland.

Rita had been readily accepted as Taketsuru's wife, but after December 1941, Pearl Harbor, things were different. Nikka's own version puts it simply: 'It was the beginning of bitter hardships for Rita. Although she was by now legally a Japanese citizen, the stigma of birth as an "enemy alien" remained. She was followed by the police and openly insulted in the street. The only consolation was Taketsuru's enduring love.'

She died in 1961, having been visited by one sister, Lucy, and in touch by letter with her mother and another sister. Nikka were well on the way to the massive success they now enjoy, and in 1990 Rita's adopted son, Takeshi Taketsuru, bought the Ben Nevis Distillery, bringing the whole sad, moving love-story back to Scotland.

Unfortunately, they don't tell you any of this at Ben Nevis's brand-spanking-new visitor centre. Instead, there is an extremely daft but enjoyable video, narrated by 'Hector MacDram', who tells the story of the distillery itself. And that's interesting enough. John MacDonald, at six-feet-four the original Long John, founded the place in 1825 after a career as a smuggler. The water which supplies the place coming from the slopes of Ben Nevis, the original whisky was marketed as Long John's Dew of Ben Nevis. Eventually, the title Long John went elsewhere, and is the name of a brand now sold by

Allied Distillers. However, Taketsuru has retained the title Dew of Ben Nevis for the current blend marketed by the Fort William distillery.

Truth to tell, it's not very nice, unfortunately. There have been a few special single-cask bottlings of ancient Ben Nevis for the Japanese market, inevitably, at prices of up to £2,000 a bottle, but the malt is not generally available. It will be, once stocks have been increased, but one can only hope it's better than the Gordon and MacPhail version I had the misfortune of tasting in a Fort William bar during a royal visit to the town. Chinese wrestlers' jockstraps weren't in it, to paraphrase the great Roy Harper.

However, the visitor centre isn't bad, the video's a laugh and there's a pleasant café with home-baking. Just don't touch the whisky until a little Japanese expertise has been brought to bear over the next decade or so. The word is that the new bottlings of Ben Nevis single will be good. We shall wait and see.

The rain was once more battering lumps out of the tarmac as I left Fort William. The orange beast's steering had apparently worked itself into a less shoulder-wrenching condition, and as both top and bottom nuts seemed tight, I was tentatively confident about getting to Oban, a place I had not visited since the great Ledaig toilet disaster of 1969, in one piece.

In fact, it's barely forty-five miles from Fort William to Oban, along a road made slick with the burnt-off rubber of a million tourists. Once over the Ballachulish Bridge and heading down the Argyll coastline, the primitive rawness of the northern Highlands seems a world away.

There is money here, in the marinas and big houses and the easy-access holiday homes. There is also poverty, as in the frequent 'new age traveller' encampments, lost would-be hippies without hope, idealism or even decent drugs and music: the drab, dope-addled grandbairns of Ken Kesey, travelling without desire, passion or the belief in change inherent in the alternative lifestyles of the 1960s. There is no joy in their bent-wood tents, their buses and wigwams. They sell scrap and beg, mongrel dogs yapping on the end of dirty string, scabby children sucking on stained dummies. Here are the young urban poor, getting not on their bikes but in their clapped-out lorries and trucks, escapees, originally from the poll tax, perhaps, from jobless family tribulation, now lost in a nomadic life of barest survival. The new age they are travelling in is not one of mysticism, witchcraft, astrology and hallucinogenics; it is the new age of the dispossessed, rootless, uncared-for poor. It is not the summer of love, but the winter of couldn't-care-less, as the redneck rage of blinkered locals exhorts unwilling policemen to move them, stop them from spoiling the lovely, lovely scenery, and the gorgeous signposts for *en suite* facilities, and the new self-catering cottages, and the interpretative heritage centre on the cleared crofters, forced off their land 150 years ago. Not that one should make comparisons. Not at all.

When I was a child, this was our holiday territory, courtesy of the Sprite Musketeer caravan my father had bought. We caravanned for years, even towing the sixteen-foot box all the way to the Costa Brava on one occasion. The continual claustrophobia of three children and two adults being crammed into that space every holiday night has left me with an absolute detestation of caravans in every shape and form.

But I remember trips north from Ayrshire, crossing the Clyde by the Erskine Ferry long before the bridge was built, then the Ballachulish ferry to head further into the Highlands. Oban was another favourite destination, although we usually stayed at the North Ledaig caravan site, over the Connel Bridge which still spans the spectacular Falls of Lora.

And there it was. Ledaig Caravan Site, much enlarged since the day of the great toilet disaster more than twenty years previously. I was a pre-adolescent, tall and gangly and sullen and hating, hating more than anything, being in a caravan over Easter with my parents and two sisters. Unfortunately, because I was also a born-again Christian, my pubescent rage at life, the universe and everything included massive dollops of guilt at feeling that way. I prayed for forgiveness and to feel better, and to love everybody.

I had, in fact, gone down to the Ledaig shore to pray, and to stop myself hammering my sisters, when the need to find a toilet became paramount. My guts went into that uncontrollable, washing-machine-on-final-rinse spasm which brooked no argument. I broke into a trot, aiming for the caravan site's toilet block.

Now my prayers had become simple, precise: God, get me to the toilet in time and I'll do anything, even accompany my father on his Sunday afternoon door-to-door evangelisation missions. I will have, as the preachers demand, a passion for souls. I will stop listening to Rolling Stones records on the radio. I also began running as fast I could without provoking disaster.

I reached the toilet block. I threw open a cubicle door. 'Thanks, God,' I breathed, silently. And that brief hesitation proved my undoing.

Well, my father found me eventually, just before he called out the mountain-rescue teams to search the moors for his missing son. Clean clothes were provided. It was explained to me that God had in fact answered my prayers too precisely, and that I should not be dissuaded from believing in Him by this unfortunate incident. He had got me to the toilets, which was, after all, what I'd asked him to do.

Becoming an atheist then would have saved a lot of heartbreak in later years, I supposed. What the experience did leave me with was a subconscious vision of God as some kind of martinet timekeeper, the kind of person to whom one second past the hour was the same as an hour too late. Either that, or the Supreme Being had the kind of sadistic sense of humour normally found amongst public school bullies. But then, maybe God was really like that.

I revved the orange beast away from Ledaig with relief. Connel Bridge was still single-track, but the disused railway which had once made it nearly impossible for our caravan to cross had been removed. Finally, I wound down the twisting hill into Oban, and found myself in hell.

Words cannot express how horrible Oban is – and it's so unnecessary. Facing a natural harbour, backed on to a huge cliff, it must once have been a pleasant fishing and steamer port. Then the Victorians came, complete with railway, and turned it into an elegant holiday resort, full of substantial houses, big hotels, a promenade and, of course, the fool's cap of what is now officially McCaig's Tower, though I've always known it as McCaig's Folly: the unfinished coliseum above the town which mocks the snarling chaos below.

Still one of Calmac's main steamer ports, with excursions not just to neighbouring Mull, but also to the Western Isles, Oban has become the Blackpool of the southern Highlands. It is still the gateway to the north as well as the islands for many travellers, and it is now, at least in the holiday season, a complete bottleneck. Traffic jams all the streets. The pavements seethe with tourists and locals, for this is a busy administrative and business centre as well. People's heads jerk this and way that, searching for something worth looking at. For Oban is also tacky beyond belief, full of disgusting shops selling Highland dancer dolls, cheap and nasty whisky miniatures and the endless bins of 'SPECIAL! SALE! MILL CLOSURE!' woollens and tweeds.

The beast and I fought through into one of the back streets, hidden behind the Victorian frontages, between the dirty back-cliff and the down-at-heel glitz of the main drag. I chained up the bike opposite a really dreadful-looking pub, and a sight which took me right back to my childhood fears of drink, instilled by dreadful warnings of what happened to families whose fathers spent their wage-packets on boozing.

Outside the pub stood a little boy of about seven, holding the handles of a push-chair in which another child, a boy of about three, sat with his head on one side, eyes staring at nothing. Occasionally the older boy would move round to the pub's door, push it open a crack and shout 'Dad!'. There would be a muffled angry reply, then the boy would return to his post at the push-chair.

I walked out on to the main promenade, which faces the sea. The old pierhead station has been woefully converted into a cheap and nasty plastic Scotrail monstrosity, and a shopping mall was being erected nearby, in the would-be ethnic shape of a series of malting pagodas. It looked quite appalling, and almost entirely unplanned. Meanwhile, cars literally raced along the wide main street, making it all but impossible to cross. I bought a newspaper, and ate, badly, in a self-service cafeteria of massive proportions called MacTavish's Kitchen.

I had planned to stay in Oban, then go to Mull for the day, return and head for Campbeltown. However, time had always been against that idea, and the thought of spending any time at all on Mull, an island so crammed with white settlers from England that it's almost impossible to hear a local accent, did not particularly appeal.

There is a distillery at Tobermory, Mull's capital, and I have to say that the vatted malt currently produced under its name, which includes some single malt Tobermory mixed with other malts, is an extremely pleasant, mild, island whisky. But I decided to abandon any thoughts of travelling there. I would stay in Oban one night, I decided, then head to Campbeltown the next morning. I finished my vegetarian broccoli pie, feeling decidedly peaky, leafed desultorily through the papers, then headed for the Oban distillery, which is slap bang in the middle of the overcrowded town centre, and quite the best thing in the whole place.

You have to hand it to United Distillers, they are really organised as far as visiting distilleries is concerned. Not only that, but the marketing of their 'Classic Malts' – Glenkinchie, Cragganmore, Talisker, Dalwhinnie, Oban and Lagavulin – has been impressive, in a kind of big-company way. As have the bottlings of other UD malts – some of them obscure, like Pittyvaich, some potentially enormous moneyspinners, like Clynelish – in the loadsamoney 'Flora and Fauna' boxed series, each showing an aspect of natural life in the vicinity of the distillery. UD know there's millions in malts.

But Oban is something special. Because it's right in the middle of 'the Gateway to the Isles' it attracts tens of thousands of tourists each year. And so the visitor centre is integrated with the working distillery in such a way that the tour makes much more sense – and is less tiring to do – than in almost any other distillery I can think of.

The distillery is cut into the 400-foot cliff which hangs over the town, and when extension work was being carried out in 1890, the 'distillery cave' was discovered, containing human bones and tools from the Mesolithic era – 4500 to 3000 BC. Barnard came here, and enjoyed Oban's 'life and gaiety'. He is terminally boring on the distillery itself, though.

Today, the (very regular) guided tours are free, but very popular, and you have to book in at distillery reception in Stafford Street for one. The videos and museum displays are excellent, as is the friendly, brief and businesslike tour. But best of all is getting your dram in the atmospheric former filling store, which is a really nice idea, all the better for Oban fourteen-year-old being a really nice dram, sort of halfway between Speyside *politesse* and Islay kick-your-head-in aggression. There's peat in there – they get their malt from UD's Ord maltings – and so it actually tastes like a real whisky. It's a Highland townie dram, though, restrained after the wildness of, say, Talisker.

I walked out of the distillery, re-entering Oban's screaming torrent of cars and pedestrians. Suddenly, on the side of the street nearest the sea, I spied a familiar bearded figure, deerstalker waggling. It was Donald Gillies, recently moved to his native Argyll from Orkney, where my abiding memory was of he and I drinking the night away in the Kirkwall Hotel while outside the biggest riot in Orkney's history took place (the two local discos closed their doors in protest at a licensing court decision, and disappointed punters went predictably crazy, attacking the board chairman's house, overturning police cars and the like). We, of course, didn't notice a thing, but then we are journalists.

Now Donald and wife Catherine were the BBC's person (half a job-share each) in Argyll, and enjoying it thoroughly, staying well outside Oban's urban tensions. 'Och no,' said Donald. 'Oban's turned into a boom town, and it's quite unbelievable. On Easter Saturday the traffic wasn't moving at all.' I told Donald I was swithering about continuing on to Campbeltown rather than spending any more time in the place, despite the esteemed presence of himself and his family. 'It's a long way on a motorbike,' he said. 'Ninety miles or so.' I continued to swither after saying goodbye to Donald, who had a package to put together for BBC Radio Highland.

It was then that I began to feel a bit strange. Was it the memory of the great toilet disaster of North Ledaig, or some kind of allergy to one of the fifteen different kinds of smoked seafood I'd consumed the previous night at the Crannog? At any rate, my guts were, once more, after twenty-three years, churning like the blades in a mash tun, and I was suddenly in urgent need of a lavatory.

The station. Brand-new and ugly, it was bound to have a toilet, maybe even one of those speak-your-requirements computerised jobs, the ones which wash themselves out after you've left, and sometimes before. I hurried to the railhead. There was nothing. No toilet. *No toilet!* I couldn't believe it. Things were getting desperate, and there wasn't even a pub or hotel handy. I considered prayer, but rejected this option on the grounds of bitter experience. Any prayer would have to be precise in terms of time, and my fevered mind was bound to make some minor error which God would take great delight in punishing. For example, I'd see a sign saying public convenience, run in delight to the decaying portacabin (and this on the Oban seafront) marked Gentlemen, and find the door locked. A small piece of notepaper would have 'out of order' written on it in ballpoint.

And that is exactly what happened.

I almost wept. Next door were the ladies' toilets, and, sweeping decorum aside, I pushed in desperation at the door, which did not have an out-of-order sign attached. It opened. No screaming women fled at the sight of a large, sweating male in leather and boots, as I leapt for one of the cubicles. The toilet pan was smashed. I tried another. There was no toilet seat. It would have to do. I tore off my trousers, and, muscles screaming, avoided disaster by millimetres. I looked up. It was only then I realised I'd left the outside door open, and could clearly see the swarming humanity of Oban passing by outside. None of them appeared to be noticing me.

Fortunately, there was plenty of toilet paper.

I left Oban in a hurry. Perhaps it was only in its vicinity that God played such scatalogical tricks. I was not going to stick around in case it was endemic, and divine revenge extended to other bowel movements. Besides, that toilet had resolutely refused to flush. It was only on closer inspection that I realised to my horror it had been disconnected. Call me paranoid, but as I drove into the blustery afternoon towards the Mull of Kintyre I was sure the Argyll plumbing police were after me.

It was a long ride. First came the climb out of Oban, then the endless coastal drag past the ludicrous artificial village of Craobh Haven to Kintraw, and the inland route to Lochgilphead, Argyll's administrative capital. The road bypassed Lochgilphead, joining the main A83 from Glasgow, which is nice and wide and modern and capable of handling any nuclear weapons required by the United States Air Force Stealth bombers reputedly stationed at Machrihanish, the air-base near Campbeltown. After Lochgilphead the weather opened out into a glorious, sunny spring day, and the ride through Ardrishaig to Tarbert was simply a joy. Loch Fyne sparkled, and when Tarbert arrived, it looked absolutely lovely in an absolutely clichéd, Para Handy, Highland film-set sort of way. It is almost perfect, set around a wide, old stone harbour, its buildings full of character and inevitably, white settlers. Who could blame them for wanting to live there, though?

After Kennacraig, the road straightens as it plunges down the Atlantic coastline of Kintyre, the stench of wrack and tangle – seaweed – overpowering. Gradually, memories of the only other time I'd travelled this road came to me: when I was six, the family had gone to Southend in a motor caravan, provoking violent car sickness in all except my father. He was to be leader at a Christian Youth Club camp, run by the Brethren assembly we then attended in Glasgow. I remembered that the seemingly ancient man in charge of the whole affair had driven a Jaguar and worn a kilt all the time, or, to my utter astonishment, tartan trews when paddling in the sea. That was also the first time I'd ever touched a guitar. They were not that common amongst born-again believers in 1965. I remembered walking up to this huge, glowing instrument, an amber sunburst model, probably fairly cheap, which I'd been forbidden to even think about looking at. And I remembered the great, singing, ringing sound it made as I gave it an almighty strum, scaring me into flight out of the school building which had been taken over by the camp, running away from that huge, wonderful noise.

That was the start of a cripplingly expensive addiction to those concoctions of wood and wire, and to the noises you could get out of them. For years all I wanted to do was play the guitar. As a full-time, living-by-faith fundamentalist evangelist, I wrote and sang songs about my faith, making records, doing religious gigs from Stuttgart to Fraserburgh, buying and delighting in a procession of Guilds, Gibsons and Fenders, preaching the word and caressing those beautiful objects at the same time. When my tenuous fundamentalism finally and spectacularly fell apart, taking a marriage with it, all I had left was a stereo system, some books, records and two guitars. You can hear dead men still living in some guitars, Clive James once wrote, in uncharacteristically serious vein. I eventually sold the scarred Gibson J40 which stayed with me through those God-fearing years. Every time I played it I could hear tunes I wanted to forget.

It had been a long way from Oban, and as the afternoon dragged on, I got colder, chilled by the icy Atlantic wind which came walloping in from the west on to the exposed, open road. Finally, at Westport, the A83 took me away from that endless rocky shoreline and south-east to Campbeltown.

Hidden away, Campbeltown appears abruptly, and entering the place is an extraordinary experience. For a start, it's virtually deserted, at least compared to Oban, and it's built on a huge, scale. The streets are ridiculously wide, the sandstone buildings huge, tenemental in the centre, with grandiose villas stretching around the loch on both sides. The harbour is framed by a grassy park and a long stretch of links to the south, and the full impact of the Gulf Stream means that palm trees and tropical plants bloom in the open air. It's a strange place, and guidebooks admit this. 'It has been called a Lowland town in a Highland setting,' says one.

The pierhead tourist office found me a room at Kildalton, a modern house built on the northern side of the bowl Campbeltown sits in. It was my first *en suite* experience of the trip, and after the 135 miles I'd done that day, not to mention the toilet trauma of Oban, I felt the comfort of my own personal, instant-access toilet and shower would be worth £15 a night. Mrs Wilson was brusquely welcoming, and the view across Campbeltown splendid.

I had two distilleries to visit in Campbeltown, two out of the forty which in the nineteenth century made this 'the whisky metropolis'. Now only Springbank – uniquely makers of two whiskies, one eponymous, one called Longrow – and Glen Scotia were left, and it was too late in the evening to do anything about seeing round them. I was a little worried about Springbank's reputation as a centre for purist excellence, and the fact that casual tourists were dissuaded from trying to see around the place. But what the hell. If I had to play the writing-a-book card to draw attention away from my increasingly dishevelled appearance, I'd do it. I had one-and-a-bit days to play with, and for months I'd been looking forward to Campbeltown. I was determined it would not let me down.

My old friend Barnard came, of course, to Campbeltown, which was in the 1880s at the height of its powers. He found the whisky city 'a pleasant place in summer for those who rejoice in a boundless sea, plenty of boating, fishing and golfing'. He also managed to visit twenty-one distilleries out of the thirty-four then operating, although there were also a few small-scale, cottage-industry stills. Yet by 1930 there were only three distilleries left and when, in 1934, Rieclachan closed its doors, Springbank and Glen Scotia were left to carry on, as they do today.

That Victorian explosion of whisky production is what gives Campbeltown its strange, empty, overgrown character. The great villas were built by distillery managers competing to see whose house would be finest. Many of the frontages on Longrow, the great wide street, lined with high buildings, off which Springbank is situated, hide the remains of malting floors and warehouses. The massive warehouse block which once aged Lochend whisky now awaits demolition, with a supermarket mooted for the spot. Lorne and Lowland Parish, the so-called 'Whisky Church', sits next door to Springbank, an extraordinary monument to the spiritual aspirations and pride of Campbeltown's Victorian distillers. The unique, perpendicular steeple, which looks like a straightened banana topped with a blob of melted ice-cream, owes its existence, along with the rest of the building, to the subscriptions of the whisky tycoons.

Why did the Campbeltown distilleries collapse so spectacularly? Many of the distilleries were small and, as the whisky industry expanded into the twentieth century, the tiny operators were simply unable to cope. The production of bad, immature malts gave the area a bad name. But Campbeltown was mortally wounded by changes in taste, which saw the mildness of Speyside malts becoming more and more popular – partly because they were simple to use in blending – and was finally killed off by the First World War and prohibiton in the USA.

Campbeltown malts are not mild. They are so distinctive that they cannot be lumped in with the product of Islay, the West Highlands, or the Lowlands, the three nearest defined whisky areas. The three Kintyre survivors, Glen Scotia, Longrow and Springbank, share certain characteristics which some feel make them closer to Irish whiskies than Scottish ones. I've heard them described as heavy, oily drams, and while frankly I think this is nonsense, there is a certain resemblance with some of the more refined Powers products. Nothing from Campbeltown is as sweet and cloying as Jamesons or Bushmills. Generically, these whiskies lack the brutal force of the classic 'big' Islay malt. Instead, they are more transparent, more delicate, allowing the salt tang of the sea, a seaweedy bitterness, and – in the Springbank whiskies – lots of peat to come through distinctively. None are common in this country, although Springbank's deliberately esoteric approach has gained them a small but fanatic following. Bob Dylan is a fan, ordering Springbank by the case from specialist dealers, Cadenheads, who buy and bottle single casks of other Scottish malts, and are also based at Springbank.

The Irish connection may partly explain why the whisky industry took off in Campbeltown in the first place. Northern Ireland is only twelve miles away, and the historic links between Kintyre with Ireland go back many centuries. Was it here that, as the story goes, Irish monks first brought the techniques of distilling to Scotland, along with Christianity? And was a spiritually blessed love of the water of life born in the hearts of the Campbeltown folk, to such an extent that they devoted their lives to making the stuff? Or was it just that there was plenty of water and grain, and a good harbour for bringing more materials and shipping out the casks? There is something mysterious about this part of Scotland, marked out as it is in ancient mounds and stones, and Campbeltown does have a certain melancholy magic, as befits the town that some say was Dalriada, the ancient, mystical capital of the island lordships, a kind of Scottish Camelot.

I had an extraordinarily good Chinese meal, my stomach having recovered from the horrors of the afternoon, and in the public bar of the Royal Hotel, right at the harbour and to be recommended, I ran through a few of the local goldies. A twenty-one-year-old Springbank was powerful, briny, complex and quite unlike any other Scottish whisky. I once said, rather extravagantly, of the twelve-year-old that it tasted of sea fog, rust and old tears, but that may have been the mood I was in at the time. Anyway the twenty-one-year-old is a more substantial dram, as I proved to my own satisfaction at the Royal after one of its nine years younger wee brothers, which seemed a little thin and edgy by comparison, not unlike a Scapa with big ideas. Glen Scotia, also at twelve years old, tasted fuller, warmer, sweeter, but still with that distinctively Kintyrish salty tang.

The sixteen-year-old Longrow, which had never before passed my lips, was a revelation. Light, almost lemon-coloured, it was like a particularly sophisticated form of distilled peat juice, without any ragged or harsh overtones at all, and with less of a salt spray attack than Springbank. It really was quite astonishing. Back at Kildalton, I slept the sleep of the surprised.

Two quick post-breakfast telephone calls arranged, after some to-ing and fro-ing, visits to both Springbank and Glen Scotia, and with a fine, blustery morning to kill, I set out to explore.

Campbeltown's museum is a splendid relic, full of eccentric items like a gilt model of Solomon's Temple, pieces of Celtic stone crosses found washed up on rock shores, enough birds' eggs and stuffed seagulls to give a conservationist a stroke, and some interesting bits and pieces from the days when whisky ruled. There is a beautifully made and perfectly usable four-gallon model of a whisky still, apparently undamaged by the Philistine excisemen. The museum has little hand-written cards attached to the exhibits, some of which are casually piled in corners, and could do with a bit of refurbishment. If they sold the feather golf balls and old clubs they have in a dusty glass case, they could probably rebuild the whole place on the proceeds.

With the weather remaining fine, I decided to take the beast, strangely light and manoeuvrable without a loaded sidecar, to Southend, to revisit the place where my guitar addiction began. Just a few miles from Campbeltown, it's a remarkably lovely spot, with a splendid beach and a really strange, massive, boarded-up concrete building called the Keil Hotel. Painted glaring, peeling white and castellated with fake 1930s battlements, the hotel mocks the natural beauty of the surroundings. Fantastically situated, it could be renovated into a luxury retreat for people who like to retreat luxuriously. On the other hand, it could be razed to the ground, which might be a better idea.

Back in Campbeltown, I wander up the lane which leads to Springbank, astonished at the building which adjoins the distillery. It is also called Springbank, but it is Springbank Evangelical Church, for which read, before the Brethren went up-market, Springbank Gospel Hall. The change of hundreds of Brethren halls to 'evangelical churches' came about from the late 1960s onwards, as the increasingly bourgeois membership stopped wanting to be associated with the 'mission' image conjured by the couthy, quaint name 'gospel hall'. People wanted, I remember someone saying to my father, to be able to tell their friends 'I go to such and such a church' without the embarrassment of having to explain what a gospel hall was, and what the Brethren were. What the upwardly-mobile Brethren missed was the self-contradiction inherent in the description 'evangelical church' because all Christian churches are, by definition, believers in the gospel, the evangel, the good news. The message conveyed by the words 'evangelical church' is therefore a weird mixture of social embarrassment and theological snobbery: our church is the only one that really believes, o ye that pass by on the other side on the way to the distillery . . . to hell. Which doesn't involve real flames, by the way, only an Absence of God . . .

Springbank, the distillery, looks ancient, and some of its buildings do date back to the place's foundation in 1828. Still in the Mitchell family after one hundred and sixty years, the manager is an evangelical of sorts, by the name of John McDougall. Only his good news is whisky.

'I love whisky, I love this industry, I love talking about it and I'd go anywhere, talk to anybody to help people understand what it's about. I'm just determined to share my enthusiasm for whisky, because for me this is not so much a job, but a hobby. I'm lucky.'

Such youthful passion is rare in the whisky trade, but J. and A. Mitchell are unique. The Springbank operation reeks of an almost religious commitment to the Cause of the Ultimate Dram, made according to traditional methods which are fanatically adhered to. Nowhere is this better illustrated than in the newly restored floor maltings which now make Springbank completely self-sufficient in malt.

'It got to the stage that we either had to tear the building down or repair it,' says John, shaggy and white-haired in his early fifties. 'And we decided to go all the way with it.'

Using their own tradesmen and with John designing things as he went along, applying many of the lessons learnt when manager at Laphroaig, the result is a three-floor maltings which burns Islay peat and nothing else, although it is hoped that supplies from a less environmentally-sensitive source will eventually be obtained.

'It's a funny business, you know,' says John, who cannot disguise his immense pride in this project. 'Here I am teaching some of these young workmen traditional methods going back centuries. But my motto is, and this applies to all aspects of distilling here: if it isn't broken, don't mend it. There is a reason for traditional methods standing the test of time.'

The rest of the tiny distillery is, John warns, 'a bit cottagey'. It isn't half. You kind of expect to find straw on the floors and a few cows out the back. The mash tun is cast iron, the washbacks larch. There are three stills, small ones, with the old peat furnace – now disused – still visible under the wash still. Unusually, the two low wines or spirit stills are heated by steam, while the wash still has a live flame applied to it.

'We feel that the live flame has the effect of sealing in the flavours of the malt,' says John. 'Anyone who suggests the use of indirect heat on that still at Springbank is in for a P45 job.'

Stepping into Springbank is like stepping into another world. The stills are not run all the time, with production being kept strictly limited, allowing such possibilities as the eccentric 'West Highland' limited edition, where everything used, even the coal to heat the stills, apparently, was locally produced. Although some distillery managers scornfully dismiss Springbank as 'a hobby distillery', the fact is that they sell what they make, often at very high prices indeed.

'We have a growing band of converts in this country,' says John McDougall, 'and markets are growing for us, especially in Germany. People's palates are definitely getting more attuned to drinking and savouring malts, I think it's fair to say that we have a wonderful product to sell, a generic product. I would like to see Scotch whisky being sold on the same kind of regional basis as French wines are – so we would be Campbeltown, Glenfarclas a Speyside and so on – and in fact we've begun dating our whiskies for the German market like vintages – a Springbank 1975, for example, making a lot of sense to them. More than saying "a ten-year-old" or "a twelve-year-old".'

The strange business of being able to produce two distinct whiskies, Longrow and Springbank, from the one distillery, is partially explained. Longrow, in the past, was made at its own plant, but the technique for producing it differs so much from Springbank that it is permissible to make the two on the same equipment. So what is the difference in technique, I inquire curiously.

'Oh, it's a matter of slightly different chemistry,' says John evasively, and won't expand, although he admits that the malt involved in Longrow is more heavily peated than that used in Springbank. In fact, according to someone who ought to know, Longrow is quite simply triple-distilled, like the Glasgow Lowland malt Auchentoshan, linking all three stills together in line and re-distilling the second distillate. That would explain the essential delicacy and smoothness of Longrow, and the fact that its peatiness, though incredibly strong, remains less abrasive than, say, in a Lagavulin or Laphroaig.

This vagueness is unusual from John, though, who is a great believer in demystifying the whole process of malt whisky production. He believes his consumers are intelligent, want to know how what they're drinking is made and have a right to be told. Except, presumably, what the difference is between Longrow and Springbank.

'There is a great deal of ignorance around about whisky, and it's no fault of the consumer. It is the fault of the industry. I just don't understand why, if people think they've got a good product, they don't believe in it and want to talk about, explain it.' This attitude, however, probably stems from John's unshakable conviction that what he is producing is the best there is. 'If you don't think that,' he says unequivocally, 'you might just as well forget it.'

The limited edition bottlings Springbank have specialised in over the years began as 'a bit of fun', but the discovery that such rarities could command awesome prices must have concentrated the mind wonderfully. For example, a thousand bottles at £150 a time of 'green' whisky, which had been matured, as an experiment, in casks which had previously contained rum, sold out by mail order as soon as it was mentioned on the Cadenheads mailing list – a list which, John reveals, is hitting the younger, cultish market I always suspected was there, waiting to be tapped. He believes Springbank malt is being discovered by an increasing number of people as something new, unique to them, and its reputation is growing by word-of-mouth.

'Because we're small, and entirely family-owned, we can do things like very limited edition bottlings because we want to, and we're not continually answerable to accountants.'

In fact, a small operation like Springbank benefits most from the low volume/high value nature of the premium malt trade. The great advantage that the Campbeltown operation has is the essential rarity and quality of its product. In Japan, the ludicrous situation exists where Scotch whisky producers are competing for the most over-the-top packaging, because there is a belief that in Japan, the more expensive, the more prestigious, the rarer the items, the more people will actually buy it. This sounds crazy, but many whisky moguls have swallowed it, so to speak, and are now out-Glenfiddich-ing Glenfiddich in presenting their whisky encased in hollow rhinoceros horn, gold dredged up from the *Titanic* and in a special presentation pack made from the skulls of Scottish clansmen killed at the Battle of Culloden. That particular one will be called Charlie's Dram, and each limited edition skull, filled with finest three-year-old grain whisky blended with a millilitre of some malt no one else wants, will actually carry the name of the dead clansman involved!

Not that Springbank would, or could, have anything to do with such activities. Their in-house bottling plant, where all the wondrous Cadenhead rarities go from cask to glass, should be painted by someone like Peter Howson immediately and forthwith, because it is just totally unbelievable. The manager laughs as he takes me to it, asking if I've been to Glenfiddich, seen their plant. I have. 'Well, this is nothing like that.'

The room is dominated by boxes and boxes of bottled whisky, Cadenhead specials with the distillery names stencilled on: Laphroaig, The Glenlivet, Caperdonich. Along a counter sit a few people, physically pouring the amber nectar into individual bottles by hand; gluing on the labels; using a primitive hand-operated vice-like thing to put the tops on.

'That's where our own whisky is kept for bottling,' says John, pointing to a giant oak vessel which looks like something Barnard might have shook his head over, tut-tutting at its primitiveness. 'It all works perfectly.'

And it does. The warehouses range from old, slightly musty, slightly warm, to cold, concrete tombs. There the whisky matures in casks which vary in origin, but these days are usually broken-up bourbon casks from the USA, remade on the premises. The product is not chill-filtered, the process which freezes out any detritus but also removes something of a whisky's character, and finings are not used to obtain sparkling purity. Springbank and Longrow, not to mention the Cadenhead bottlings, are about as natural as you can get.

You get no freebies at Springbank, and one would hardly expect it. This is a serious, purist distillery; no messing about, and although the smallness of the operation gives John the impunity to lash out at the conceits of the whisky industry's big boys, sheer *joie de vivre* tempers the near-arrogance with which he fights his corner. If Springbank were a car, I ask him, what model would it be? He looks perplexed at such a question. A Jaguar? I prompt. Or maybe an Aston Martin? Something imbued with classic British hand-made individualism?

Eventually, the perfect image of Springbank occurs to him. The light of absolute certainty shining from his eyes, he leans forward. 'We,' he says, 'are a Ferrari Testorossa.'

That night I once more eat Chinese, and contemplate sheltering from the rain in Campbeltown's astonishing art-deco cinema, a copy of the Graumann Chinese Theatre in Hollywood made all the more Californian by the palm trees and tropical plants which line the grass verge outside. But Barbra Streisand and Nick Nolte do not appeal, and instead I drop into the Royal for another Longrow sixteen-year-old. It is, I decide, the best whisky I've ever tasted. But the problem is one of time and place; maybe Longrow is the best whisky you'll ever taste when you've just spent the afternoon visiting the distillery, when you're soaking wet and gazing out on to a blue misty Campbeltown night. And maybe not. But that's how it was for me.

Severely breakfasted, I packed, paid Mrs Wilson and headed for Glen Scotia, which was in the middle of a refurbishment programme and smelt strongly of paint. Never mind, Glen Scotia has a real, dead ghost, the spirit of a former manager who, consumed with financial and other worries, threw himself into Campbeltown Loch, presumably with the words of the song 'Campbeltown Loch, I wish you were whisky' running through his head. I looked for him, but all I found was the very much alive and thoroughly welcoming Roy McKinven, a local Campbeltown boy who had worked his way up through the distillery ranks to his present post of manager. He offered me coffee and sticky buns in his tiny office at the very foot of Glen Scotia's massive, and mostly unused building.

'They say there's Irish blood in us all hereabouts,' says Roy, who's in his thirties and who exudes boyish enthusiasm. 'Campbeltown folk tend to be a bit of a mixture. In the eighteenth century this was a place people came to hide, and many of them just stayed.'

Glen Scotia is owned, along with the Littlemill Distillery at Bowling near Glasgow, by a consortium involving French and Canadian interests. Local supermarket tycoon Jimmy Gulliver bought the place in the 1980s, but had to close it in the face of an industry-wide overproduction crisis. This was the period when reliance on cheap blends for cash-flow nearly ruined many distillers.

Now, Glen Scotia, which began production in 1832 as plain old Scotia, is working five twenty-four hour days per week, employing ten people, and things are going reasonably well. With about 60 per cent of production going for blending, the rest is bottled at twelve years old as a single, with some going to make up the vatted malt, Royal Culross. The demand is there, Roy says, for Glen Scotia twelve-year-old, and that is where the marketing push will be in the future, particularly in France, but Glen Scotia does not rely on exports for survival.

I wonder if there is any rivalry between Glen Scotia and Springbank. Roy smiles. 'We're quite friendly, but really we're aiming at different markets. There's no malice, and everyone respects one another, on the whole. They're dependent on the export market, and don't distil all year round as we do.'

Roy has no truck with mystique, reminding me in this respect a wee bit of Jim Robertson at Highland Park. I wonder where they get their water from. He grins: 'The same place as Springbank, and Campbeltown Creamery – from the local industrial water supply! I bet John McDougall didn't tell you that!' Although this means that the metered water has to be paid for, the supply is completely free of additives, unlike the ordinary tap water, and comes from Crosshill Loch above the town.

We tour the empty distillery, which seems industrial compared to Springbank, but is actually fairly standard, with malt as usual being brought in from outside. The gregarious warehouseman Bobby, on hearing that I'm writing a book, asks if there's anything that has particularly interested me so far. I tell him about the illicit stills, and he laughs.

'I was up on holiday one year, in the West Highlands, and I came across this still, in a wee croft house, but you could smell it for miles around. Absolutely unmistakable smell, it was a wonder they didn't get done. I said to the wife, they're not making jam in there.'

Bobby is curious about my motorcycling attire, and on hearing I have a combination, he laughs again. One of the now retired Glen Scotia workers, he says, used to ride one, and on one occasion took his wife on the pillion and mother-in-law in the sidecar on a trip to Glasgow.

'The whole thing came apart at Anniesland Cross,' he says, 'quite literally, the mother-in-law went one way, he and the wife went the other.'

Glen Scotia matures in 'whatever casks we can get, really', which I suspect is true of more distilleries than will admit it. Roy offers me a dram, but it's too early in the morning, and by this stage in the trip I'm into liver protection. We have another coffee and sticky bun instead before I take my leave, heading into Campbeltown for a few souvenirs. In a bookshop more disorganised than any I think I've ever seen, I procure a copy of Norman Newton's useful little booklet *Campbeltown's Distilleries*, then visit the wonderful Eaglesham's delicatessen and off-licence for a half-bottle of Longrow at vast expense.

I'm loath to leave, because Campbeltown, with its odd, lanky, overgrown architecture, its history, its fine seashore and harbour, and most of all its whiskies, has partially seduced me with its down-at-heel charm. Barnard liked it too, even finding time to pick up a good wee joke. It goes against the grain to quote the old bore again, but here he is telling it:

> A capital story is told of an aged woman who resided near Hazelburn. She was a rather doubtful character and was charged before the sheriff with smuggling. The charge being held proven, it fell to his lordship to pronounce sentence. When about to do so, he thus addressed the culprit, 'I daresay my poor woman it is not often that you have been guilty of this fault.'
>
> 'Deed no Sheriff,' she readily replied, 'I haena made a drap since youn wee keg I sent to yersel.'

As I start the bike, a taxi arrives from Machrihanish with two American Air Force men in it, heading for Glasgow on leave. Campbeltown's quotient of Americans is small, although I had come across three Hemingwayesque types launching a boat at the harbour, presumably for off-duty impersonations of the Middle-Aged Man And The Sea. The guys who emerged from the taxi were not into sea fishing, by the look of them; they carried ghetto blasters and wore street clothes straight from a rock video, with unlaced trainers Scottish kids would kill for. I wondered about going up to them and saying, hey, wassappenin', you doods flying any Stealth fighter bombers from your top-secret section of the Machrihanish base? Is it true that you bombed Saddam from Scotland during the Gulf War? That's what people are sayin' man, wassdavibe? But I'm a shy sort of soul, and no good at American accents.

Instead, as I ripped at the outer edges of the MZ's envelope (about 50 mph) up the Atlantic coast of Kintyre, I sang the songs which I'd learned as a six-year-old child during that last trip to Kintyre, at the CYC camp singalongs, when I'd heard a guitar jangle in the same room for the first time:

> Climb, climb up sunshine mountain
>   heavenly breezes blow
> Climb, climb up sunshine mountain
>   faces all aglow oh oh oh
> Turn, turn your back on doubting
> Look up to the sky
> Climb, climb up sunshine mountain
> You and I . . .

My singing was lost in the snarl of the orange beast, as a cold sea mist swept in from the west and the stink of rotting seaweed filled the air, and I remembered my mother's distinctive contralto filling that swaying hired caravanette.

> We are marching up the hillside and the trail leads home
> We are marching up the hillside and the winding trail leads ho ho ho home
> Sometimes, we're finding, that the trail is a winding
> But we don't care NO!
> No we don't care NO!
> For the trail leads home
> We're on the homeward trail (we're on the homeward TRAIL)
> We're on the homeward TRAIL!
> Singing, singing, everybody's singing,
> GOING HOME!

There's nothing at Kennacraig but the Calmac pier, the shipping office, a waiting-room and a carpark. Lines of lorries and cars are already there, waiting for the Islay ferry, when I arrive in a cloud of nostalgic nonsense songs that, on reflection, sound suspiciously like something the Hitler Youth might have bellowed, smiling with menace. I pull the bike into one of the loading lanes, noticing as I do so an unkempt green Mercedes 28OE, one of the old ones with pillar headlights. It is driven by a tall woman with long blonde hair who, as I watch, climbs out, obviously weary after a long journey with the two small children who are strapped into childseats in the back.

She's very attractive, I think to myself, stumbling a little as I swing on to static ground from the silent bike. I decide to go over and speak to her, which is probably quite sensible, as the blonde woman in question is, in fact, my wife.

Chapter Nine

ISLAY

As I was using up all my holidays in the service of liver and brain damage, it had been arranged that wife and family would join me for a three-day sojourn in Islay, where I could conduct a leisurely investigation of the seven distilleries packed on to the peaty archipelago while she and the kids did whatever people do on holiday.

The car journey from Cromarty to Kennacraig had not been without incident. Our one-year-old male human, a bad traveller, had encrusted his childseat and everything within a range of about three feet with vomit. The four-year-old had girned fitfully ever since spying, in Oban, a model back-hoe excavator he wished to add to his collection of heavy earthmoving equipment. His mother had refused this request.

'Oban,' she said, 'is the toilet of Scotland.' I could only agree with this sentiment. If only it had a few more toilets, though, working ones.

We sat for half an hour watching someone who looked like Ian Gillan from Deep Purple using a battered tractor unit to haul lorry-trailers on to the MV *Claymore* at great speed. Then Isolde the sexistly named green Merc was waved aboard, followed in due course by the orange beast. We believe in symbolising the healing of the east-west divide in our family transport, hence the vehicles from the two Germanies. Well no, actually the real reason is that my wife fell in love with the twenty-year-old Merc, which had been tarted up by an unscrupulous pensioner from Nairn to look immaculate, and bought it in the face of environmentalism (a 2.8 litre fuel-injected petrol automatic) and good taste (our friends variously described it as a dodgy antique dealer's car, something a South American dictator drives, or a Jerusalem taxi). Inevitably doomed, especially in the accident-prone hands of my wife, Isolde remained resolutely reliable, with the great advantage that, despite her patina of rust, she could comfortably drive straight through the average, say, Ford Sierra and come out the other side with passengers and dignity unscathed.

Two hours of cheerfully greasy Calmac food and consequently heaving stomachs later, the *Claymore* arrived at Port Askaig. The weather had changed from relatively horrid to absolutely foul, with a gusting wind and icy rain, as I followed Isolde off the boat and on to the isle of my forebears. Across the Sound of Islay, the famous Paps of Jura were completely obscured by psychotic-looking clouds. Welcome to Islay.

Ancestors don't interest me as much as perhaps they should. My sister once conducted a search through the Morton family background, hoping to find a connection with the Earl of Morton and the Douglas clan dynasty (very dodgy Border cattle-thieves) but the trail went cold in the eighteenth century with endless lists of Mortons whose sole occupation seemed to be that of carter. On my mother's side, the line seemed to halt at my grandfather, who had left Islay as a child. That was all I knew. He had gone on to become a railwayman and a salesman of Singer sewing machines, dying at fifty of heart failure after running for a bus. He had been a famous preacher amongst the Brethren of central Lanarkshire, spending all his spare time moving among the smoke and grime of the steelworks and pit bings, from tin-shack gospel halls to some other 'gathering of the saints'. His son, a frequent and influential presence during my childhood, went into what seemed to me that most romantic of professions, journalism. He also played in a rock band. Later I went on to imitate him in both respects.

Would I find any family roots on Islay? My grandfather had left the island with his family in about 1910, moving first to Inverkip, then to Lanarkshire. I had no exact birthdates, no idea which part of Islay he had been born in. But maybe I could pick up a flavour of the MacCalman heritage, the only lump of the *Gaidhealtacht* in my polluted bloodstream.

The van ahead of the Merc managed to misjudge a turn climbing out of Port Askaig, a place which looked, in the disgusing weather, very wet indeed, and ploughed into a thick hedge of hawthorn. No one was hurt, so Isolde and the beast formed a convoy across to Bowmore on Loch Indaal, an indentation on the west coast of the island.

Bowmore's famous white, round church dominates the village. Built, the story goes, without any corner for the devil to hide in, it loomed out of the driving rain as our convoy of German vehicles climbed the hill past the distillery. By this time, despite oilskins and my usual bad weather gear, I was colder than I'd been at any time during the trip. I hoped my wife knew where she was going. We passed two pedal cyclists, plodding in Gore-Tex and misery through the rain and our convoy's spray. It struck me that things could be worse.

We were bound for a place called Kintra, a farmhouse bed and breakfast, and I already had the deepest misgivings. Booked blind, I was sure it would be cold and basic and without any hope of decent food and drink. Still, it was too late to do anything about it.

Out of Bowmore is 'the Long Road', something like eight miles of arrow-straight tarmac across some of the most desolate moorland outside of Siberia. This the peat-bog country where the barnacle geese roost, where peat is extracted, to the despair of conservationists, for whisky production, and where, over on the 'machair', the sandy grassland at Laggan Bay, one of Scotland's greatest 'wee' golf courses surrounds the Machrie Hotel.

Kintra is actually on the edge of Laggan Bay, but you have to double back from Port Ellen, on the south coast of Islay, to get there. Numbed, I followed my wife along what seemed like endless roads and dirt tracks, until finally we arrived at a big, isolated farmhouse. This was our destination.

Kintra turned out to be perfect. Although slightly distracted by the pressures of the lambing season, Mrs MacTaggart, one of the dwindling band of native Gaelic speakers on the island, swept us into the massive farmhouse, lit fires, made sure we had tea, cakes, hot water and towels, and generally welcomed us as heroic travellers. Could we get an evening meal? No problem, any time we wanted food, the Old Granary Bar and Restaurant would be open. Bar? Restaurant? Oh joy! Beautifully converted from, yes, an old granary, heated by two peat fires, the Old Granary was everything you could wish for in flagged-floor traditional pub-stroke-eaterie. Kids were allowed, it was part of the B&B, and they had all seven Islay whiskies.

After a thawing bath and general ablutions involving the children, I decided to telephone a few distilleries to see about tours the following day. A brochure, entitled *The Islay and Jura Whisky Tour*, is available, but don't be misled. If my experience is anything to go by, getting to see around Islay's distilleries is not easy. With the exception of Laphroaig and Bowmore, where regular morning and afternoon tours are run in spring and summer, you have to telephone for an appointment. Ardbeg, run by Laphroaig, is judged unsuitable for visitors, and Bruichladdich discourages them. All the others – Caol Ila, Bunnahabhain and Lagavulin, which offer tours, refused to show me around. They were too busy. No one was available. I had decided not, on this occasion, to sell myself to the managers as intrepid, book-writing, motorcycling, lunatic, piss-artist Tom Morton, but simply to be a typical tourist, partly because I had the family with me. On Islay, it seems, tourists are only tolerated by distilleries when it suits them – despite the whisky industry being one of the island's major attractions.

In the flickering peat-light of the Old Granary, we ate and drank cleanly and politely while the children gorged messily and noisily, causing not even a raised eyebrow. Stone floors are easily cleaned, I suppose. As we counted our blessings for choosing Kintra and not some shake-and-vac hotel with floral nylon curtains and a landlady with a dust neurosis, two of the wettest figures I have ever laid eyes on trooped in.

We all fell silent as they passed us, like two sea-zombies trawled from the deep. Together they stood at the fire, motionless, as steam came from their clothes and water gathered in pools about their feet. Eventually, one of them spoke, in a strong Birmingham accent. 'Nice day for cycling,' he said.

These, then, were the two intrepid Gore-Tex-clad riders on the storm we had spotted coming out of Bowmore. Were they staying at Kintra?

'Well, yes,' said the taller one. 'We're just wondering where we should pitch our tent.' We just looked at them. Outside, the wind and rain continued unabated. I knew from my own experiences over the previous fortnight that continued exposure to vicious weather could turn your head a little. In fact, I only put my retention of at least some sanity down to the ingestion of the liquid invented by Scots to cope with this kind of weather. It seemed that these two pedallers, who did look like mild and bitter men, had not spirits taken sufficiently. Now they were planning to camp, and were obviously in need of psychiatric treatment.

I capped the day's evil weather with suitable drams: Ardbeg, reopened in 1989 without its floor maltings, alas, but with the ten-year-old available certainly still benefiting from on-site peat malting. Halfway between a Laphroaig and a Lagavulin, it has all the thick, iodine kick of a class Islay, pungent and smoky. Then, from the depths of my Joy Bag, I extracted a miniature of Port Ellen 1971, bought way back in Elgin at Gordon and MacPhail and one of their Connoisseur's Choice series. Now closed, the Port Ellen distillery buildings line the road from Kintra into Port Ellen itself, but are overshadowed by the huge, modern United Distillers maltings, one of the industrial variety which supplies malt to several of the local distilleries, including Lagavulin, Caol Ila, and to a small extent Laphroaig and Ardbeg too. UD could reopen Port Ellen if they had a mind, and they should, if the old bottlings are anything to go by. The 1971 is drier than some of the other Islay drams, but remains typical of them in its seaweedy potency. If anything, the peat is more pronounced than in the heavyweight Lagavulin.

After bringing to bear the forgotten skills necessary for bathing and bedding children, we retired to Mrs MacTaggart's wonderful lounge, and pored over a massive collection of Scottish and Gaelic history books as well as a selection of guides to Islay. Why had Islay become such a centre for whisky production? After all, other places had water, peat and barley. And Islay didn't really have that much barley of its own, did it?

I found the answer in the Islay and Jura marketing group's visitors' handbook, an admirable publication. In an anonymous, very short 'History of Whisky on Islay' the following paragraph explains all:

> The answer lies not in climate or geography, but in political economics. After the Union of the Crowns in 1707, the Scottish Board of Excise was set up and its officers collected duty (or tried to) on all whisky produced. For some reason Islay was without an excise officer for the following ninety years. During this time it was left to the laird to levy and collect duty. It was, of course, in his interest to have a thriving whisky industry. Unhampered by crippling taxes, the industry grew up, the skills were entrenched by the time and excise officer arrived and successive governments have done very well out of it ever since.

Next day, after one of the great breakfasts, we departed *en famille* for Laphroaig, the whisky I'd fallen in love with all those years ago when malts first began to impinge on my tastebuds. Like all the Islay distilleries, with the exception of Bruichladdich which is a road-width away, Laphroaig is beautifully situated on the seaside. Like nearly every Islay building, it is painted white, and lies a little way eastwards along the rocky coast from Port Ellen. Lagavulin and Ardbeg are virtually next door.

At first, we were alone with our guide, a jolly woman called Mrs Henderson who seemed particularly well informed about distilling in general and Laphroaig in particular. We were being shown round the light-airy maltings – always for me the most enjoyable part of the whole whisky-making process, partly, I think, because it's so slow and primitive and goes back, unchanged in technique, to the dawn of civilisation – when we were breathlessly joined by two more families, both youngish and English.

Unlike the every-fifteen-minutes Speyside whisky tours, those offered by Laphroaig and Bowmore come at set times, one in the morning and one in the afternoon, and if you miss the start, that's tough. As we continued on to the malt-mill, which was in operation, several of the children in the group, including, inevitably, ours, demanded to be taken away from the infernal racket. And so it was that my wife found herself back in the carpark, talking to another woman who had been banished from the tour with her offspring, about the perils of whisky widowhood.

As it turned out, the two fathers who were even at that moment being told by Mrs Henderson that only about 30 per cent of the malt used by Laphroaig was actually produced on-site, the rest coming either from Ireland or Port Ellen, were not whisky junkies; they were distillery addicts.

'Everywhere we go on holiday, there has to be a distillery,' my wife was told. 'Then off they go and tour them, leaving us with the kids, or dragging us around with them.' These men were not professionally involved in the whisky industry, not great drinkers, not social historians or even journalists. They just liked distilleries. If pushed, I would admit there is a seductive aspect to the smells, the warmth, the alchemical magic of making spirit from grain. But much of the technology, identical as it is from one place to the other, I find terminally boring. These men, though, like Barnard, loved the mash tuns and the spirit safes, the spirit receivers and the automatic cask-filling computers, no matter how many they saw. I got excited about floor maltings because I saw so few of them. They thrived on a millimetre's difference in still sizes.

They had, it turned out, had the same problems I had experienced in getting to see around Bunnahabhain, Lagavulin and Caol Ila, despite having been on Islay all week. So it wasn't just me.

Back on the Laphroaig tour, and rather flying in the face of my casual disdain of differing distillation techniques, I was absolutely astonished to find shining stainless-steel washbacks, rather than the larch or oregon pine amost universally used elsewhere.

'They're easier to clean, and you can control the levels of carbon dioxide coming off,' said Mrs Henderson. 'We've got wooden washbacks in Ardbeg, which is run from here, and that's one of the reasons visitors wouldn't want to go round the place. The tun room is absolutely stinking.'

Certainly Laphroaig is immaculate, clean as a new pin and most definitely not in the least bit niffy, unless you count the ubiquitous peat reek. Mrs Henderson is proud of the place, not least because her husband Iain is the manager. She pointed out her house, which overlooks the sea and the distillery.

'We get all our peat for nothing, and we don't have to cut it,' she said, pointing at the massive store of cut peat for the maltings. 'With a smell like this, peat and distilling, and a view like this – I always say, if heaven's like this I'll be happy!'

Laphroaig is much sought after for blending, its strong character meaning that a little goes a long way in the oceans of dull old grain whisky. But that 70 per cent of 'blending Laphroaig' (which is matured in sherry or wine-treated casks, with the single malt ageing exclusively in bourbon wood) is matured elsewhere on the island. Only the single malt and, at Japanese insistence, any Laphroaig destined for the Suntory blends, is matured on site.

With no reception centre to speak of, there was no complimentary dram. However, everyone was given, free, *gratis* and for nothing, a miniature Laphroaig ten-year-old, worth all of £2.00. This compares with the 'free drams' you get at some distilleries which are about one-twelfth of a gill. A miniature being roughly a double, Laphroaig does the visitor proud. Mind you, so, in this respect, does Glenfiddich.

Mrs Henderson had been watching my surreptitious note-taking, and as I was about to leave, asked if I would like to meet her husband. It turned out that a deputation from Allied Distillers, Laphroaig's owners, had been expected that day, but had cancelled their visit at the last moment. I was suspected of being a secret Allied agent, sent to check out the distillery.

I revealed that far from being a management spy, I was, in fact, merely a reporter in search of tittle-tattle and scandal. This seemed to relieve Iain Henderson, who plied the whole family (my wife and kids had been rescued from the carpark) with coffee and biscuits, and me with some expensively printed brochures which told the Laphroaig story in rather tedious detail. Inevitably, the place has had a few moments of crisis and upheaval, like the attempt to imitate Laphroaig at nearby Lagavulin, which involved stealing Laphroaig's brewer, duplicating the stills and other frenzied imitation. But even with the same peat, the same barley and the same water, it could not be done.

What else? Well, one of the first owners died after falling into a vat of pot ale, or burnt ale; the blend Islay Mist was born in 1928 after the Laird of Islay House asked for whisky to be supplied for his son's coming of age, and Laphroaig itself was thought 'too heavy for everyone's taste'. And, of course, there is the mysterious tale of Bessie Williamson, the secretary, who was left the distillery by Mr Iain Hunter, her managing director (and no funny business has ever been suggested) in 1954, running the place until selling out to Long John in 1967 and even then remaining as chairman and director until 1972. She was the first woman in modern times (and, it seems the last) to run a distillery. United Distillers made a tremendous fuss when Liz Stewart became a mashperson at Dalwhinnie, the spectacularly situated mountain distillery in the so-called 'gulag' south of Kingussie, the highest in Scotland.

Liz was hailed as the first woman to enter the male bastion of Scotch whisky production, but Bessie Williamson was just a little earlier, and a bit more senior than she.

Iain Henderson and his wife were enthusiastic hosts. Laphroaig was a cult whisky, he said, and that could have unforeseen problems. One Friday, as everyone was about to pack up and go home, a yacht was spotted, apparently in difficulties offshore. Eventually, a small boat was seen to leave the vessel, which had finally dropped anchor, and a party of several tired, cold and wet French students landed at the distillery.

'They said they had come on a pilgrimage just to see round Laphroaig, which was their favourite whisky,' said Iain. 'Well, what could I do? Of course, we took them in, dried them off and showed them round. They were thrilled to bits.'

Laphroaig, according to Iain, is the number four best-selling brand in the world 'or possibly number five', after Glenfiddich, Glenlivet, Glenmorangie and (maybe) Macallan in that order. That's the ten-year-old. The fifteen-year-old, difficult to get except from the distillery and specialist shops (the exceptionally rude staff at the Bowmore off-licence told me it wasn't made) is something else again.

Smoother, peatier, more sophisticated than its little brother, like a sweeter, less austere Longrow, Laphroaig have one very important customer for whom the fifteen-year-old is kept aside. Prince Charles was visiting Brora, where he was performing some official function, when he was offered a pre-prandial dram. 'I'd like a malt,' he was reported as saying. 'What do you have?' And all they had was Glenfiddich. Not even Clynelish, for goodness sake! Quick as a flash, a reporter asked him what his favourite malt was 'Laphroaig fifteen-year-old,' came the alleged reply. Was this true, I asked Iain.

'I'll show you the photocopy of the cheque from the palace if you like,' he said. I took his word for it. I mentioned that my interest in Laphroaig had been sparked off by its presence in almost every chapter of John Fowles's *Daniel Martin*. He informed me that it also makes frequent appearances in the novels of Dick Francis, and that John Simpson of the BBC put his survival through the stresses of reporting from Baghdad during the Gulf War down to a bottle he happened to have with him. Which, incidentally, he wouldn't have got into Saudi Arabia, far stricter on drink than nasty old Iraq.

Laphroaig's status was perhaps most fully affirmed by the visit, in December 1991, of nine generals from the (then still) Soviet Army, flown in secretly by their British counterparts for a little rest and recreation during a trip to the Faslane nuclear submarine base. Could this be the beginning of the post-Glasnost marketing of Laphroaig in the Community of Independent States? The generals went home with plenty of Laphroaig to share, equally no doubt, with their people.

I asked Iain what made Laphroaig so special. He found it a difficult question. 'Who knows, really? We use the same water as Lagavulin, and they have the same design of wash still. At Ardbeg we have the same malt . . . and yet Laphroaig is completely different from either.'

On that shoulder-shrugging note we took our leave, with me exulting in the fact that I didn't have to clamber into yellow oilskins and kick a recalcitrant motorbike into stuttering life. As we took the kids, who had spread biscuit crumbs all over the beautiful leather settees of the Laphroaig boardroom, out to Isolde, Iain asked me where I was bound after Islay. I mentioned Bladnoch, Scotland's most southerly distillery, and was immediately swept back into the office to look at picture albums.

'I was manager at Bladnoch before I came here,' he said, 'and my wife set up the visitor centre there. We built the whole thing from scratch.' And the photos are there to prove it. 'You'll like Bladnoch,' he told me. 'It's a smooth malt, kind of like Armagnac, and in a beautiful spot.' I got the the hint of some regret that he had left. He and his wife shook their heads, but with more than a touch of nostalgia.

'No. You've got to move on in this job,' said Iain. 'Laphroaig's a more important whisky.' It is, too. It also tastes about 100 per cent better than Bladnoch, which in the one brief snifter I'd had of it, bore no resemblance to Armagnac – or at least, to good Armagnac – whatsoever.

That afternoon I took the orange beast into Bowmore while wife and weans, sealed securely against water ingress, pottered around Kintra's fantastic beach. In good weather, Kintra must be paradise, and even in bad it wasn't unpleasant. Unless you were camping. The mad cyclists had departed, never to be seen again.

I arrived at Bowmore, to my intense annoyance, half an hour too late for the afternoon tour. However, the apologetic Angela, one of the guides, told me I could join a special tour which was being arranged the next morning, Saturday, for a party of golfers from the Machrie Hotel. Fair enough. Islay was not proving an easy place to actually see around distilleries, although in one sense, why should working factories bend over backwards to have hordes of ignorant tourists wander around, getting under their feet, and then expecting free booze at the end of it? It is good PR, and there is the distillery shop, which can shift a lot of stuff in a good week. But there is a definite atmosphere on Islay redolent of the 1960s in the rest of Scotland: that sense of putting up with tourists, taking their money and then kicking them out. Not at Laphroaig, not at Kintra and not at Bowmore, but prevalent nonetheless.

As I discovered on my return to the various bosoms of my family, my wife had made the hilarious discovery of a café in Port Ellen which had apparently informed her that they allowed 'no children especially small ones'. My sentiments exactly, except that children have to start somewhere, and they usually start small. We stuck with the Old Granary, where the service was, it had to be admitted, slow, but the kids were more than tolerated and the food good.

It didn't suit the English family ('I can't understand a word they're saying' . . . 'that's because they're all Scotch') who had stayed one night and were now going to the Machrie Hotel 'for a bit of luxury'. I hoped the Machrie were as understanding of their habit of sitting up late drinking while their kids rampaged around, apparently ignored.

But maybe I'm just too much of a Calvinist at heart. I hate to see children in pubs as adjuncts to serious drunkenness-seeking, and that has been one of the spin-offs of more liberal Scottish licensing laws on the English model. There used to be a 'café-bar' on the south side of Glasgow, the only one for miles where kids could be taken to sit with their parents as they drank to distraction. Push-chairs would pile up outside, taxis would disgorge families from outlying housing schemes, and the end result inside was like something from a Victorian Band of Hope magic lantern show, warning of the evils of drink: fathers asleep, their kids trying desperately to wake them. And the management ringing the tills with relish.

I turned up at 10.30 a.m. for the special trip around Bowmore, together with five stunning young women who were apparently on the island for a pre-nuptial hen party with a former inhabitant. No golfers appeared, and so Angela, the friendly guide, showed us the Bowmore video, which is really exceptional as distillery videos go. Which isn't very far, actually.

At eleven o'clock the golfers arrived, young, upper-middle class, English and arrogant in an army-ish, public-school sort of way. Most were either still drunk from the night before, severely hungover or, at the sight of women, loud, yappily erect and obnoxious in the way yuppies used to be before the recession. They were clearly all of a type, and apart from being all golfers, I couldn't work out what it was that unified them. There was a preponderance of short hair, so maybe they were all military, or secret agents, or backslidden Mormons or something. Those I talked to claimed to be on 'a sort of stag golfing weekend' but wouldn't say any more.

Bowmore's floor maltings are not quite as classically open and beautifully maintained as Laphroaig's, but remain pretty impressive. Angela makes a mistake with her unruly party as we watch Martin, one of the maltmen, turning over the germinating barley with a big, flat wooden shovel.

'Martin's available for stripping, at a price,' she tells the hen party girls. The golfers overhear and snigger. Martin, his back to us all, takes no notice whatsoever. But the golfers now realise that Angela's game for a laugh, haw haw, and insist on her demonstrating her shovel technique 'to show us how strong you are'. Embarrassed but gritting her teeth, she does, and receives a round of ironic applause. At the kiln, Angela explains that Bowmore, in an effort to conserve the peat stocks of Islay, have taken to using peat 'caff', slightly damp, powdered peat, instead of the more usual machine-cut bricks.

This means, according to Angela, that 'we use two tonnes a week instead of ten tonnes' thus pleasing Professor David Bellamy and others who protested at the removal of peat from a barnacle goose roosting site.

Well, maybe. I am later informed by a cynical distillery insider that the environmental PR benefits are wholly incidental, and that the real reason this change has taken place is that you can get much more smoke from caff much more quickly, thus saving the more precious commodities of time and money.

The golfers make lots of imaginative jokes about one of their number who is called Pete ('You chuck peat in there, do you? In you go then, Pete'), we pass by the copper-topped mash tun and then have make an abortive visit to the mash room, where the former stainless-steel washbacks have been ripped out and replaced with larch ones, in an interesting reversal of habits at Laphroaig. Unfortunately, it is quickly realised that the floor of the mash room has just been varnished, and we beat a hasty, if sticky, retreat amidst much honking, braying public-school laughter.

By the time we reach the still-house, none of the golfers is paying much attention to Angela, and instead are talking handicaps and hangovers. One pulls on an Arthur Scargill mask and insists on bellowing, 'But are you *unionised*?' at every opportunity.

Angela is becoming annoyed. 'It seems some of you find this funny,' she says icily. 'I have no idea why.'

I tell myself not to be racist. I know plenty of Scots who habitually behave in ways as bad, if not worse, than this, and many of them are journalists. Maybe it's the unremitting maleness of this heavy, stupid humour which is so offensive. The all-boys-together heartiness. I half expect them to get their willies out for a length-and-colour competition at any moment. But they're slightly too well brought up for that, at least this early in the morning. And I imagine these particular willies would be very, very small anyway.

A swift visit to the warehouses, some of them actually below sea-level, and then we return to the reception centre for our free dram. The golfers perk up at this. 'I still don't have a clue how whisky's made,' says one. 'Who cares?' asks another.

Bowmore, as served at ten years old, is lighter than either Lagavulin or Laphroaig, less abrasive, but still very much an Islay whisky. I find it a wee bit glossy, a wee bit tame. It's reminiscent at times of Highland Park, without the northern openness and bite the Orkney whisky possesses. You might imagine it would appeal to a bigger audience than Laphroaig, which, of course, it doesn't, perhaps illustrating that milder tastes do not make up the majority of consumers. On the whole Bowmore's nice, and that's about as far as I'd go.

I'm being picked up in Isolde by my wife, and while waiting I take a look at Islay's only public swimming-pool, the MacTaggart Pool, which has been built in one of Bowmore's disused warehouses. It is heated using waste energy from the distillery itself, again pleasing the conservation lobby, and seems very nice, if you like public swimming-pools. Which I don't. As Orson Welles used to say, how many people do you think have pissed in this pool before me? Give me the sea any time, sewage and radiation notwithstanding. However, the MacTaggart Pool does offer a laundrette and sauna as well, in case you need to sanitise your smalls while sweating out the effects of all that good Islay malt . . .

That afternoon, chauffeured by my wife and armed with a pocketful of miniatures and some mineral water, I went on a tasting trip of Islay distilleries, which were, of course, closed to my enquiring tastebuds. After a typically deep-fried and microwaved lunch at the otherwise pleasant Port Askaig Hotel, I consumed a 1977 Gordon and MacPhail Caol Ila at Caol Ila, the Paps of Jura grey and unbreastlike across the sound on Jura. Caol Ila tastes less assertive than Laphroaig or Lagavulin, but lacks Bowmore's subdued, rather dull niceness. Lots of seaweed and peat, though with other more extravagant characters on offer locally, it's hard to get excited. Even while gazing over at Jura, it's a pleasant experience, but not a transcendent one, particularly given the rather ugly, tin-hut design of Caol Ila's buildings. Strangely, Caol Ila whisky was supposedly so popular in the nineteenth century that it had to be rationed.

The winding, dead-end road to Bunnahabhainn is spectacular, and so is the distillery itself, which has its own beach and pier and even its own luxury self-catering cottages to let. I have consumed Bunnahabhainn many a time and oft, because if you want to drink an Islay malt in large quantities, this is the one to go for. It retains the scent of island life, the essential qualities which go to make up an Islay whisky – the sea, the seaweed, the salt, the peat – but in a delicate, much less obtrusive way than the others. Neither does it have Bowmore's rather obvious sweetness. Bunnahabhainn is light but characterful; definitely and dangerously quaffable. Fortunately I only had a miniature with me of the fairly common twelve-year-old. They say it's a good introduction to Islay and I'd go along with that. It's also the one to drink with hot smoked fish, like mackerel, which sounds crazy but is, I can assure you, a truly remarkable and wonderful experience especially in the open air. It's worth trying the whole range of smoky whiskies with smoked foods such as salmon. However, the Shetland Smokehouse's unique, much imitated Gravadalax (salmon pressed in dill and cognac) works better, conversely, with the mountain sharpness of the underrated Dalwhinnie (better, in my opinion, than any Glenlivet).

We had thought of going over to Jura for a few hours, but, aside from travelling to Barnhill, where George Orwell, battling against the illness which finally killed him, wrote *1984*, there seemed little point. There's not a lot else there. The Jura distillery is not generally open to visitors, and it's a dram I dislike, because I'm convinced it's a manufactured whisky entirely calculated to appeal to this mythical monster with the bland palate, bearing as it does hardly a hint of island character. Unlike Bunnahabhainn, it is not that easy to drink, either, having such a bland, rather olive-oily taste that you end up geting fed up with very quickly. I know because I have tried to drink a lot of it, having had access to a free bottle or three. What do I mean by 'a lot'? What do you mean, what do I mean?

Bruichladdich, over on the western shores of Loch Indaal, isn't quite as spectacularly situated as some of the other Islay distilleries. Perhaps the gentler, grassy land behind it is indicative of a lack of peat in the water supply. At any rate, this is Scotland's most westerly distillery, and the tall stills produce a light, clean spirit which has only the merest hint of Islay about it. The first time I tasted the stuff (somebody bought me a bottle), I couldn't believe it actually came from Islay. I kept waiting for the inevitable blast of sweaty-socks-belonging-to-someone-undergoing-treatment-for-a-foot-complaint that I love so much. It never arrived. Of course, I managed to polish off the bottle eventually, with help, but Bruichladdich, to me, is a disappointment. I keep feeling I should be adding some crumbled peat or essence of seaweed to it, to make it taste how it ought to. Biased, me? Damn right. Anyway, I finished off the five centilitres I happened to have on me, listening to BBC Radio Ulster's outrageous Saturday afternoon satirical show, which is liable to get somebody shot, and the earth did not move. At least not because of the whisky.

Our time on Islay was running out, and still the only thing I knew about the MacCalmans was that there were five MacCalmans and one McCalman in the local telephone directory. Should I phone them up and say, as some American heritage-hunters are inclined to during trips to Scotland, 'Hello, I may or may not be your fourth cousin twice removed . . . nobody ever mentioned a MacCalman household which left the islands in 1910 or thereabouts, give or take a decade or so, I suppose? . . . Hello? Hello?'

I didn't do that. However, at the excellent Museum of Islay Life, just along the road from Bruichladdich at the excessively bonny village of Port Charlotte, I pored over a few books and discovered that yes, the MacCalmans had lived in Islay for several hundred years, and that one, Janet, whose second name had been spelt in the parish register as NcKalman, had been quite famous. Janet, it seemed had been prone to casting spells, of the 'may your butter turn mouldy' variety, and was in 1697 called before the local kirk session to answer charges that she had been up to such minor-league occultism. She did not appear, and could not be found at first because it turned out she was officially homeless. When finally dragged before the elders, including the beadle, also called MacCalman, she was found 'to be so stupid no sense could be gained from her' and was admonished.

I wondered what my mother would have made of that. Euphemia Jones Adam MacCalman would probably have laughed, then gone serious and said something like, 'You know, the MacCalmans have always had that second sight.' She did sometimes speak of meeting people whose faces she had seen in dreams. But then she'd have noticed we kids looking at her, saucer-eyed, and she'd have snorted with laughter: it's all a bit different from a daft old woman who told people she wished their butter would go off, she'd have said. And we'd have relaxed.

There was a time when witches and demons were all too real to me, when, with my first wife and two eldest sons in tow, I took the rapidly disintegrating faith of the Brethren and full-time fundamentalist evangelism into a strange, strange port. In a castle overlooking Dumbarton, filled with the acrid smell of the area's maltings and the sweeter distillery reeks, we lived 'in community' with tongue-speaking, prophesying, healing, demon-casting, hand-laying Christians; believing in it all; participating in it all. Until one day a prophetess told me, in tears, that she'd seen me, in a vision, with a woman who was not my wife. And I knew she, or God, was right. And then the whole edifice of religion and family, my whole life up to that point, disintegrated. Because for me there was only ever a choice between belief and its implications, or the absence of belief and what that implied. Consistency, for some reason, seemed important. At the time. Or maybe it was just selfishness, marginally justified theologically.

Back at Kintra, Mr MacTaggart was grey with tiredness, having been lambing all day. The weather had turned again from bright, artificial-looking sunlight to wind and heavy rain. 'I had a lamb who wasn't for coming out just there,' he said. 'And I thought, well, if I were you I wouldn't be for coming out either, out of that nice, safe, warm place into this filthy rain and cold. But we got him out eventually.'

I told Mrs MacTaggart of my rather desultory search for my MacCalman roots, and she agreed with my theory that the MacCalmans might originally have come from Ireland. 'In Gaelic, "MacCalman" would mean "Son of the Dove", and it would have been a priest's name, a holy name,' she said. It was still my middle name, even if its meaning now seemed more than a little ironic.

That night, I took my last miniature, a sixteen-year-old Lagavulin, down to the road beside the distillery, just along from Port Ellen, and duly drank it. It was dark and wet and dreich and there wasn't much atmosphere to absorb but the typically bad Islay weather. Still, I uncorked the tiny bottle, poured it into a glass I'd brought from Kintra, and drank the stuff down.

Lagavulin is not to be messed around with. I doubt if anyone could casually drink a lot of it in the way you could Bunnahabhainn or even Talisker. It is the biggest, the toughest, the meanest, most evil son-of-a-bitch whisky you can imagine, so dry and so peaty and so seaweedy it knocks your head horizontal. Yet its complexity is amazing, and finally, so is its warmth. Full of fusel oils, someone had said, full of all the things other distilleries discard. Well, maybe, and if so, it is likely to provide the worst hangover of any whisky outside supermarket rye. I don't advise anyone to seek a Lagavulin hangover, though. It is a whisky which should be treated with respect. And in my case, affection, even if the bastards wouldn't let me see round the distillery.

Next day we loaded Isolde and the beast and, once more in convoy, drove to Port Ellen for the ferry back to Kennacraig. The weather had been awful, but we had all enjoyed Islay, with the four-year-old son building sandcastles in conditions which would have defeated the SAS. Now wife and weans were going home, and I would head for Ayrshire, using the tiny ferry from Claonaig on the eastern coast of Kintyre to Lochranza in Arran, then hopping across from Brodick to Ardrossan. All courtesy of a Calmac Hopscotch ticket, to which I was introduced by the entire Calmac office staff at Kennacraig, carrying myself and the bike to Ayrshire as well as to Islay and back for £47.

As you leave Port Ellen on the steamer, the white splashes along the coastline of Laphroaig, Lagavulin and Ardbeg leap from the coastline, no matter how dull the weather, their names painted in large black letters finally fading with distance.

'Are we going to Shetland on this ship?' asks four-year-old son, giving both my wife and myself a pang of nostalgia. Both of us wish it was going to the islands we, for some reason, mostly my fault, no longer live on.

'We're going to Shetland soon,' says my wife, 'so that Daddy can write his book.' Ah yes, the book. The original idea was to write it in the evenings while I was travelling. This has not worked out too well, but I've got some great notes. Some of them are even legible.

Kisses and goodbyes are said on the car deck, and I watch as the green Merc sweeps away, the occupants waving as I await instructions to remove the orange beast. Black clouds had been poised above Kennacraig as the *Claymore* nosed up West Loch Tarbert, and as we docked, on time at six p.m., it was abnormally dark. Now the seamen are waving, and, alone again, I bump over the stern ramp and back on to Kintyre.

Chapter Ten

OLD HOME TOWNS

Bad weather is boring. I was entering my third and final week of travelling and swallowing, and the weather had been, with occasional exceptions lasting a matter of hours, diabolical. Such is early spring in Scotland, I kept telling myself. But people I met, at filling stations, in shops, in pubs, would all shake their heads and say things like 'worst April in years'. Now it was nearly May, and the weather was about to go completely bananas.

The blackness overhead should have warned me. It's only a matter of six miles across Kintyre from Kennacraig to Claonaig, and I had an easy forty minutes before the last ferry to Lochranza. But at Gartavaich, about halfway there, one of the worst hailstorms I've ever experienced nearly put me off the road.

In agony (oh, the stupidity of that open-face helmet) and blinded in what had become a white-out, I stalled the bike going up a steep hill, having to keep from slipping backwards by holding the front brake on. Two very minor problems had developed with the beast since the steering débâcle in Skye. One was finding neutral with the foot-operated gear selector; the other was starting from hot whilst the rider was emotionally upset, angry or panicking.

It took five minutes of increasing fury to get the bike into neutral, signified by a flickering white light in the middle of the speedometer, and another ten to actually start the reluctant engine. By that time, the hail had gone off, and a blink of startling sunshine appeared. The weather had gone schizoid. Or manic. Or both.

After about a mile, the blackness returned to the sky, and the hail swept down. I tried to continue, passing two very serious-looking racing cyclists who were wrapping their tiny, lycra-clad bodies in what appeared to be polythene bags. Eventually I had to stop. Once more, the whole landscape was transformed into a black-and-white film watched on a badly tuned TV. The cloud above had changed into an arrowhead of pullulating menace, and it felt like the penultimate, demons-breaking-loose scene from *Ghostbusters* was being re-enacted for the benefit of myself and the two unfortunate cyclists, of which there was no sign. Oh God, I cried through gritted teeth. If I opened my mouth it filled with hailstones. Oh God, I know you hate me, but have a heart. Think of those two poor cyclists.

Despite, or perhaps because of such hysteria, the hail suddenly lifted again, and I was able to throttle down to Kintyre's east coast. For a second, I glimpsed the peak of Goat Fell across the water, then it vanished. All that could be seen was . . . well, nothing. A grey-white amorphous sky met the steely sea just offshore. Arran, indeed the whole of Scotland, might not have existed.

I parked the bike on the slipway, just behind two cars, both crammed with large men in Pringle sweaters. Then I beat a retreat from the returning hail to a wooden shed which offered basic shelter to waiting foot passengers.

Inside was an old lady, who smiled as I burst in, shedding hailstones in all directions from my grimy oilskins.

'Terrible,' she said. 'Terrible. You know, I was just out for my evening walk, when this came on. Lucky I was able to take shelter.'

English-accented, she was, she claimed, 'a local'.

'This is a lovely spot, you know,' she told me, 'when the weather's less inclement.' I took her word for it.

Just then, the two poly-bag-clad cyclists entered. The little ferry *Loch Ranza* had just emerged from the glaur offshore, and they whistled jointly with satisfaction.

'Aye, that's good. Thought we might have to wait for the next one.'

But there isn't a next one, I said. The summer timetable doesn't begin until tomorrow. They looked at each other, as if the thought of spending a night on Kintyre was the end of the world.

'Fuckin' hell, that was close then,' one said in a broad Glaswegian twang, with apparent disregard for the sensitivities of the old lady, who smiled in a friendly fashion. I asked where they had come from that day.

'Tobermory,' said the other cyclist. They were interchangeable, small, hard-muscled men in spray-on cycling gear, their polythene coverings not to be laughed at. They seemed perpetually angry, their voices something of a threat, a so-what-is-it-to-you question in every word. They were Glaswegians in the country. Tobermory to Claonaig was a hell of a way on a pushbike, I ventured.

'Och, not a bad ride. Just one stop, not counting the ferry. Just as well we're getting this one, though. Want to stay in Arran tonight, boat home from Brodick themarra.'

I didn't ask what the attraction was in Arran. They seemed driven by an internal force I knew nothing about, something fierce and frustrated that only the pain of pedalling could assuage. The ferry, empty, had arrived. I said goodbye to the old lady, wondering what had brought her to become 'a local' in Claonaig, and wearily trudged to the beast.

In the saloon of the *Loch Ranza*, the Pringle-sweatered men were drunkenly toasting each other from a trophy, which one was continually refilling from a bottle of Bells. 'Golfing at Machrihanish,' said one to me. 'Great weather down there, actually. Hellish, this. You on a motorbike, too. Just hellish.' Was this some kind of annual competition then? 'Foursomes, yes. Bloody good.'

I left them to their toasting of eagles and birdies and other obscure golfing fauna and went up on deck. Suddenly, the world had changed. Arran was revealed in that low, temporary evening sunshine, a black knot of cloud still lurking over its peaks. I had been to Arran exactly twice, once on a Saturday for a Sunday School trip, once, during my brief post-evangelism stint as a religious affairs producer with the BBC, to make a film about a group of modern-day pagans who were worshipping in the woods. The pagans, who included a former North Sea diver, were nice people who drank quite a lot, seemed to have sex frequently and liked to frolic naked in their 'pagan glade', the location of which we were sworn not to reveal. One woman had long blonde hair and played the harp.

The sun was still shining as we landed at Lochranza, and I bumped ashore behind the golfers who stopped at a local hotel for further refreshment. The two cyclists had removed their polythene, but could not keep up with the awesome power of the mighty orange beast.

I was bound for Brodick, where I could not, I had lately discovered, hope to catch the last ferry for Ardrossan that night; I had therefore booked a B&B called Allandale House and resigned myself to a night in Arran's 'capital', which I recalled as being almost Hebridean in its lack of fun-factors.

The trip from Lochranza to this Stornoway of the south was, however, amazing. They call Arran the Highlands in miniature, and, following the A841 through Glen Chalmadale and Glen Sannox, I understood why. Herds of deer roamed next to the road, mountain peaks soared into the clouds, and the scenery was generally spectacular in that compact, easily-got-to way that makes the Lake District so appealing. Past Mid Sannox, I followed the coast to Brodick, seeing from an unfamiliar angle an Ayrshire shore I knew well: Ardrossan, Saltcoats and, just visible, Troon, town of my education and upbringing.

Allandale House turned out to be a modern building on the hill above Brodick Pier, run by Valerie and Muriel Young in what seemed to be a continuous theatrical performance. I wasn't sure if the mistress-of-cere-monies who met me at the door was Valerie or Muriel, but her luminescent dress matched the vibrant, not to say vibrating, decor of the house. Still, it was clean, there was a telly in the room, I had 'en-suite facilities, own bath' and it was only £16 a night.

Food was required, so I ventured, on foot, down into Brodick in search of sustenance. Brodick is basically a strip of decaying hotels and a few shops strung out along Arran's least attractive shoreline, with a castle and a few more hotels stuck in some woods at one end. Nothing seemed open. Admittedly it was a Sunday night, but at the end of April, one might have expected a little activity. The fish and chip shop exuded an aroma not of hot fat, but of cold, desolate fritters scattered in the doorway. The hotels looked worn, hungry and desperate, a mixture calculated to put off even the most bedless of tourists. I found this strange. Arran had, indeed has, a reputation as a centre of wild, youthful drunkenness, music-making, drug-taking and promiscuity, and yet Brodick looked like an abandoned film-set for an A. J. Cronin story: dour, poor and joyless.

A bar called Duncan's had blackboards outside offering a variety of real ales and live music, so I wandered in. A large notice on the wall ordered: 'NO

CHILDREN AT BAR'. At the bar sat a middle-aged man and a young boy of about nine, who was munching one of those outlandish, patented items of gruesome convenience bar-food only the British would be stupid enough to eat. A Bocadildo, or some such name: an extra-long hot-dog sausage magically inserted in a piece of uncut French bread. A tired-looking barmaid listened to a decidedly unlive Tom Petty as she drank coffee, as barmaids all seem to do when they have a moment. But can you get them to make you a cup when you want one? Huh.

There was no one else in the place.

'How ye doin, uv seen you afore, huvntah?' said the man as soon as I'd sat down. I don't think so, I replied, cautiously. 'Och aye, am certain,' said the man, who was thin, red-faced and none too sober. 'Lissen, see this wean?' I regarded the healthy-looking child, who was finishing off his bizarre meal with some relish. 'Can't feed him enough. Just can't stuff enough food down his throat. Fish and chips? Lissen, we go, his mam'n'me'n'him, o'er to Ardrossan, and lissen, you cannae get decent chips here innis dump, no way, so we always, always get chips. An this wan here'll have pickled onion, pickled egg, chips, fish, you name it, he'll bloody eat it. Ah cannae afford it man, telye, not in this life. Not in this bloody life.'

I ordered a Murphy's and muttered 'growing lad, eh?' What the hell, I'd try one of these sausage things. I ordered with all the bravado of a Costa Brava tourist trying his first paella. After a few minutes, it came, a mad cow special, wrapped in tissue paper and steaming gently. I bit.

'Whadye make of that, then?' asked the man with the small boy, who was eyeing my sausage hungrily.

'Better than what you get at the fair, anyway,' I said, although actually I was none too convinced of that. The sausage was barely lukewarm, and at least you had the option of watery onions with fairground hot-dog barrows.

'Ach well, he likes them anyway,' said the man, nudging the boy. 'He could eat four at a time, coon't you, Jum?' The boy smiled, nodded.

'Ach well, let's go, son. Need to get that set of bagpipes so you can learn them.' The father and son, as I supposed they were, slid off their stools. 'He's learnin' the pipes,' the man said to me as he headed for the door. 'He's musical as hell.' And they were gone.

The barmaid, whose name was Fiona, said the weekend had actually been quite busy until that day. 'I don't know what's happened,' she shrugged. Outside, the weather darkened again, and the skies prepared to unleash another barrage of hail or rain, or perhaps some Egyptian plague like blood or insects or worms. At least it would make a change. I noticed, amongst the rather fine selection of malts on the Duncan's gantry, a bottle of Cameron Brig, the only readily available single-grain whisky you can get apart from The Invergordon. A dram was cheap, and the taste not as bad as I'd expected. Woody, grainy, but with the sandpapery edge of the spirit held in check by ageing, it was bearable, but only just. I bought a Mars Bar to take the taste away and headed back to the Allandale to watch TV.

Next morning I checked the bike in for the 11.05 crossing to Ardrossan and wandered Brodick collecting what useful items I could find, such as newspapers. I'd seen better shops in the most obscure corners of Shetland, and the whole place felt like a ruined resort somewhere in Siberia. At breakfast, either Valerie or Muriel had told me that there was little to do in Arran 'except walk', but that the place had been so busy the previous weekend that no one could even do that. 'There were over two hundred bikers here on a rally,' she said, 'and dozens of police to watch them.' I was a bit miffed that she obviously didn't count me as a biker. Perhaps it was the way I didn't write on the walls or piss on the carpet, as bikers are supposed to do.

The waiting-room at Brodick is like something from the 1950s period of British Rail comfort provision: concrete floor, hard seats, no heat. Outside, it was, as usual, cold and wet. I read the papers, and, as I pondered the political numbness of Scotland, a small and wretched family came in, trailing unhappiness like a banner. There was a gorgeous blond boy child, about three, and his weeping mother, who looked ravaged and thin and at the end of her tether. A huge, lumbering, red-faced young man, blond like the child, was with them, embarrassed, mumbling, ripping a polystyrene cup to shreds in his hands.

'I just can't,' said the woman. 'I just can't cope with this anymore. I can't . . . I'm sorry, coming to disturb you at your work, I'm sorry, but he just wants everything, he just wants everything he sees, he keeps *asking*, we're in a shop and he just *takes* something off the shelf and I can't, I can't buy it.' She turned to the child. '*What do you think you're doing to me?*' She was screaming at the beautiful little boy, who, obviously used to this, smiled at her. '*Leave me alone!*'

The big man screwed up the bits of cup in his hands, and mumbled something about a playgroup. The woman kept on sobbing, as the child, unconcerned, rocked back and forth, sitting on his hands.

'He just, he just messes up the playgroup. They don't want him there. Nobody's said it, but I know they don't. He hit a little girl, a sore one, last week. But I've got to work. What else can I do? *What else can I do?*' Finally the big man got up and murmured, uneasily, that he had work, that he'd speak to her later, after work. The woman looked up at him, then down, shaking her head over and over again. And the child kept on smiling.

The ferrymen insisted I tie the orange beast to the side of the MV *Isle of Arran*, as they were expecting 'a wee bit of rolling'. I headed up to the cafeteria for the by now familiar Calmac bacon sandwich, and for fifty-five minutes the sea remained remarkably calm. The rolling only began as we neared the treacherous entrance to Ardrossan Harbour, which is surrounded by artificial breakwaters and closes frequently during winter storms. The steamers have to go beam on to the prevailing tide to get in, and the result can be alarming. Warnings are broadcast over the ship's Tannoy, instructing passengers to leave the decks and sit down, but, as a veteran of spine-jarring Force 10 trips to Shetland on the *St Clair*, I felt it incumbent on me to stay outside and see what happened. Nothing much did. The boat wallowed a bit, then we were inside the breakwater and that was that. In a January gale, though, I could see that things might get a little traumatic.

Ardrossan. As I accelerated up the main street, I passed the gospel hall where my mother and I used to go and sing as part of the Bethany Hall mixed choir. I was thirteen and almost a bass, and the choir outings were fun. We used to entertain at the Saturday night 'soirées' (for years I thought the word was 'sworry', because that's how it was pronounced) different Brethren branches would have to encourage themselves, get out the house, meet members of the opposite sex and, supposedly, evangelise the unconverted. In reality, hardly any heathen ever came along, although there was always a speaker of varying quality.

Such occasions were used to blood young, inexperienced preachers, before they were permitted on to the big-league Sunday night gospel meeting circuit. I remember one young man attempting to break the ice with the joke about the nervous young actor with only one line to say: 'Hark I hear a pistol shot.' Except he gets it wrong, and says (cue hilarity) 'Hark, I hear a shostle pit.' This junior Billy Graham, quaking with nerves, made a slight error in the telling. 'He wandered on stage,' he told the congregation of behatted old women and doomy-browed men, 'and he said . . . he said . . . "*Hark*! I hear apostles *shit*!" ' That was the end of his preaching career.

I headed south, through Saltcoats and past the Nobel explosives factory at Stevenston, on to the dual-carriageway which bypasses Irvine New Town, a place I have a distinct soft spot for. As a student, I once landed a summer job organising a bizarre bunch of visiting entertainers for the children's playschemes in Irvine. There was Hampe and Lola, the husband and wife trick-cycling team who must have been in their late sixties. Hampe suffered from back pain, so sometimes they just did balloon sculpture. There was a family of trampolinists who were so amateurish the children they were supposedly entertaining could perform more tricks. And there was a banjo-playing clown called Mr Hoppity who was so bad-tempered he would physically remove any of the (sometimes less than impressed) Irvine kids who created any disruption at his school-hall shows, shouting and screaming all the time. God knows where they came from, these poor, pathetic show people. The kids hated them.

Anyway Irvine now has some nice modern houses, a good (if sewage-prone) beach, some great golf courses, interesting old buildings, a fantastic sports centre, the Magnum, an excellent shipping museum and a couple of good pubs and restaurants. It also has dreadful unemployment and a plethora of social problems, but don't let that put you off building a factory there.

I used to cycle to Irvine from Troon to get bits for my pushbike from Harry Fairbairn's tiny cycle shop. He went on into motorcycles, and then opened a Fiat car showroom. Now Fairbairns is one of the biggest BMW-dealer networks in the country. In those days, behind the dunes at Barassie lay Dundonald Camp, where boy soldiers from the Junior Tradesman's Regiment were taught how to be chefs and mechanics, how to fire machine-guns and get drunk. It has disappeared now, but Hillhouse Quarry, where again I had a student job before unemployment wiped out such luxuries, still churns out roadstone, ready-mixed cement and tar. Some of the things which went on when I worked there are just unthinkable, like the workman who took delight in throwing stones at fused, dynamite-packed blasting holes while some of his workmates ran for cover. Or the young labourer who deliberately smashed a bottle over his arm so he could have the day off 'sick' to make a court appearance.

I made a sentimental detour from the A78 down into Troon, just to see what the place was looking like. Apart from a huge outbreak of ticky-tacky houses on the outskirts, remarkably little had changed. Marr College, the green-domed school set up with Walker whisky money but long since a Strathclyde Region comprehensive, had sprouted an ugly concrete extension, but the purple and gold blazers remained the same. A couple walked hand in hand up St Meddan's Street, he with long, straggly black hair in an ex-RAF greatcoat, she wearing the miniest of skirts beneath that amazing blazer, and knee-length boots. I felt like a first-year again, back in 1968, when couples like that were the gods and goddesses of our despised pre-pubescent playground existence. They used to meet during breaks by the golf course whin bushes outside the playground, sharing cigarettes and endlessly practising great dribbling kisses. First-years would spy on them, occasionally shouting excessively rude things like '*Tits!*' at them and then running away in hysterical laughter. I didn't though, because I was a Christian.

I avoided Portland Street, where Bethany Hall was now called Seagate Evangelical church, a name-change which had provoked bitter divisions in the congregation. One particular man had apparently argued that the word 'Sea Gate' derived from the fact that sailors had once drunkenly wound their way along the street from the harbour, vomiting all the time, and was actually 'Sick Gate'. Still, I couldn't resist a look at the prom, where every summer Sunday afternoon and evening the Brethren would set up camp amidst the near-naked holidaymakers, bellowing the gospel into the seagull wind with a loudhailer and an accordion to help. And the kids too, of course. Dressed up to the nines in miniature suits and ties, we little boys would sing choruses, being rewarded with wrapped boiled sweets, choruses nothing could erase from my memory:

Store your treasure in the bank of heaven
Where no thief can steal away
There you'll find it safely waiting for you
When you get to heaven someday . . .

I got out of Troon fast.

My aim was Bladnoch, down near Wigtown, the former pride and joy of Mr and Mrs Henderson from Laphroaig. I passed Ayr, where my now retired and remarried father stayed when he and my stepmother were not at their house on the Costa del Sol. I knew they weren't at home, though, because I'd arranged to see them at their timeshare lodge in Dunkeld later in the week, on my way back north. We met but rarely. Still a member of the Brethren as Dad was, my extravagant backsliding from the faith had caused him such never-discussed pain that it was easier for us both not to see each other.

The A77 Ayr-Stranraer road is one of the great, bad highways of Scotland, a two-lane high-speed deathstrip full of neurotic holidaymakers and gruff lorries bound for Belfast. Flat out at 50 mph against a strong wind, the beast was suffering, and I was being hassled by angry drivers who couldn't get past. At Maybole, I took a tiny unclassified road which looped through the overgrown and lovely valley of the Water of Girvan until it joined the B741 at Girvan itself. The scent of the grain distillery there filled the air, but with the Ladyburn malt distillery long ago dismantled, it seemed pointless to stop. Instead, I climbed out of Girvan on the A714, and into the Galloway Forest Park.

Galloway is the great ignored section of Scotland. In fact, so ignored was it in the 1970s that plans were made to build a nuclear-waste dump near Loch Doon. This was virulently opposed by the local MP, and the proposal was eventually withdrawn in 1981, after a public inquiry. That MP, Ian Lang, later became a suddenly and decidedly pro-nuclear Secretary of State for Scotland.

Galloway has everything, from mountains to forest to wonderful beaches, although there is, of course, the radioactive pollution from Sellafield in Cumbria to watch out for. Kirkcudbright, Creetown, Wigtown itself – all are beautiful, virtually unspoilt and easily accessible. Yet the tourists continue to bypass Galloway and head north to the *en suite* delights of the Highlands, or south to the Lake District. It amazes me.

It stayed dry for the ride to Newton Stewart, across mountainous, forested country which was strangely reminiscent of alpine Germany, minus the incandescent white peaks. Past Newton Stewart, which is reputed to be, after Dumfries, the most heavily pub-provided town in Scotland, I rode due south to Wigtown, a silted-up port that looks so much like Cromarty in its Georgian bonniness that I felt quite confused. Less than a mile down the road I came to the most southerly distillery in Scotland, Bladnoch.

I could see why the Hendersons had loved the place. Bladnoch is nothing but a crossroads with a pub, a distillery, a river and a bridge. The day had turned schizoid again, and, as I neared a genuine turning-point in my journey, after which it would be northwards all the way, a bleary sun made the old stone distillery buildings shine. I had barely got off the beast when I was politely approached by a uniformed girl wearing a badge which said 'Fiona'. Would I like a tour? I would indeed.

I set off with a middle-aged English couple and Fiona to see around what is a small, well-kept United Distillers place which betrays strong evidence of its 1814 farmhouse origins. Built around a courtyard, like many distilleries, Bladnoch's honey-coloured stone gives an impression of cosiness, of warmth. Inside, the equipment is almost completely computerised, with the only automatic spirit-safe I've ever seen. Sensors detect when the middle cut, the purest spirit, is coursing from the spirit-still, and automatically divert it through the steel spirit-safe to the spirit-receiver using compressed air to move the pourer. No stillsman with his nose trained to detect the higher alcohols is needed here.

Only three per cent of Bladnoch's production is matured in plain oak casks, and bottled, at eight years old, as a light 'n' easy single malt. Tasting it, as outside the weather turned again and hail battered down, it seemed quite sharp, almost grainy in some respects. I liked the distillery – the Hendersons' reception centre is light and airy and welcoming – but I didn't like the whisky. Unlike Mr Lang the local MP, who is thought to have saved Bladnoch from closure through discreet lobbying of United Distillers – and by saving his seat in the face of Scottish National Party certainty that he would lose it – and who used to drop in for the occasional dram before he assumed higher authority in the land.

Wigtown reminded me too much of home, so I went into Newton Stewart looking for a bed. The tourist office there fixed me up at what turned out to be the bargain of the whole trip. Corsbie Villa, run by George and Betty Graham, charges £15.50 for bed, usual massive cholesterol breakfast, and dinner, which for me was home-made vegetable soup, fried salmon steak with tatties and two veg, hot apple pie with ice-cream and coffee. It was very good too, and the place seemed popular with Telecom workers and reps – usually a good sign.

Newton Stewart itself looked much too small to be a town, and far from the dozens of pubs I'd expected, there seemed only a handful. In one, the Black Horse, I was welcomed virtually with open arms, served Lagavulin sixteen-year-old at £1.15 a measure, and asked: 'Are you a local, then?' It turned out the owners had just moved in, and I was their first customer. 'It's awfully quiet here,' the woman behind the bar said, rather nervously. 'Do you think local folk will come in here eventually?' It was a nice, ordinary pub, all stone floors and a good pool table, so I reassured her. The Star was more up-market (it had a carpet) and I tried a Glenkinchie, the UD Lowland flagship malt from Pencaitland near Edinburgh. Soft and rather sticky, I didn't like it. But then, after a Lagavulin, little else can measure up.

Next morning, as I navigated out of Newton Stewart towards New Galloway, I discovered the half of the town I'd completely missed the previous night. Sure enough, there were pubs everywhere. Maybe I'd misled the woman at the Black Horse, as there seemed to be more than enough bars to go round, for both locals and tourists.

The trip north took me through the spectacular hydro-electric schemes of upper Galloway, hidden away amongst the forested hills and fells. The road from New Galloway onwards, the A713, brought back memories of long Sunday morning drives from Troon to Kirkcudbright to 'support' the tiny Brethren assembly there. Only one man, a local craftsman potter named Tommy Lochhead, attended the tiny church, which met in an ancient building in the middle of the village. The rest of the 'two or three [literally] gathered in My Name' were women, which meant they could not actually contribute to the worship. Myself and one other Brethren boy from Troon, girfriends and anyone else we could come up with, used to go along to help out, and to enjoy a fabulous lunch courtesy of Mrs Lochhead in their hand-built house next to the pottery. It was this road we took, roaring back and forth, singing worshipful choruses at the top of our voices, quite confident we were the Lord's emissaries, that Kirkcudbright would be revived.

At Dalmellington, I left the main road for the winding B741, and found myself suddenly in the remains of Ayrshire's mining industry. Partly overgrown pit bings towered above me, and while new-born lambs skipped in the ruined mine buildings, the smell of sulphur grew in my nostrils, and the little burns by the side of the road ran red and brown. The landscape's innocence was lost long ago, but at New Cumnock, it is suddenly being raped all over again, and this time on a massive, shocking scale. These were the open-cast strip mines which had taken the pits' place, great black scars across the land, employing hardly anyone, taking advantage of a depressed economy desperate for jobs, any kind of jobs, to rip the countryside to shreds for a few years. There was dust and dirt in the air, and money for a few. Not for New Cumnock itself, though, which stands shabby and scabbed by decades of neglect. The open-cast mine company headquarters were well outside the village, with four-wheel-drive pick-ups standing outside, and the taste of exploitation everywhere. It was like something you'd expect to see in the Third World, in the Zambian copper belt. Not half an hour from the Galloway Forest Park. No doubt promises of reinstatement have been made, promises that someday the second Euro Disney will bloom on this gashed earth, that trees will grow and orchards bloom, and Mickey Mouse bless the people of New Cumnock with his holy fertility. Sure.

Big new roads had been built in this part of Ayrshire since my last visit, many years ago, and soon I was in the village of Mauchline, not far from

Kilmarnock, and I was hungry. There I found a street where, side by side, three tea-shops competed for business from the housewives and shoppers. Each tea-shop had a window-display of home-made cakes, and rows of push-chairs were parked outside. I entered the smallest, least extravagantly decorated of the three, and had the best piece of chocolate and hazelnut sponge cake I'd tasted in decades. All three tea-shops were virtually full. Perhaps there is some kind of study to be done on the cake-eating habits of the Mauchlinese, the Viennese of south-west Scotland.

Kilmarnock, home of the Johnny Walker empire, has a bottling and blending plant you can tour if you so wish. I didn't, and turned my head towards Glasgow, my old home-town.

Half an hour after joining the worn old four-lane A77, I was entering Newton Mearns, the great swathe of suburbia that forms Glasgow's southern border. Stopping at a telephone-box, I arranged to meet an old photographer pal for lunch, and consequently ended up spending the afternoon on a high-speed, Mansellesque tour of Rutherglen and Hamilton, delivering pictures to some of Stewart's clients in a Saab 900i. Lunch, in the form of food, never made an appearance. Stewart was so grossly offended by my avowed intention to stay in a bed and breakfast that he almost threw me out of the car (which at approximately 115 mph would have been unpleasant), before using his cellphone to contact partner Sandie and tell her he'd invited me to stay with them. Back at Stewart's office, I stumbled shaking from the Saab, whose wheels were smoking and which smelled strongly of burning rubber. Photographers. Can't live without 'em, can't shoot 'em. Shouldn't ever let them drive.

I had two important people to see for tea, namely my two eldest sons, products of the religion-founded marriage which had collapsed along with my short career as an evangelist. Aged eleven and nine, they are simultaneously scourges and connoisseurs of Pizzaland, where they know every twist and turn, every special offer and shade of garlic bread. Scorning the children's menu, they can out-eat a too-slim Sumo wrestler on crash weight gain. We talk of films, computer games, school, and vaguely of their mum's new husband, whom they like. When I take them back home, their mother tells me they've been asking about changing their surname from Morton to her new one. And there's nothing I can do about it, she says. And she's right, too. I don't have to like it, though.

Back at Stewart and Sandie's, their two-year-old Roddy is in fine fettle; I am not. After a few beers, I open with some ceremony the half-bottle of Longrow I bought in Campbeltown, and Stewart and I spend the rest of the night drinking it, revisiting old joint triumphs when we took on the wonderful world of rock 'n' roll and occasionally won, talking of families and money and growing old without growing up, or was it vice versa? Eventually, we just sit and listen to old Rolling Stones records. The Longrow seems to expand as you drink more of it, into a welcoming, cushioning, healing spirit, the distillation of the sea and land I already miss in this big, hustling city. It reminds me of the Shetland I ran to after my options in Glasgow had narrowed to the rock business I'd learned to despise, of a place where people and peat smoke and moorland and the sea and the biggest skies in the world gave me a welcome I didn't deserve, and a chance to remake my life as a journalist. And having done that, inevitably, I went back to the mainland, by that time with another family reluctantly in tow.

When I woke up, astonishingly, my head was clear, although my limbs were noticeably reluctant to follow the instructions it was giving them. Stewart was similarly undamaged from the neck upwards, and I noted another Longrow quality: its hangovers were in a different class.

I persuaded Stewart to take the day off, and fuelled up on coffee and bacon rolls, I decided to offer him the chance of a lifetime. He could be my first passenger, I told him. He could come with me and take some pictures of me doing Marlon Brando impersonations at the Littlemill Distillery in Bowling. He could, for once, have me scare him to death with my roadcraft. Amazingly, he agreed. The Longrow effect once more.

Clad in a leather flying-jacket and scarf, Stewart's presence in the sidecar excited more than passing interest that morning as I gradually got used to having something heavier than luggage to drag round left-hand bends.

'*Yer bum's on the groon*!' was shouted not once but many times by small boys as we sat at traffic lights on the way to the Clyde Tunnel. People waved. An old man came up to us at a junction and said, 'You know I haven't seen a sidecar for years.' Mothers pointed us out to their children. It was like being famous.

The Clyde Tunnel was terrifying. In its narrow confines, you feel like you're doing about 200 mph, and the road's curved camber makes steering a combination a mysterious exercise in remote control. We shot out of the top into the open air, Stewart opened his eyes and said, calmly, 'That was interesting.' Which is how he'd described the Soweto riots he'd once covered.

Bowling Basin is one of Glasgow's great hidden assets, unfortunately about to be capitalised on by its owners. The western terminus of the Forth and Clyde Canal, it was until fairly recently a lost village of old, rotting boats, of houseboats containing people no one knew existed, of people with decade-long dreams of converting that fishing boat into a yacht, in which they'd travel the world, leave Glasgow behind for ever. Now it's being upgraded into just another leisure marina, with proper moorings and toilet facilities and plastic company boats used for entertaining clients and screwing secretaries. Long gone is the original puffer which was used as the *Vital Spark* in the BBC Para Handy series. It used to lie, half-sunk in the inner basin, and I remembered summer escapes from the Charismatic Castle just up the road, picnicking in dishevelled, secret Bowling, as local kids dived into the canal from the disused railway bridge, dicing with gastroenteritis as they did so.

Just along the road from the basin itself, near the oil storage tanks, is Littlemill Distillery. Uniquely, its still-house is on one side of the road, a busy one, while its cask-filling and maturing takes place on the other. This means that the spirit-pipe which, remember, according to customs regulations must be in plain view, travels across the road, about twenty-five feet in the air, much guarded by wire mesh but definitely vulnerable to upper passengers on a double-decker bus.

David Anderson, Littlemill's manager, laughed off suggestions that the pipe might be a little exposed. 'We haven't lost a drop yet,' he said. 'If a lorry can get under the railway bridges, it can get under the pipe, so we haven't had any problems with it.'

Littlemill, along with Glenturret near Crieff, has claims to be the oldest distillery in Scotland. The date 1772 adorns the main building, but it's thought this could refer to the brewery which operated on the site before it became a distillery. The genial David showed us the unusual, bottle-shaped stills which only just qualify as pot-stills, using as they do a system not a million miles away from Mr Coffey's continuous version. They are not Lomond stills, like Scapa, but were the invention of a Mr Thomas, who also operated the Loch Lomond Distillery in nearby Alexandria. The stills there, however, are now traditional. And frankly, I'm not going to even attempt to explain how they work, other than that they use a technique called, I think, reflamation to give a much greater degree of control over what kind of spirit you can actually obtain. 'You can get more than one type of whisky,' said David, 'and distil up to 90 per cent alcohol content.' But only one type is actually made, at a much lower strength.

The disused maltings contain another of Mr Thomas's inventions, a special malt-turning machine, and on the whole Littlemill is something of a fascinating eccentric among distilleries. There are dark stories, too, about its past, with tales of large-shouldered, mysterious American 'meat barons' from Chicago coming over to Scawtland when they owned the place, to like, uh, check out their little, uh, investment. Nearly all production goes for blending, along with that of sister distillery Glen Scotia in Campbeltown, but a little finds its way into bottles at eight years old. I'm not a fan of Lowland malts, and one might wish Littlemill tasted as eccentric as its production process and history. Light, fresh and almost sweet, it's swiggable, but not particularly memorable.

We posed the bike above some barrels for a few daft pictures, and then set off for Auchentoshan, which is part of the Morrison Bowmore group and used to have a flourishing visitor centre. Situated in Clydebank, this is a really bonny distillery in a surprising, industrial setting. Technically a Lowland malt, its water comes from the Kilpatrick Hills, which are technically in the Highlands.

All we really wanted to do was take some photos, but the assistant manager had to be consulted for permission.

'Are you Tom Morton?' asked Glen, the assistant manager. For a moment I froze. Had I been put on a distillery black list? Had warnings been sent all over the country about my mission? No, it was worse than that. Glen remembered me from my days as a singing evangelist. I had apparently performed/preached at his church on several occasions. And yes, he'd be delighted if we took some pictures. We didn't discuss the past.

Auchentoshan is immaculate, just as its older brother Bowmore is in Islay, and plans are afoot to build the mother and father of all reception centres there. This is a good idea, as it's my bet the whole of Glasgow will want to have a look around the place. And there might even be money in it. Because, I discovered, the nearest competitor in the distillery tour stakes near Glasgow, Glengoyne, charges £2.00 a skull for a visit, and £5.00 for what it terms 'a tutored nosing'. How many drams do you get for that, I ask? If Auchentoshan can put something really good together, I suppose no one would mind them charging a couple of quid as well. In one sense it's absolutely amazing that the Speyside whisky trail distilleries don't charge for tours. I mean, I can't begin to describe how guilty I felt taking all those free drams . . . You know, those firms are on the verge of making, oh, less than a couple of million a year, and there I was, taking the bread from the mouths of the owners' children, wherever they are, at Eton, Harrow, Glenalmond, Barlinnie . . . wherever.

Look at those shops at Glenfiddich and elsewhere. Plenty of moolah changes hands there. And the PR value of tours to people like United Distillers is obviously enormous. On balance, perhaps charging for visits takes malt whisky production one step away from the indigenous industry it has been for centuries, and one step further into the murky world of tartan tat, tourism, Harry Lauder and wee docken, Doris. I think the traditional approach, laced with a genuine welcome, that I found, say, at Dalmore, pays dividends in the end. Surely there is a way of making this approach available to the wider public without dressing up that welcome in tartan and stained oak-cladding, spurious militarism, Spode and Caledonian kitsch of every description? Surely?

We zoomed once more through the Clyde Tunnel, Stewart by this time claiming to be enjoying himself. On the way back to his house, where I'd decided to stay for another night, we stopped at a supermarket for copious supplies of liver-repairing mineral water, determined not to repeat the previous night's excesses.

'Well, that was fun,' said Stewart as we dismounted, cramped but thankfully dry, outside his house. 'It was . . . interesting.'

'More interesting than South Africa?' I asked.

He thought for a moment. 'Not quite as, mate.' Oh well. So much for my spirit of adventure. I obviously still had a long way to go.

Chapter Eleven

THREE WHITES AND A GOLDIE

Despite my 1,500-odd miles of experience, battling the orange beast around Scotland, I was still officially a learner rider, and banned from motorways. This meant that my northwards exit from Glasgow had to be via the Clyde Tunnel, Bearsden, Milngavie and Strathblane. A soft, even gentle but undeniably wet rain was falling as I passed Glengoyne, which is being marketed, forcibly, as 'The Unpeated Malt'. You might as well say it isn't really whisky at all, in my opinion. Yes, I have tasted it; no, I don't like it.

The distillery is particularly lovely, and I assume that for £2.00 a tour you get a decent dram at the end. I decided not to unwrap myself from my wet-weather gear to find out, though, because frankly I was fed up with distilleries. I was even, it has to be said, fed up with alcohol, and the previous evening's mineral-water-only ruling had been something of a relief.

As I sailed through the fine, even slightly warm spray, past the rich half-Highland commuterland beside the Lake of Menteith towards Callander, I pondered the question of alcohol and its associated -ism. Should I give up drinking? Was I drinking too much?

Yes, and yes. I'd often given up drinking, mostly swearing eternal allegiance to temperance in the throes of mind-bending, stomach-churning hangovers of a journalistic origin. But, at least until this trip, my consumption had been going down and down, courtesy of a virtually teetotal wife and an increasing boredom with the effects.

Was I, generally, drinking too much? More than the advised twenty-one units a week. Some weeks, a lot more. Some weeks hardly anything at all. Some weeks nothing at all.

I knew an alcohol counsellor, on a social drinking basis, and although by no means a pisshead, he could easily take the odd bucket or two and frequently did so. Interestingly, he told me that outside of the Alcoholics Anonymous, trust-in-your-own-concept-of-God, complete teetotalism approach, most alcohol counselling had as its aim a return to moderate drinking; and that this was proving successful.

Maybe. I had known one or two heavily dependent drinkers in my time, though, and their concept of abstinence had been drinking sweet sherries and half-pints of heavy, as opposed to whiskies and pints. Moderation for them was only getting drunk in the evenings. Some held down stressful, responsible jobs in the midst of this maelstrom of moderation. Others gradually toppled into soiled-pants, falling-over wretchedness.

Here I was, planning a celebration of Scotland's spirit, and ignoring the fact that it was also Scotland's curse. The memories came flooding back: the drunk man threatening to commit suicide in our kitchen; the child with foetal alcohol syndrome; the mother perpetually down the pub, her young son left screaming in the rain outside, forgotten; the fights I'd seen; the endless, stupid court cases I'd reported – murders, assaults, child abuse, theft – all involving drink. 'My client has only the haziest recollection of the evening in question, My Lord, as he had consumed a large amount of alcohol.'

Laughing with the problem drinkers: I remember doing that too, to my eternal shame. Buying them drinks, watching them get arseholed, congratulating myself that I could handle it. And the days when I couldn't.

Once, years ago, I sat in on the dissection of two brains, one normal, one a heavy drinker's. It was for some forgotten TV programme, and as the doctor sliced a cross section through the grey blancmange, he said, 'Notice the difference in size. Long-term drinking causes shrinkage.' I shook my head and heard the knocking.

The Scotch Whisky Association's little booklet, *Questions and Answers*, has an interesting section on health. Is alcohol good for health? Yes, comes the reply, in moderation it has been proved beneficial.

'This has been endorsed in a report by the British Medical Association which states that up to 30 grams of alcohol a day – the equivalent of four single whiskies – can help prevent heart disease.' Alcohol, the book goes on, 'can help relieve stress, and promote appetite and sleep.' Note the 'up to' and 'can help'. Current medical thinking is that one single whisky a day may help prevent some kinds of heart disease; four would almost certainly cause dozens of other problems. The Scotch Whisky Association does admit that 'misuse of alcohol can not only damage health in a number of ways, but may cause domestic and financial problems', but goes on to make the amazing assertion that 'in Britain the incidence of drunkenness, alcohol-related illnesses and drunk-driving is amongst the lowest in the world, and official figures indicate that less than two per cent of those who drink alcoholic beverages have a drinking problem'. On a UK-wide scale that is merely misleading. In Scotland, it is dangerous rubbish.

Two-thirds of Scotland's adult population is officially classed as drinking heavily, and one-third of those drinkers are estimated to be alcohol-dependent. Two-thirds of children taken into care are there because of events linked to alcohol abuse. Alcohol is a feature in 60 per cent of all suicides, a half of all murders and 80 per cent of all deaths by fire. It is the biggest cause of absence from work, and is recognised by health professionals as the biggest threat to public health after smoking. In Scotland, alcohol abuse is the third biggest cause of death after heart disease and cancer, and it is involved in both those conditions as well.

No wonder, then, that 'for many years the Scotch Whisky Association and individual whisky companies have sponsored research aimed at discovering why it is that there are those who seem unable to control their drinking'. In fact, alcohol 'cure' centres and dependence programmes get a lot of their funding from the not-very-guilt-ridden whisky industry where, post-dramming, the problem of alcohol abuse amongst its own workforce has apparently diminished.

'In many cases,' wrote sixteen doctors to *The Lancet* in 1907, 'it [alcohol] can be truly said to be truly life-saving owing to its power to sustain cardiac and nervous energy while protecting the wasting nitrogenous tissues.' Oh yeah?

Alcohol kills the brain, damages the liver, gives you stomach cancer and heart disease, and, in men, can cause 'feminisation, including the development of breast tissue, shrinkage and atrophy of the testicles and impotence'. It also makes a few people and governments rich. Perhaps it would be a nice idea if distilleries, all of them, did charge for tours, then ploughed the money into alcohol-dependence research and treatment. But alcohol kills things other than the body. It also kills political will. The gin subsidies of nineteenth-century England are well documented attempts to dull revolutionary zeal. In Scotland?

The best writing Neil Gunn (with whose work I have a love-hate relationship, as those paying attention will have discerned) ever did is in the chapter called 'The Descent' in *Whisky and Scotland*, in which he traces the development of the temperance movement out of the social squalor caused by the Industrial Revolution, and the consequent plague of alcohol-dependence. Two blazing paragraphs are worth quoting:

> All that concerns us here is that the folk, who had to have some sort of escape if they were to save themselves from being permanently debased, found that escape in whisky. Whisky took them out of themselves, it liberated them to blasphemy and fighting, it lifted their heads to shout a final challenge, a Yea hideous in the mouth but affirmative, it caressed them, and finally made of the gutter a bed of forgetfulness.
>
> Whisky . . . was the drink of the people; the national drink. At this hideous period whisky became the national whore and lost her reputation so utterly that to this day even English Chancellors of the Exchequer continue to squeeze the last shilling of her immoral earnings out of her with an exorbitant shamelessness.

This was cheap grain, the watered-down product of Thomas Coffey's still. Yet the argument still holds. Gunn spots the terrible irony behind the spurious, drunken spouting of Burns's famous line 'Freedom and whisky gang thegither'.

> Poverty, social justice, degradation – the memory of so vast an impertinence has to be drowned before the soul may rise into freedom and breathe its native air and eject its spittle of laughter on what are still designated in the feu-charters of our lives as 'superiors'.

And so in the pure spirit of Scotland, shall memory and will be dulled, pain forgotten? And shall we be baptised, reborn for a revolution where freedom shall reign, poverty disappear and the drinks and the talk be very, very cheap? Or shall we just drink and drink and talk and talk while our brains shrink and our livers expand and the problems of the world, and of our country, just fade away? Make mine a large one . . .

How, then, can I defend my enthusiasm for malts? I take my stand for health on the grounds that malt-drinking is not about drunkenness-seeking, but about taste and history and geography and, yes, the wee jag of the spirit beneath. The drunk will not taste the difference between a malt and an under-proof supermarket turpentine-substitute. And I think in malt whisky, in the craft of its production, in its traditional methods and the joy of the practitioners who still love the art of the making, in its essential Scottishness, its parochialism, in the need to attend to history but to adapt to change, there are lessons for our future. Despite the fact that the distilleries are owned by almost everyone but Scots . . .

Glenturret is owned by Highland Distillers. A nice Scottish name. And who, in the end, could mind the hefty presence of Remy Martin and Cointreau in such company? The Auld Alliance and all that?

Just outside Crieff, Glenturret trumpets the fact that it is the oldest distillery in Scotland, supposedly going back to illicit distilling in 1717, which, in fact, almost any distillery could if it troubled to do the research. There was an 'official' distillery there by 1775, but Littlemill's buildings are older and Glenturret has certainly not been in continuous production. The stills were dismantled in 1921, American prohibition having killed the place off, and all whisky removed by 1927. Thirty years later, James Fairlie bought the place and began a remarkable revival.

The idea was visionary for the 1950s. Glenturret would be operated as a small craft distillery with tourism integral to its development. So what you have now is probably more visitor centre than distillery, with a restaurant, huge shop, bars and the usual videos and displays. When I arrived, Glenturret was heaving with bus parties, and I almost went on my way, unwilling to frighten the elderly tourists with my increasingly muddy appearance. I had learned that another peril of an open-face helmet in wet weather was a face like a coal-miner's.

I bravely ventured in, though, only to find that I was expected to pay £2.00 for the privilege. Something in me revolted at the idea. The place was so obviously a tourist trap that all my rationalising on the question of charges disappeared in a puff of whisky snobbery. Had I not been around several dozen of the blasted things, only paying once, and that to see the dead Dallas Dhu?

'Och well,' said the woman at the reception desk, eyeing me sympathet-ically, 'you've missed the first five minutes, anyway, so you might as well go ahead for nothing.' So I did.

This whisky tour was pure professionalism, smooth and jokey and rather glib. The party including children and old people was so big, and the actual interest in the process so tenuous, that I suppose it was inevitable. Not to mention the hundreds of thousands of visitors who pass through the place each year rather blunting the guides' enthusiasm.

The malt, inevitably, comes from elsewhere. But what about the Glenturret mash tun? At first I thought I was seeing things. Clad in fake plastic wood-grain effect externally, brand-spanking-new stainless steel inside, the mash tun is tiny, the size of a jacuzzi. And there are no blades to churn up the mash, no motor to turn the blades. Instead, there's just a man with a pole, who stirs it like a giant pot of porridge.

When Barnard came here in the 1880s, he found 'the inner workings of the distillery are of the oldest fashion, plan and type'. Yes, well, but this is ridiculous. A manual mash tun in this day and age is simply a conceit, a regressive kind of tourist-technology. Because that's what it's for.

I realised that James Fairlie's integration of tourism and distilling went much further than I had imagined. The whole enterprise was clearly geared to easy observation rather than efficiency, and I found that rather fake and rather sad.

The tour was speedy. The tun room, with its tiny washbacks, the still room, neat and tidy and absolutely traditional, then the spirit store and then, very quickly indeed, into the second, massive part of the visitor centre. There we were given our drams of Glenturret eight-year-old – very small ones, too, I thought, if you were paying the entrance fee – which tasted like a rather sweet Speyside malt. You know, bland, creamy, smooth, etcetera. The guide chided me vociferously for adding water. 'That's sacrilege, you know!'

'Well, there's not enough whisky to actually taste it, is there?'

I was directed to the bar.

This was the first distillery I'd been to with a bar, and it was packed. Seething, in fact, with pensioners well on their way to liquid leglessness, via, oddly enough, draught beer for the most part. Glenturret specialise in limited-edition bottlings of their whisky, ranging through eight, ten, twelve and fifteen-year-old singles to frankly ludicrous money-spinning efforts such as '5000 days', a cask-strength fifteen-year-old and too many other very old and moronically expensive varieties to sensibly mention.

For a set fee you could get a dram of about five varying Glenturrets. I decided to pass. On the basis of the nondescript eight-year-old, I was sure it would be a waste of my time and money. The whole marketing tack was the same as John MacDougall's at Springbank/Cadenhead: low volume, high value. But the crucial difference lay in the target market. Sure, some of the older Glenturrets may be very good, if you like a bland whisky sherry-flavoured and concentrated with age, but most of the sales at Glenturret would be to visitors with money and ignorance to burn, souvenir spend-thrifts for whom a £60 Glenturret, untasted, is bound to be better than, say, a Clynelish, a Laphroaig and a Lagavulin, three for the same money.

However, you can't knock the Glenturret experience as a successful tourist attraction. Well, yes you can, actually. It's the symbolic overtones which worry me. This whisky is tourist-dependent, subservient to the needs and requirements and desires and pockets of the casual customer. There is nothing proud about Glenturret. It is picturesque, pleasant and far too nice for comfort. The dead distillery cat, Towser, is in the *Guinness Book of Records* for supposedly catching 28,899 mice. I rest my case.

The bike's steering seemed to be loosening again, but the lower nut was still tight. I cut across country via the picturesque mini-glen of Strathbraan, heading for Dunkeld, and a reunion with my father.

He is on his own, as we are slated to have a man-to-man talk about various family matters, and he is dressed in fluorescent pink trainers and a mauve track suit. Apart from our somewhat contrasting taste in clothes, we are looking more and more alike as I get older and he, bearded and bespectacled and now jogging and cycling, appears to get younger. He makes me some lunch, tinned mince, beans and tatties, and I start, stupidly forgetting to allow time for grace to be said. Dad silently shuts his eyes and gives thanks, while I munch on godlessly.

We fence, talk at and around but not to each other, miss various points, remember too much, forget too much. For the first time, I realise how badly my fall from grace has hurt Dad, how anchored he still is to the tradition instilled by that gospel hall beneath the steelworks, how I am bound for hell and how much that really concerns him. And how his religious friends must tut and gossip about my disgrace, and poor him with a son like that, a tragedy, let us all pray for that saddened father. How petty, subtle revenges have been taken against him for my sins, and how he has been powerless to respond.

There is too much which cannot be said. Eventually, we stop trying to say them or avoid saying them, and talk instead about my trip, about computers and cars, my sons and the possibility of two of them no longer being known as Mortons, which absolutely infuriates him. But there is nothing we can do but talk about it, which hurts too much. So we stop.

I agree to stay the night in his timeshare apartment, which faces on to a rigorously Victorian riverscape, and depart for a look round Edradour, Scotland's smallest distillery, a few miles up the A9 at Pitlochry. I will see Dad and his wife for dinner.

The A9 is potentially super-fast, modern, straight and deadly. However, the main route between Inverness and Perth changes continually from dual to single carriageway, and it's on those sections that the frustrations caused by slow-moving heavy goods vehicles and caravans often lead to accidents.

I wound the MZ up to 55 mph and found the road, for the first time in my life, relatively exhilarating, with few lorries or even cars to contend with. Next day, on the same stretch, a motorcyclist would be blown into the path of a lorry and killed.

Pitlochry, nine miles from Dunkeld, is modernised Victorian Highland kitsch, half grey houses and shops selling knitwear and walking-sticks, half giant hotels with spires and pretensions to castlehood. It was once a spa town, and misleadingly, the United Distillers Blair Athol malt is made in the town, and not in the village of Blair Atholl (two ls) six miles up the road. Michael Jackson's *Malt Whisky Companion* asserts that Pitlochry 'is not far away' from 'village and distillery'. It's a rare factual error in what is an excellent and exhaustive, if over-generous book. I'd tasted Blair Athol eight-year-old in the past, and couldn't remember a thing about it. The distillery is fantastically ugly from the road, offering the passer-by only a sight of its warehouses. However, once past this forbidding entrance, some nice old buildings are revealed.

Blair Athol is a big part of the Bell's blend, and has a typically expansive and expensive UD reception centre. I merely popped my nose in and departed. I didn't have the time to spend on the place, and frankly, I'd thought it was in Blair Atholl too.

To get to Edradour you turn up a hill in the middle of Pitlochry, and climb through rolling meadows and hills. At the farm of Edradour, there is absolutely no sign of the distillery, and it is only when you follow the tiny, winding road down into a hitherto-invisible cleft, a wrinkle in the landscape, that it reveals itself – and then only when you're right on top of it.

Edradour is a joy and a delight to see round, and probably more attractive to tourists than the likes of Glenturret. It is tiny, almost a model distillery, working on the traditional lines which give its owners some justification for calling their whisky 'hand-made'.

The cleft which hides it would have been the perfect site for illicit distilling, and there is no doubt that much went on in the area before a group of local farmers founded Edradour as a co-operative in 1825, as a way of making high-value products from their own malted barley. More than any other distillery in Scotland, Edradour gives the visitor a clear, unpatronising, very genuine look at traditional methods of whisky-making. Even the malting barn, now a museum and tasting room, has the best displays, particularly on smuggling, I'd seen anywhere. There's nothing fake about Edradour. It's like a timewarp, though, to find that the tiny stills (at 500 gallons each, the smallest permitted by the customs – anything smaller would be 'portable' and thus illegal) use burn water in concrete tanks as condensers, with genuine old-fashioned 'worms' bringing the vapour through the water and into low wines and spirit. The mash-tun – a real, mechanically-agitated cast-iron one, not a hand-operated pretend one like Glenturret's – is tiny, and the wort is cooled in the last remaining Morton Refrigerator in the whole whisky industry. These Mortons get everywhere.

Water can be a problem, with midsummer droughts regularly provoking temporary shut-downs. The worst year in living memory was 1990, and consequently, in the year 2000 there will be a shortage of ten-year-old Edradour; not that it's widely available at the best of times. The three employees produce only a thousand gallons a week, and even then, a lot goes for blending the famous (and weird, matured as blends in cask) House of Lords whiskies.

The guides at Edradour are a class act, too, retired gentlemen from the area who have a genuine interest in whisky. Mine told me that Edradour came number three on his list of favourites, after Glenlivet and Balvenie. And you get a decent dram, before the tour itself, while you watch an excellent video about the place.

Is Edradour a decent dram? Well, actually, it's not half bad in a Glenlivety sort of way, with a bit of Highland force coming through, a touch of peat and weather. Edradour is one of those whiskies which used to use the Glenlivet name as an appendix to its own, and you can still find that stencilled on its casks. An eccentric habit, considering how far from Glenlivet Pitlochry is, but there are similarities in taste, and even in local topography.

The tales surrounding Edradour are remarkable. The dramming days, now long gone of course, used to see each worker being provided with a daily ration of three drams, all raw, white spirit straight from the still, and a final, going-home dose of matured, golden whisky. This was known as 'three whites and a goldie', a brilliant name for a folk song or even a book; much better than *Spirit of Adventure*, in fact. Now, as in all other distilleries, the workers get their monthly bottle and discount on company products, which in this case is Clan Campbell, now a subsidiary of Pernod-Ricard. Who are French.

The rather tortuous history of Edradour's ownership throws up some interesting things, like the reputed Mafia connection (c.f. Littlemill and Glen Scotia) and the quite definite popularity, before offers were allegedly made that could not be refused, of whiskies made by William Whiteley and Co, then Edradour's owner, amongst the bootleggers of American Prohibition. The story goes that House of Lords and King's Ransom, the two blends produced by Whiteley using Edradour as a base malt, were exceptionally popular at the Cotton Club and other New York speak-easies. As the official Edradour history puts it, 'it was timely that Whiteley had designed a rather special square bottle for his premium blends, "as tough as possible and as light as can be" '. Production, it seemed, 'flowed smoothly to cope with unexpected American demand'.

There were 32,000 speakeasies in New York during Prohibition, as opposed to only 15,000 official bars before the Volstead Act rang the curtain down on legal imbibing. Whiteley whisky was fired on to Long Island beaches in hollow torpedoes, brought into deserted harbours – rather like today's cocaine runners of the Florida Keys and the Ullapool reaches – aboard fast launches, and even in former German U-boats – a technique today's coke runners don't seem to have cottoned on to yet. It seems hard to believe that the quiet, rural atmosphere of Edradour could ever have had any connection with such nefarious goings-on. And then you remember the place's own near-invisibility, and its roots in smuggling of a different kind.

I bought a bottle ('tough . . . light') of House of Lords for my father and stepmother, and returned to Dunkeld, bearing a gift which was gracefully accepted. These days, the drinks cupboard in my father's house is not locked, and the occasional millimetre of whisky is even consumed, on special occasions.

We ate in Dunkeld, my motorycle jacket being unsuitable for the more luxurious timeshare restaurant, and I talked about how the whole question of illicit distilling fascinated me. It was like the abominable snowman. Everybody said it was there, but finding any hard evidence was almost impossible. Then Dad said: 'You know that one of your relatives had a still?' I just looked at him. 'I better not tell you anything else. It's not the kind of thing I'd like to see in print.' I assured him that I would not identify the particular blood-relative involved, and pleaded with him to tell me more.

It was an interesting tale. During the war, one of my reasonably close relations had apparently owned a pub on Clydeside. 'It was down by the docks, and all the sailors used to come in, I know that,' said Dad. 'Anyway, he had a still, down there, and he used to make his own spirit, and sell it. All I can remember clearly is that he used to colour it brown with cold tea. He was never caught, either.'

Ah, so I wasn't the only skeleton in the Morton closet. I felt quite cheered. We went on to talk about the Brethren, gossiping about characters from the past. A litany of deaths, divorces, suicides, preachers-turned-thieves and drug addicts came to light, as I dragged from Dad the details of scandals I had only had hints of as a child: a sidelong glance there, a hissed 'be quiet, not in front of the children' from Mum there. Even now, he didn't want to tell me, and I got no hint of *schadenfreude* as I heard the conclusions of old, strange stories, of the reasons certain people had suddenly vanished from our childhood lives. I was the sorrow he had had to bear, and no one else's troubles made it any easier.

As I tried to get to sleep that night in my father's temporary house, which was like a hotel suite, still bearing the tobacco fumes and scents of the former occupants, I thought of the Brethren, and how it had seemingly spawned just as much scandal and shock amongst its members as any other comparable group of human beings. And then I realised that it *was* just another group of human beings, like a bowling or tennis club, except with that great guilt-and-sin magnifying God of ours twisting and exaggerating every social transaction out of normality, into a neurotic, hysterical, pressurised existence.

I'd tried to tell Dad about this already, about how I felt my upbringing had put incredibly metaphysical pressures on me, and he'd shook his head. 'I don't remember you being like that at the time, Tom. You weren't pressurised by us. I think you've reinvented your childhood. It wasn't like that. You're wrong.'

And maybe I am.

Two more days, and it would all be over. It also seemed, as I vibrated along the A926 east of Dunkeld, that there might be an abortive end to my trip, if I couldn't sort out the bike's steering. Every time I took one hand off to signal or wipe rain away from my goggles (yes, that's right, it was pissing it down again) the bike began leaping about like a startled rhino in heat. Turning, even with both hands firmly on the controls, became a battle against the bucking steering. I was heading across country from Dunkeld, aiming to join the main A94 Aberdeen road at Finavon and then shoot north to Glengarioch, my last distillery, at Old Meldrum just north of the Silver City. But things were getting, quite literally, out of hand.

At Kirriemuir, I stopped, and for the dozenth time felt the lower nut of the steering column, the one which also held the sidecar on. Tight as it had been ever since that fright in Skye. Casually, I removed the plastic cover from the top nut, and the whole assembly came away in my hand.

I sat stupidly, just looking at it for a minute. No wonder there had been a bit of a wobble. Again, I marvelled at the forgiving nature of the by-now considerably beaten-up beast. That damp hesitation near Forres, the Skye incident, and now this. Any one could have been terminal, either to the bike or the trip or to me. Yet the MZ had soldiered on. I hadn't even checked the plug.

In a Kirriemuir ironmonger's I spent £12 on an extra-large Mole wrench, that brilliant tool which falls somewhere between pliers, an adjustable spanner and a vice, and within minutes had the steering back together again and tightened up securely. Once more, the handlebars needed the strength of the Incredible Hulk to move them. But at least they no longer wobbled. And at least the front wheel wasn't going to come adrift.

As Aberdeen approached – very quickly as it turned out, the A94 being both fast and safe – the sun came out, blessing my second-last day of travelling with a wan kind of heat. At Stonehaven, where the obscure Glenury Royal used to be made, I turned off for Banchory, intending to circle Aberdeen through the hinterland villages of Echt, Kintore and Inverurie until I reached Oldmeldrum.

That was a mistake. I should have gone straight through the city, as my detour took ages, and involved frequent crossings of busy commuter roads. The countryside was essentially uninteresting, although it featured constant reminders of the oil wealth which leaves Aberdeen property prices untouched by any recession: the Porsche and BMW in the driveway of a former manse; the child playing in a garden in a motorised miniature car; the boats sitting on trailers outside double garages. I wondered if the orange beast smelt home. Originally registered in Aberdeen, Balmedie, its last residence, was within easy striking distance. I considered arriving at the doorway of the anonymous person I'd bought the MZ from and telling him I'd had to pay the asking price over again and another £100 to make the thing roadworthy. If you could call this brute-force-and-ignorance steering roadworthy, that is. But he was probably offshore, watching videos and eating triple T-bone steaks and praying for his two weeks off to come more quickly.

I finally reached Oldmeldrum just in time for lunch, nerves jangling after numerous encounters with high-speed repmobiles, some of their drivers yelling into cellphones as they cruised one-handed on back roads at 90 mph. And in the Meldrum House Hotel I had my best bar lunch since the Croft Inn way back on Speyside, several lifetimes ago. Home-made steak pie, home-made chips, carrots *al dente*. Only the rather suspicious, 'Southern Comfort'-style demeanour of some other Friday lunchtime *habitués* of the public bar made me feel a little uneasy. Ho, stranger. What brings you to town. Best be mosying along, if you git mah drift.

I mosied, a bare hundred yards through the cramped centre of Oldmeldrum, which is every inch a grey Grampian farming village, to the gates of Glen Garioch. Beside the distillery were the famous greenhouses where excess heat from the distillation process helps grow prize-winning tomatoes, just as Bowmore (part of the same company) heats the local swimming-pool and Tomatin (whose managing director is the legendary Scottish Football Association board member Jock 'hero of Copenhagen' McDonald) used to, ahem, breed eels. There is, by the way, money in eels, with Scottish slitherers fetching huge sums abroad. So Tomatin knew what they were up to. Japanese-owned Tomatin, with its twenty-three stills the biggest malt distillery in Scotland, is actually a very nice dram indeed: robust, peaty and not to be messed around with. A bit like Jock McDonald, in fact.

'We make a little bit of money out of our tomatoes,' said Glen Garioch (pronounced Glengeery) manager Willie MacNeill, a harassed man. A lorry, belonging to a transport company unused to Glen Garioch requirements, had been stopped on the motorway by police who found it overloaded to the tune of four hogsheads. A tortuous Friday afternoon rescue operation was now underway, involving hired transport. 'This is all I need,' said Willie.

Glen Garioch not only has its own floor maltings, it was also the first distillery to be connected to North Sea gas, and its kilns use gas and New Pitsligo peat. Due to fears about the accumulation of carcinogenic enzymes during the malting of certain varieties of barley, handfuls of sulphur have to be added to the kilns, without, it appears, significant effects on the malt. Varying periods over burning peat are employed depending on who wants the malt, because Glen Garioch's maltings are much in demand by other distilleries. Exactly who is a closely guarded secret, but even the mighty Moray Firth Maltings have certain specialist jobs done at Glen Garioch. The malt destined for the distillery's own whisky is lightly peated for four hours, and is made from local barley.

Bob Clark's local dialect, all loons and quines and fit likes, is hard to decipher at first, but eventually the white-haired and boiler-suited maltman makes perfect sense. Glen Garioch don't do conducted tours anymore, unless you claim to be writing a book or have some special interest in tomatoes, but Bob, twenty-two years at the place, is the ultimate guide. And malting is his special subject.

The listed, beautifully kept Glen Garioch maltings are a joy. 'We had Free Polish troops billeted here during the war, after Dunkirk,' says Bob, 'and that's why you can still get the windows open. They used to have rope ladders they would throw down as fire-escapes. One of them carved his initials on a beam. I can't mind which beam, though.' We gaze fruitlessly into the darkness of the malting-barn's roof, but nothing can be deciphered.

Bob takes me through the whole malting process, pointing out that Glen Garioch is currently using local barley exclusively. 'And the yields we're getting out this year's crop are unbelievable,' he says. 'Just unheard of in the industry, I would say. About 411 litres of spirit per tonne of barley.'

So there are advantages to remaining intensely parochial in terms of materials, it seems. Despite that nasty little enzyme. In the tun-room, only one wooden washback remains, blackened and skelfy amidst a clutch of eight dully glittering stainless steel, younger, more efficent relatives. 'That's coming out next week, that wooden one,' says Bob. Any regrets? He shrugs and says nothing.

So what does Glen Garioch taste like? I've only tried the eight-year-old, and you can't help feeling, that with their own maltings and using local barley, something a bit more substantial, a bit more characterful could be marketed. Mind you, the older versions, even the ten-year-old, are reputedly much bigger and smokier. I don't know. Maybe I'd been expecting too much from Glen Garioch because everything about the distillery was so . . . *right*. But the malt, at least at eight years old, is bit throwaway.

Into Aberdeen, then, past Dyce Airport, furiously buzzing with North Sea helicopters. I'd decided to treat myself to a proper hotel for my last night, so from Oldmeldrum I'd booked the Brentwood, negotiating a half-price rate (£28) because it was a Friday. It was central and modern and I needed a shower.

I hit Aberdeen city centre as the rush-hour started. It was a nightmare, and it was hot, and the beast began to heat up and stutter and generally misbehave in a most uncharacteristic way. Finally, just outside Aberdeen Art Gallery, the clutch cable stretched its way out of adjustment, and suddenly I had no clutch. Traffic piled up behind me. I had to haul the beast on to the pavement for emergency, gut-wrenching repairs, mostly involving a lot of swearing under my breath. Is this how it ends, I kept thinking. Clutchless for the sake of a centimetre's extra adjustment, and stranded one day from home. Much twisting and bloodied fingers later, I was mobile once more.

Not to put too fine a point on it, at the Brentwood I was treated like some kind of scum which the rain had washed up on the doorstep. It's not even that good a hotel, merely an expanded guest house with recessed spotlights, staff name-tags and pretensions. How would I be paying? Cash. Could, I, umm, please pay in advance then, stuttered the receptionist, eyeing my rain-lashed, dirty face and leather jacket nervously. I paid. No one offered help with my things. I'd no sooner entered the room than the telephone rang. It was reception, demanding that I move the orange beast from its place of well-earned rest in the carpark. 'You've parked in a car space, and the manager says we'll need that tonight for . . . a car,' said the receptionist. I determined to ignore this request, but eventually compromised on squeezing the MZ a bit nearer to the wall. One scrape and I'd sue, I promised myself, though how I was supposed to tell which, amongst the beast's many blemishes, was the fault of a drunken parker, was uncertain.

Cadenheads had an office, or so some of their bottles indicated, at 18 Golden Square, Aberdeen. I couldn't find it, and it seemed an unlikely place for a whisky empire based far away in Campbeltown. I later discovered that the whole operation had been moved to the Mull of Kintyre, but it had proved a bit difficult to change all the existing labels, particularly as they were already stuck on bottles.

That night I went arty. Aberdeen is real city, as compared to Inverness, which has half the cosmopolitanism of, say, Lerwick with four times as many supermarkets. Aberdeen has, it must be admitted, oil and consequently money. It has a relatively sensible group of local politicians in power. Relatively and comparatively, that is. It has, importantly, a university and several polytechnics. It is a seaport. It has an excellent popular theatre. It has real shops, a real music scene, top-line bands and drama companies every week of the year. Interesting people like Michael Clark, Annie Lennox and . . . some others come from the place. Aberdeen Art Gallery is a real art gallery, with an internationally acclaimed collection including an important Francis Bacon. And that's where I was going. To the opening of the 58th Annual Exhibition of the Aberdeen Artists Society, as sponsored by, surprise surprise, Shell. It's amazing the posters you notice when you're trying to repair a clutch cable.

You can get into these things without an invitation if you're (a) smartly dressed, which I, of course, was not; (b) know one of the organisers, which, as it turned out, I did, or (c) are a card-carrying member of the National Union of Journalists, which may be the worst-organised and most expensive to join union in the world, but does provide you with a yellow-and-black card some people seem to be impressed by. Well, hardly anyone, to be exact, and certainly not the very sussed staff at the Aberdeen Art Gallery. So it was just as well Deirdre, one of the exhibition organisers, was an ex-journalist acquaintance from way back.

Once inside the massive marble halls, I realised this was no blue-rinsed-spinster-with-watercolour-set exhibition. Nine galleries had been set aside for three hundred paintings, prints, tapestries, textile collages and sculptures by professional or semi-professional artists from all over the north of Scotland, including, loyalty bids me mention, Cromarty's very own John McNaught and Gillian Jones.

Very few of Aberdeen's aesthetes, I thought, knew me, so as the halls filled up with the great, the good and the drunk, I found myself in the ideal position for some systematic eavesdropping, which, as you may have gathered, is both a habit and a career with me. I armed myself with a glass of red wine, freely provided by Aberdeen City Council, and set off. I was disappointed.

Beneath the chattering, buzzing, echoing noise of a big crowd fuelled by free drink, I picked up only snippets of conversation and comment as – with the exception of the art students, who were draped outside on the balcony, bored, beautiful and smoking – hundreds of people did a slow, circular dance around the walls of nine galleries, looking everywhere but at each other.

'Oh yes! yes! *yes!*' ejaculated a women dressed in finest Nextisms, gazing at C. J. Bailey's amazing sculpture *Wail! Whale*. Was it sex or was it art? I couldn't tell. Bob Batchelor, who was quite famous for his flower prints and paintings, had a small oil called *Purple Irises* on show, and a flamboyant middle-aged couple stood before it, shaking their heads so slightly you could hardly see the movement. 'So obvious. So, so *so* obvious.'

The woman took up the lament. 'Yes, flowers. I mean, all those bloody flowers. What does it mean? I mean, flowers. *Where is the reality in that?*'

Two elderly men stood in the middle of this kind of thing, which I must admit, I quickly got rather fed up overhearing. 'Where's Jim?' asked one. The other looked at him for a second before replying.

'Jim's dead.'

'Oh. I'm very sorry to hear that.'

'Yes. I thought you'd have known. It was two years ago.'

Just then, a small, bespectacled, balding figure I vaguely recognised came up to me. 'Excuse me, I'm sorry to intrude, but are you Tom Morton?' This was usually a cue for really embarrassing reminiscences from people who'd once heard me preach or sing religiously. I'd once been forced to sign a man's bible, as if in some way I was its author. What do you put on a bible? Sincerely yours? In the end I wrote 'Every blessing, Tom Morton'. I feel awful about it even now.

But no! Joy! This leather-jacketed exhibiting artist was one George Cheyne, former drummer with excellent punk/funk band APB, whom I had championed to general disinterest in the mid-1980s, when I was writing reviews for the rock weekly *Melody Maker*. APB were a small-scale phenomenon. They all came from the village of Ellon outside Aberdeen 'apart from me', George reminded me. 'I'm frae Methlick', and released an independent single which, freakishly, became the toast of New York's black underground dance radio stations, where they were originally thought to be black, as once the Average White Band had been. Flown to America, they became stars on the New York club scene, playing sell-out concerts of two and three thousand people. But in Britain, partly due to a refusal to move from, gulp, Ellon, no major record deal materialised and the gigs remained minor league.

'I'm really glad to meet you again,' said George, 'because I always wanted to thank you for all the support you gave us. You were about the only one, wi' Bob Flynn at the *NME*, and we really appreciated it.' This was the kind of thing I'd only ever heard from one other rock band, namely Runrig, and one folk group, Capercaillie. Journalists are less than dog-shit to successful pop stars, and seen merely as tools to aid the climb to success by those on the up and up, or down. Or just hated anyway for the hell of it.

So what had happened to APB? George, a trained artist, had left the group to concentrate on his painting, with some success. The rest had formed another group and were still plugging away. Did he miss it? George's face furrowed, and suddenly he was far away.

'I wish you'd seen what it was like Tom, in New York. Nobody over here ever saw what it was like, and it was amazing. We were stars. Four wee loons frae Ellon and Methlick, and we were walking down these streets, and playing these halls that were sold out. Just playing in New York was so exciting, something I'll never forget, that feeling. But I suppose I've had the chance to do that. Not many people have.'

I had a look at George's paintings later. They were all of New York.

Dave Jackson is another musician, a jazz-folk guitar player whose love affair with Shetland has taken him to many folk festivals and inspired much of his painting and conceptual art. His massive 1991 installation *The Slockit Light* (the light which has gone out), inspired by a transcendentally powerful fiddle tune by the late Dr Tom Anderson, was a roomful of material, banners and paintings and cases of found objects, relating to the changes in crofting lifestyles over a century. It was profoundly moving, and he was exhibiting one print, also called *The Slockit Light*, at this mammoth show. I really liked it, but I was damned if I was going to pay show prices for it.

We talked music for a while, and Shetland, and how he was giving the island's folk festival a miss because he felt it was going stale on him a wee bit, or he was going stale on it. He had some work in Orkney planned which was likely to take up most of his time.

'All right, Dave,' I said. 'Name your price for *The Slockit Light*. I like it. I've got to have it.' I was gushing like an art junkie. Such personal negotiations are just not the done thing at all at group exhibitions, but after several glasses of council wine I was past caring about artistic etiquette. We agreed a figure, I drunkenly wrote out a cheque, and suddenly I felt like an art connoisseur, a patron.

'This is the end of my journey,' I told Dave, my new-found protégé. Wrongly, in fact. 'And I don't even have a whisky.' It was time to leave art and search for higher things, like food and spirits.

After an excellent Turkish meal, the lack of whisky was put to rights, by the application of several large . . . oh no . . . Glenmorangies, the only malt the restaurant possessed. They went down like white wine. Suddenly I was back in Tain, back in the St Duthac, cruelly shouting and laughing at Doug Scott as he tried to tell me how his hopes for socialism in an independent Scotland were in tatters, how we were powerless to change our destiny, how Scotland's spirit of adventure had turned to vinegar in all our mouths, how the dark ages stretched ahead. I was shouting and laughing because I knew he might be right.

But in Aberdeen, I drank quietly, not to forget, but trying to keep the memories of the previous three weeks as clear as possible. Here I was, a purchaser of art, a consumer of Turkish food and whisky, a resident at an expense-account hotel. What was adventurous about that? Where was my own, personal spirit of adventure? Should I go down to the docks, take in a few dubious strip shows and then stow away on a freighter bound for the Arctic? Or should I try and remember what had happened during three weeks' intensive travelling the length and breadth of my native land, learning about drink, drinking in the atmosphere, and just drinking? And see if there was any spirit of adventure left in either Scotland or me?

That sounded like a pretty tiring task. So I went back to the Brentwood. Feeling mischievous, I tried to find the fire alarms. I'd set them off, get put in jail, cause a stushie and a scandal and have to be bailed out by my incandescent-with-rage wife! What a great ending to the book! But I couldn't find the fire alarms. I was too drunk.

FINALE

I woke up at seven, got dressed, got on the bike and went home.

I didn't bother with a Brentwood breakfast. I picked up Mars Bars, orange juice and crisps at a filling station and gradually regained contact with reality. Which was just as well, as I think I was trying to ride a motorcycle at the time.

Irresponsible? Still over the limit after the previous night? Probably. It's no mitigation, but I was sick of travelling and I wanted home. Anyway, God had his final revenge on me. He and the weather were always close.

Just outside Inverurie, the rain started. And then, as I climbed into the grim Grampian mountains, God started firing the hail at me like buckshot, in small, gusty surprise attacks. I was determined not to stop, but in Huntly, I ground to a halt. Shivering from the cold and the hangover, I found a café run by an ex-oil-rig cook, who supplied, without question, two mugs of coffee, two egg and bacon rolls with two eggs on each, plus a selection of home-made cakes. I began to feel less dead.

This was the notorious A96, but early on a Saturday morning there was little traffic. I was in Speyside, with distilleries to the right and left of me, but even when I passed through Keith, with the spatterings of hail now turning to unremitting rain, not the smallest vestige of my conscious thought turned to pot-stills and mash-tuns and malt-barns and spirit-safes. I'd had enough. I wanted out of this grey, wet, cold, hateful country. I wanted to go home, to a house where I could shut it all out. All of it, the weather, the drink, the people, the politics, even the bloody religion. Maybe after hassling me from Caithness to Galloway and back, God would put away his hail gun and try and impress me with some good weather. But I doubted it.

At Elgin, the bike began to stutter and stammer in rain which seemed, again, heavier and wetter than anything I'd come across before. A pool of rainwater settled warmly inside the seat of my oilskins, and a mile out of Nairn, the orange beast died.

I pumped the kick-starter desperately for half an hour. A passing driver, a woman who said she owned RD Motorcycles in Nairn, offered to get a mechanic out. I shook my head angrily, spraying her with undeserved, ungrateful rainwater.

Finally, the rain went off. Shaking with cold, I took off the plug lead. The connecting cap was full of water. I blew on it, wiped it, shook it, put it back on. And the bike started first time.

Those 150 miles from Aberdeen to Cromarty were the worst of the whole trip. It seemed that way, anyway. So it was that way. Partly it was all self-inflicted, through the previous night's over indulgence, partly it was the weather. But once I'd crested the hill out of Rosemarkie, barely hanging on, sodden, to those heavy, heavy handlebars, the rain cleared miraculously and that wonderful vista opened up: Ben Wyvis, the Cromarty Firth, the oil rigs and the spidery structures under construction at Nigg. My gloves were heavy and wringing wet. Only my bottom, soaking in a warm pool of body-heated water, had much feeling left in it as I vainly attempted to find neutral outside our house, where Isolde was parked, disdainfully ignoring the beast and me.

I switched off, and climbed stiffly on to relatively stable ground. I rang the doorbell and waited. There was nobody in.

Later, there was a party to celebrate my safe return. My wife ceremoniously tore up the famous life insurance policy. I drank nothing but mineral water. And some champagne. And a few Glenfarclas 105s, a measure of which I poured into the beast's petrol tank. I kept the bottle of Aludrox my wife had bought strictly to myself. No blood in either urine or stools so far: a triumph.

David Alston, curator of the local museum, was there. He telephoned two days later to say that my talk of illicit distilling had sparked off a vague memory that the last case recorded in Ross-shire might have been in Cromarty. He had done some checking and indeed, forty years ago, a famous local drouth had vanished for four days over New Year. When found, he was unconscious in his own house. Revived and apparently none the worse, he had blamed his 'wee turn' on the work of a neighbour, a retired engineer who had been distilling his own spirit on top of his cooker, using a home-made still he'd concocted out of boredom.

And so the last still found by the authorities in Ross-shire (and there may be one or two still going today, hidden in the depths of the Black Isle) was duly removed and broken up.

From our house.

Sandness,
Shetland,
June 1992